NATIONS OF THE MODERN WORLD

CEYLON — S. A. Pakeman

Formerly Professor of Modern History, Ceylon University College. Appointed Member, House of Representatives, Ceylon, 1947–52

ENGLAND — John Bowle

Professor of Political Theory, Collège d'Europe, Bruges

MODERN INDIA — Sir Percival Griffiths

President, India, Pakistan and Burma Association

MODERN IRAN — Peter Avery

Lecturer in Persian and Fellow King's College, Cambridge

JAPAN — Sir Esler Dening

H.M. Ambassador to Japan, 1952–1957

MALAYA — J. M. Gullick

Formerly of the Malayan Civil Service

PAKISTAN — Ian Stephens

Formerly Editor of The Statesman *Calcutta and Delhi, 1942–1951 Fellow King's College, Cambridge, 1952–1958*

SOUTH AFRICA — John Cope

Formerly editor-in-chief of The Forum *and South African Correspondent of* The Guardian

SUDAN REPUBLIC	K. D. D. Henderson *Formerly of the Sudan Political Service and Governor of Darfur Province, 1949-1953*
TURKEY	Geoffrey Lewis *Senior lecturer in Islamic Studies, Oxford*
THE UNITED STATES OF AMERICA	H. C. Allen *Commonwealth Fund Professor of American History, University College, London*
YUGOSLAVIA	Muriel Heppel and F. B. Singleton

NATIONS OF THE MODERN WORLD

MODERN INDIA

MODERN INDIA

By

SIR PERCIVAL GRIFFITHS

FOURTH EDITION

FREDERICK A. PRAEGER, *Publishers*

NEW YORK · WASHINGTON

BOOKS THAT MATTER

Published in the United States of America in 1957
by Frederick A. Praeger, Inc., Publishers
111 Fourth Avenue, New York, N.Y. 10003

Second Edition 1958
Third Edition 1962
Fourth Edition 1965

Library of Congress Catalog Card Number: 65-14181

Printed in Great Britain

TO

MY MOTHER

Preface

THE WRITER of a book on Modern India is beset at the outset with three difficulties. First there is the old question of whether to assume the necessary background of knowledge, or to give a brief and therefore unsatisfactory sketch of Indian history and religions. As this series is intended for the general public, the latter alternative had to be chosen, but the limitations of a procedure which allows under five thousand words for a summary of Hinduism and a few pages for an account of the impact of Britain on India are obvious.

The second difficulty lies in the speed of change in modern India. Any study of Indian affairs at this point of time resembles an attempt to take a still picture of a fast-moving scene. There are, however, certain long-term trends discernible and if the writer has succeeded in analysing them, it will matter little if the details are overtaken by events.

The third difficulty arises from the fact that some of the matters discussed in this book arouse strong emotions in India and there is always the risk that a frank account of them by a non-Indian may give offence to a people whose newly-won independence has heightened their natural sensitivity. The writer nevertheless hopes that, since India stands in his thoughts and affections only next to his own country, he may be permitted to write about the doings of her leaders as freely as he would about the British Cabinet.

This book is based mainly on close observation of India's politics and administration over a generation and on innumerable discussions with many Indian friends – politicians, officials, business men and members of the professions. To them all, the writer is grateful, but particular acknowledgments must be made of the help of a distinguished Indian friend, who in view of his high position prefers to remain anonymous, but who has contributed much to this book by his acute, though friendly, criticism of the manuscript.

ix

Finally, thanks arc due to Miss D. Hammond for her competence and patience in the secretarial work involved.

Wentworth, Surrey   P. J. GRIFFITHS
1957

*   *   *

THE ISSUE OF a fourth edition has provided the opportunity of bringing the story of modern India up to date.

October 1964   P. J. G.

Contents

Maps

SECTION I

THE HISTORICAL BACKGROUND

Introductory

ODERN INDIA presents a spectacle of unity in diversity to which history provides no parallel, except perhaps in the Roman Empire. The diversity has existed from time immemorial and has been the subject of many books, whereas the unity is of recent growth and still takes observers by surprise. That growth, however, was only rendered possible by certain facts of history and geography. The great barrier to the north makes India what a recent geographer has called 'an intelligible isolate' – an entity sufficiently cut off from the outside world for long periods to allow its inhabitants to develop characteristics of their own. Under these favourable geographical circumstances, Hinduism was able to build up throughout India a common culture and a uniform way of life. For centuries the people of India were included in the fold of caste and subjected to the disciplines of a hierarchy whose main gradations were acknowledged throughout the country. The foundations thus existed on which, under favourable political conditions, a structure of true unity might be erected. British rule provided the necessary conditions. The uniform rule of law, the administration of India as a single country, the use of the English language and, above all, the nineteenth-century liberal thought which all educated Indians absorbed with such avidity, gradually gave rise to a sense of nationality and then to a feeling of ardent nationalism, in which militant Hinduism had a large part to play. The controversies and disturbances in the fifties over the formation of linguistic states may warn us not to exaggerate the strength of the new unity, but it is nevertheless true to say that the deepest political emotion of the great majority of educated Indians today is pride in their Indian nationality.

In the course of the psychological struggles which have led to this new unity, Hinduism has had to meet a great challenge. Many writers on Indian affairs have dwelt on the absorbent capacity of Hinduism – its power to assimilate alien beliefs and feelings without undergoing radical transformation itself. Greeks, Scythians, Arabs, Mongols, Persians and many others have exercised dominion and left a mark on India, but it could not be said that the main structure of Hindu thought has been changed by their advent. A far greater challenge to Hinduism has risen from the impact of European civilisation, principally through the medium of the British, during the past two hundred years. The Englishmen who influenced India in the formative years of the nineteenth century were characterised, first by a rugged, individualistic Christianity and secondly, by a frank devotion to the attainment of material prosperity. In this latter aim, the great superiority of Britain to India in the mechanical arts and sciences made success certain, and the prestige earned by this success to some extent transferred itself to the Christianity which the all-conquering British preached. A reaction against Hinduism, which was in a somewhat decadent phase at the beginning of the nineteenth century, set in strongly and educated Indians began to question their own traditions. This reaction did not affect the masses and even amongst the upper classes the phase soon passed. Towards the end of the century a movement back to the old Indian faith gathered strength and early in the twentieth century militant Hinduism was in full force.

In the meantime, the rugged Christianity of the mid-nineteenth-century rulers of India had been replaced by the scepticism or the vague half-belief which characterised so large a proportion of young Englishmen in the early years of the twentieth century. Scepticism is always infectious and it has proved a more seriously corroding influence on educated Indian society than the early attacks of rival religions. This influence, however, was only strong in the top stratum of society. At levels below that, religion began to be seriously influenced by politics and a somewhat aggressive Hinduism received popular support, mainly because it was not of foreign origin. Along with the *Swadeshi*[1] movement, it was part of the apparatus required in the struggle for independence, and not unnaturally it lost some of its appeal when that aim was achieved.

[1] Literally of one's own country – applied to the use of indigenous products.

It is difficult to assess the residual strength of these various forces or to state what their resultant is today. Indian society is clearly divided between those who believe whole-heartedly in Western values and those who cling tenaciously to the traditional thought and culture of India. The division cuts across differences of occupation, rank, habits of life and even party, but amongst those with whom most foreigners come into contact – Indians with an advanced education of the Western type, perhaps holding superior posts in British business firms or in Government service – the Westernisers are in a majority. The foreigner is thus apt to get the impression that scepticism, indifference, or a hazy idea of postponing thought about religious matters until one has more leisure, is as common in India as in Britain. In reality, these Westernisers are only a small minority and amongst the majority of ordinary folk, even in the cities, religion still counts for a great deal, though it differs considerably, both in social practice and in belief, from the Hinduism which Raja Rammohan Roy strove to reform early in the nineteenth century.

In the villages and small towns, Hinduism is strongly entrenched. The Brahman priest and the Pandit still have great authority and the influence of the older women is strong in support of the ancient religion. Villagers still gather round to hear the reading of the Hindu epics or the sacred books and so preserve the traditional means of religious instruction throughout the ages. Even in the villages, however, forces are at work tending to modify Hindu thought and practice. The young men go to work in the large towns and soon find the strict observance of caste rules difficult in business or official life. They acquire, too, the more materialistic attitude of the townsfolk and when they return to their villages are apt to find themselves a little out of tune.

✓ It is impossible to guess what will ultimately emerge from the melting-pot of modern India. The present writer is sufficiently conservative to hope profoundly that Hinduism will endure as a powerful force, but his Western-educated Indian friends often discourage this hope and express the view that humanitarianism and social service must, in the years to come, replace orthodox Hindu thought and aspiration. Shorn of fine words, this would seem to mean a spiritual vacuum, into which

Communism would shortly move. The connected question as to whether Hindusim is likely in any case to be a bulwark against Communism can only be posed, and not answered here. An answer would have to allow for the fact that belief in the importance of the individual, which is the only true antidote to Communism, is not inherently strong in Hinduism.

The emphasis in this chapter on Hinduism would not be justified but for the fact that, in spite of Nehru's secularism, partition has left India virtually a Hindu country. There are, indeed, a very large number of Muslims[1] in India, but they do not count greatly in Indian life and thought. Partition has, in fact, strengthened India politically and psychologically, by giving it greater homogeneity.

The economic effects of partition on the other hand have in some respects been deleterious. The food problem has become more difficult; important raw materials such as jute and cotton are now lacking or in short supply; and India has lost an important market in those parts of the sub-continent which were formerly supplied from Calcutta, Bombay or Amritsar, but which are now in Pakistan and seek their supplies of many commodities from countries other than India. This economic loss would be less serious if India and Pakistan became good neighbours, but there is no sign that this is likely to happen. Some of the causes of friction will be discussed in this book, but it looks as though the world will have to accept a situation in which the long-term relations between India and Pakistan will be rather like those which prevailed in the Balkans before the First World War. This parallel is, to some extent, misleading, since the conflict in South-east Europe at that time was an aspect of the struggle between two empires, whereas Indians regard their dispute with Pakistan as really a family row. As one distinguished Indian put it recently: 'It is something like a quarrel in families in India. Partition of property has not always been a final solution; bickering goes on for quite a long time, sometimes for one or two generations; then the quarrels subside.' It must, however, be remembered that this is not the view taken in Pakistan, where feeling is more bitter than in India.

---

[1] At the time of the 1961 Census there were 47 million Muslims in India.

The creation of Pakistan was part of a settlement which, while leaving India completely free to frame her own constitution and to decide on her ultimate relations with Britain and the Commonwealth, established initially a federal, parliamentary form of Government and left India a full commonwealth member. India, thereafter, was free to choose for herself with regard to both these matters. In a country with a population of about 330 million at that time and equal in area to two-thirds of Europe without Russia, federation was perhaps inevitable, but it is a striking tribute to British influence that Indian politicians almost took it for granted that their constitution must, in the main, follow the British rather than the American model. Parliamentary government is indeed working on somewhat different lines from those which prevail in Britain, in the sense that there are no signs of the emergence of a true two-party system. The parliamentary system nevertheless commands the respect of the entire country, apart from the Communists, and it seems likely to endure. The machinery of the ballot box is proving more satisfactory than the most optimistic student of Indian affairs expected, and a largely illiterate electorate has not proved as susceptible to extremist propaganda as was feared. It could reasonably be claimed that Britain's political legacy to India was sound.

In economic affairs, too, Britain left India in a strong position. In the last few decades before the transfer of power, the example of British enterprise had been followed by many Indian business men and the increase in productive capacity between the two wars was impressive. By the end of the Second World War, India had attained a considerable industrial status and her leading men, with the exception of Gandhi, had come to believe that still further industrialisation must be the basis of the increased prosperity which they were determined to achieve. This conviction, together with a desire to reduce the disparities between the rich and the poor, led to the concept of 'planning', which was first given definite shape by a group of India industrialists and has dominated Indian economic thought ever since. At a later stage in this book we shall discuss the National Plans. They are the warp and woof of modern Indian thought and are indeed an aspect of the faith in the possibility of progress which Britain bequeathed to India and which has taken the place of her age-long fatalism. Indians today believe that the destinies of their country lie in their own hands and the creation of this belief may prove to be the most enduring result of the British connection.

That connection has not been snapped by independence, though its character has changed. The ties of affection between Britain and free India are strong and, in spite of her determined nonalignment, India today is a willing and loyal member of the British Commonwealth.

Chapter 1

Hinduism

I N SPITE OF the strong impact of Western ideas, Hinduism
is still the dominant influence in Indian life, and a brief
study of it is an essential preliminary to any understanding
of modern India. One of the difficulties of such a study is the
necessity of including three separate levels of religious thought
and feeling. The lofty concepts of the Brahman philosopher,
the more emotional, personal religion of the devotees of Vishnu
and Siva, and the crude, dark superstitions of the fear-haunted
villager, are all equally entitled to a place in our account, since
those who entertain these divergent ideas are, by reason of
their membership of one of the castes, all included in the
Hindu fold. In this chapter we shall endeavour to consider,
though necessarily in summary fashion, firstly, the principal
beliefs and practices of educated Hindus; secondly, the caste
system; and, lastly, the religion of the Hindu masses.

Our approach must necessarily be historical, but for our
purpose we need not go back to the great pre-Aryan civilisation
of the Indus Valley. It will be sufficient to start at the stage
when the ancestors of the early Hindus broke away from the
parent 'Aryan'[1] stock, perhaps in the beginning of the second
millennium before the Christian era, and moved down into
North-west India, driving the Dravidian inhabitants to the
south. At a later stage, Dravidian religious ideas were to influence Hinduism considerably, but in the early centuries after
the immigration the beliefs of the Hindus developed along
natural lines, with little outside interference.

The Hindu sacred literature, written in the Sanskrit language, provides a panorama of the unfolding of the human
spirit – from the first, almost instinctive tendency to worship,

[1] A term used loosely, since it properly denotes a linguistic, not an ethnic
grouping.

23

up to the most profound theological speculation – unparalleled elsewhere. The first of the sacred works is the Rig Veda, a collection of hymns composed during the course of several centuries, the earliest of which can perhaps be assigned to about 1500 B.C., or a few hundred years at most after the coming of the Aryans to India. Nobody who has experienced the vividness and impressiveness of natural phenomena in Northern India will be surprised at the poetic feeling and sense of beauty underlying the early Hindu personification and deification of natural forces. The indescribable beauty of the dawn; the infinite, pitiless sky; the terror of the storm; the cooling, life-giving rain at the beginning of the monsoon – these must indeed have seemed divine and the outpouring of wonder and adoration before them is expressed in the Rig Veda in passages of the highest poetry. There is an exuberance of spirit in these hymns in marked contrast to the pessimism of later Hinduism. The gods themselves, of whom there are many, are seldom malignant; they are described again and again as the Devas or Shining Ones, and altogether the reader of the Rig Veda forms the impression of a joyous, active religion. It is true that if the gods are to exert themselves on behalf of men they must be propitiated with sacrifices. 'Here is butter, give us cows', is an oft-quoted phrase typifying the relationship between men and gods – but the gods ignore, rather than harm, the man who neglects his duties towards them.

As the centuries passed, the gods resolved themselves into a kind of hierarchy, though the pre-eminence was not at all times assigned to the same deity. The concept of natural law and of moral order also began to emerge and to be associated in particular with the god Varuna, as in the twenty-eighth hymn of the second book of the Rig Veda:

. . . . : the rivers run by Varuna's commandment.
These feel no weariness, nor cease from flowing:
    swift have they flown like birds in air around us.

Loose me from sin as from a band that binds me: may we
    swell, Varuna, thy spring of order.
Let not my thread, while I weave song, be severed, nor
    my work's sum, before the time be shattered.

Far from me, Varuna, remove all danger: accept me
graciously, thou holy sovran.
Cast off, like cords that hold a calf, my troubles:
I am not even mine eyelids lord without thee.

Gradually the idea of the oneness of nature began to pave
the way for the sense that God, too, must be one and in the
famous Song of Creation in the Tenth Book, the Vedic seer
seems to be groping, still a little uncertainly, towards monotheism.

'Who verily knows and who can here declare it, whence it
was born and whence comes this creation?
The gods are later than this world's production. Who
knows, then, whence it first came into being?

He, the first origin of this creation, whether he formed it
all or did not form it,
Whose eye controls this world in highest heaven, he verily
knows it, or perhaps he knows not.'

This trend towards monotheism developed in a direction
somewhat different from that followed by the Jews and led,
not to their dualistic concept of a creator standing outside his
creation, but to a rigorous monism according to which God and
His creation are one. The soul, it was said, must be permanent
and unchanging; the same in our waking moments as in dream-
less sleep; and empty therefore of all content. The soul cannot
perceive what is not in it, or it would be itself subject to
change. It must therefore be identical with the unchanging
World-Soul, which is itself free from all causality and change.
The World-Soul and the individual soul (Brahman and
Atman) are both the one ultimate reality, approached in one
case objectively, and in the other case subjectively. This is, in
fact, the way by which the Upanishads, in which this doctrine
was expounded, fought shy, to quote Radhakrishnan, of the
conception of an omnipotent mechanic fashioning pre-existing
matter into the universe. Nothing is fashioned, and there is
no mechanic, since everything is one undifferentiated, timeless, self-existing whole. Of nothing else but the World-Soul

can positive existence be predicated. Separateness from this single world-entity is an illusion, productive of misery; salvation consists in abandoning the illusion, losing one's imaginary, separate self in the World-Soul and so casting off the bonds of unhappiness by ceasing to think that one exists. Not by any means all Hindu thinkers have accepted this monistic view and it is indeed rejected by several of the six orthodox systems of philosophy. It has nevertheless been the dominant *motif* in Indian philosophy since the Upanishads.

Side by side with it grew up the belief in metempsychosis which has thus been stated in philosophic terms – 'ignorant of its identity with the World-Soul, the soul is entangled in the perishable world and as it itself is imperishable is condemned to a perpetual series of changes. Once dragged into the *Samsara* or vortex of life, it passes from one existence to another without respite.' Death is merely the release of the soul from the body to which it is temporarily attached. It is then, perhaps after an interval, reincarnated, and the form in which it is born is inexorably determined by its *karma* or the sum of all its past actions, good and bad. In the words of one of the Upanishads – 'Accordingly, those who are of pleasant conduct here – the prospect is, indeed, that they will enter a pleasant womb, either the womb of a Brahman, or the womb of a Kshatriya, or the womb of a Vaisya. But those who are of stinking conduct here – the prospect is, indeed, that they will enter a stinking womb, either the womb of a dog, or the womb of a swine, or the womb of an outcast (*candāla*).'

The wearisome round of rebirths is the result of the illusion of separateness from the World-Soul. Once the individual soul loses this illusion, the bond of *karma* is broken; death will then be the final deliverance, the absorption into the World-Soul.

To the Western mind, this desire to be freed from individual existence appears, like so much of the Brahmanical teaching, to be fundamentally pessimistic and conducive to resignation rather than to an active, purposeful life. It is wholly at variance with the exuberance of the Rig Veda and no satisfactory explanation of this great psychological change has ever been given.

The question naturally arises as to whether the transmigration of souls is merely a doctrine of philosophers and scholars, or whether ordinary Hindus believe it in a practical sense. This matter was the subject of a particular inquiry in the 1901 census of the United Provinces, and it was reported that the doctrine of *karma* 'was one of the firmest beliefs of all classes of Hindus', though the idea of salvation was, as a rule, not absorption in the World-Soul, but the attainment of happiness and comfort in heaven. It was also reported that divination was still resorted to from time to time when a man died, in order to ascertain what his next life would be. The report went on to say that a man and woman will bathe together in the Ganges with their clothes tied together, in the sure and certain belief that this will ensure their being again husband and wife in a future existence. Even today it is still true that the Brahmanical doctrines of monism[1] and metempsychosis are the very essence of the spiritual thought and feeling of the great majority of caste Hindus.

By themselves, however, these cold conceptions are not sufficient to satisfy the yearnings of the average man and so side by side with them there have grown up two great devotional religions, whose adherents respectively worship Vishnu and Siva. We must emphasise that *Vaishnavism* and *Saivism*, are not revolts against Hinduism, but form an integral part of it. Hindu thought is infinitely flexible and little given to rigorous definition, and a Vaishnava would find no difficulty in reconciling worship of Vishnu as the Supreme-Spirit, with a belief in the monism of the philosopher, or with the doctrine of the illusion of all separateness from the one World-Spirit, the only reality. Vishnu and his worshippers exist only in the fog of illusion, but within that fog they stand in the relation of God and His creatures.

Vishnu is the most popular deity in modern India and is regarded by many millions of Hindus as the saviour, the friend, the comforter, the very present help in time of trouble. These human qualities have been strengthened by the incarnations in which he has been manifest. The Hindu belief in *Avataras*, or incarnations of God for some purpose of deliverance, is thus set forth in a discourse of Krishna in the Bhagavad Gita:

[1] Though not all schools of Hindu philosophy accept this doctrine.

'For whensoever the law fails and lawlessness uprises,
O thou of Bharat's race, then do I bring myself to bodied birth.
To guard the righteous, to destroy evildoers, to establish the law, I come to birth age after age.'

This doctrine made possible the identification of the Vedic god Vishnu with a very ancient hero-god Krishna, as well as with Rama, the central character of the great Hindu epic Ramayana, and so led to the foundation of a cult of personal devotion of great power and beauty. The great characteristic of Vaishnavism, or the worship of Vishnu, has always been earnest piety of a rather emotional kind, well illustrated by the following hymn, written by Ramanuja in the twelfth century.

'The vessel of a thousand sins, and plunged
    Deep in the heart of life's outrageous sea,
I seek in thee the refuge of despair;
    In mercy only, Hari, make me Thine . . .
But for Thee I am masterless; save me
    There's none to earn Thy mercy. Since our fate
Weaveth this bond between us, Master Mine,
    O guard it well and cast it not away . . .
Lord Madhava, whatever mine may be,
    Whatever I, is all and wholly Thine.
What offering can I bring, whose wakened soul
    Seeth all Being bond to Thee for aye?'

Siva is a god of a very different character – the personification of 'the cosmic force which changes and in changing both destroys and reproduces' – a worthy successor to the Vedic deity *Rudra*, the roarer. Hindus have always understood that death and reproduction are inseparable and equally important aspects of change, and have not been afraid either to recognise destruction as a divine function, or to associate sexual, creative activities with the deity. Not only is the symbol of Siva the phallic emblem, but it is in connection with him that the conception of *Sakti*, or the female creative energy of the gods, has been most highly developed. The spouse of Siva is the form in which his power is made manifest and as Kali, Durga,

Mahadevi, or by one of her many other names, she plays a more dramatic part than any other deity in Indian life. She is often malignant and the sect of the Saktas, which is particularly associated with her, has given cover to much that is evil and repulsive, and to the grossest sexual orgies. Under other aspects, however, the goddess can be mild and benevolent, and the Durga festival in Bengal is comparable, as a season of happiness, goodwill and family reunion, with the Western Christmas. Siva himself, too, has different aspects. As Bhairava, he is a terrible destroyer; as Bhutesvar, he haunts cremation grounds, wearing a string of skulls for a necklace; while in another aspect he is mild and jovial. If this were all, his worship might long since have passed away, but he is also God and Father, and devotion to him has inspired some of the finest religious poems in South India. In the Tiruvaçagam we hear him addressed in terms of true religious fervour:

'With mother-love he came in grace and made me his';
'To thee, O Father may I attain, may I yet dwell with thee';

or again:

'What the soul desires is deliverance from matter and life with Siva and this he grants by bestowing grace.'

If, however, the unwary Western reader is here inclined to draw a parallel between these aspirations and those of a Christian, the best correction can be supplied by O'Malley's account of the ceremonies in the temple of Lingaraj at Bhubaneswar. 'The god is represented by a natural block of stone 8 feet in diameter, rising 8 inches above the ground, and encircled by a stone ring, which represents the *yoni* or female organ. Bells are rung at early dawn to awake the god from sleep and a lamp is waved in front of the stone. The cleaning of his teeth is symbolised by pouring water over the stone and rubbing a stick on it, bathing by pouring water over it, and dressing by putting clothes on it. There is a succession of meals, which need not be described; there is an afternoon siesta, from which he is woken up by loud strains of music; an afternoon meal is served, after which there are a bath and change of clothes. The stone is draped in costly vestments, and flowers and perfumery are placed on it. Finally, after other offerings of food, a bedstead is brought in and the god has a night's repose.'

This is as far a cry from the theism of Ramanuja as that was from the Brahmanical teaching of the immanence of deity. There is, in fact, nothing clear cut about Hinduism and it offers to every individual either transcendental philosophy, or a theistic devotionalism, or something little removed from simple idolatry, according to his needs and spiritual capacity. Even temple worship is not obligatory, and indeed the most important religious exercises of the laity are the ceremonies performed daily or periodically in their own homes. In many houses there is either an image or a picture of Krishna, or a *lingam* or a *salagram* stone symbolising respectively Siva and Krishna, and before these idols worship is conducted morning and evening, by the head of the house, or by the Brahman family priest. More important even than this daily worship are the rites in connection with the naming of a boy, or with the assumption of the sacred thread which it is the privilege of the higher castes to wear, or the *sraddhas* or death ceremonies which no good Brahman will neglect. Those ceremonies, which are intended either to facilitate reincarnation, or to secure admission to an intermediate heaven, continue for a fortnight after death and are repeated at intervals during the next year and thereafter annually as long as the eldest son of the deceased is alive.

These domestic rites are the vital elements in everyday Hinduism and the man who observes them may believe what he likes and still be a good Hindu, provided, of course, he keeps the rules of caste. To that subject we must now turn.

In early Vedic days, sacrificial ceremonies had been regarded as voluntary acts, pleasing to the gods, in return for which they could be expected to be friendly. Some centuries later, these sacrifices came to be regarded first as obligatory, and, secondly, as acts compelling the gods, whether they liked it or not, to perform their part of the contract. The correct performance of the rites thus became of supreme importance and the priests, who alone knew how the ceremonial should be conducted, grew in power. After a long period of struggle, the hierarchical precedence of the Brahman, or priestly class, over the Kshatriyas or warriors, was established and before long a

fourfold order of society, in which the Vaisyas, or merchants
and agriculturists, and Sudras, or servants and menials, constituted the third and fourth classes, was recognised. A super-
natural origin for this division was in due course discovered
or invented, and in a very late Vedic hymn it was declared that
the Brahman, the Kshatriya, the Vaisya and the Sudra came
respectively from the mouth, the arms, the thighs and the feet
of Purusha, the personal and lifegiving principle in all animate
beings.

Although most authorities would agree with the foregoing
account of the origin of Brahman supremacy, widely different
views are held as to the origin of the caste system in its more
general aspect. Some, emphasising the fact that the Sanskrit
word for caste is 'varna' or colour, have regarded it as the
consequence of the great gulf between the conquering Aryans
and their Dravidian or aboriginal subjects. Others have considered it primarily as an economic, functional division of
society, which gained permanency and rigidity because of its
convenience. The two views are not incompatible, and it is
certainly the case that caste barriers became more definite as
the Aryans first extended their conquest over the Dravidians
and then came into contact with the relatively uncivilised
aborigines. Caste thus became, and has remained, the central
feature of Hindu society.

Occupational differences and social feuds have throughout
the centuries led to the splitting up of castes, and today,
instead of the four *Varnas* of the Vedic period, there are well
over two thousand castes or similar societies in India. Between
the castes there is a fairly well recognised grouping according
to precedence, but it is less rigid than might be supposed, since
lower groups are constantly striving to secure a higher status.
This may be achieved, not by any formal act, but by the
adoption of some custom normally characteristic of a caste in
a higher group. In certain districts of West Bengal, for example,
the members of a particular low caste were striving hard some
years ago to reduce the period of mourning for a father from
thirty to eleven days, since the latter period was that observed
by Brahmans.

Caste customs vary so much from place to place that no
general account can be more than approximately correct. It

may, however, be said that a caste is a social group consisting solely of persons born in it, who may not marry outside the caste, who are severely restricted with regard to eating and drinking with members of other castes, and who are subject to the discipline of the caste in all social and personal matters. Sénart, the classical European authority on this subject, has thus defined caste – 'Figurons-nous un groupe corporatif, fermé, et, en théorie du moins, rigoureusement héréditaire, muni d'une certaine organisation traditionnelle et indépendante, d'un chef, d'un conseil, se réunissant à l'occasion en assemblées plus ou moins plénières; uni souvent par la célébration de certaines fêtes; relié par une profession commune, pratiquant des usages communs qui portent plus spécialement sur le mariage, sur la nourriture, sur des cas divers d' impureté; armé enfin, pour en assurer l'empire, d'une juridiction de compétence plus ou moins étendue, mais capable, sous la sanction de certaines pénalités, surtout de l'exclusion soit définite soit révocable, de fair sentir efficacement l'autorité de la communauté; telle en raccourci nous apparaît la caste.'

Caste discipline is very much of a reality in the villages of India even today, and the individual who obstinately flouts it is liable to excommunication. Nobody will then eat or drink with him, or supply him with food, or perform any service for him, and in the self-contained villages of India, life under such conditions is almost impossible. The offender soon has to submit to whatever penalty the caste *panchayat*,[1] or gathering of the elders, may impose. As a rule, the powers of the *panchayat* are exercised justly and there can be little doubt that, on the whole, caste discipline makes for morals and good order. This is an aspect which is frequently forgotten by modern writers who condemn the caste system as oppressive and reactionary. A more balanced view would appear to be that throughout the centuries it gave Indian society stability, and so partially compensated for the lack of large-scale political genius displayed in much of the Hindu period. It was conservative rather than progressive in its tendencies, but conservation was perhaps what ancient Indian society most needed. Caste was in fact the vehicle in which almost everything of permanent value in Hinduism was carried.

[1] Literally, a body of five persons.

Unfortunately, the system developed two serious abuses. The first, which arose at an early stage, was the unjustifiable discrimination between one caste and another in the matter of elementary rights – a disparity well illustrated by the principles laid down in ancient Indian law books. Manu, for example, declares that under no circumstances whatever could a Brahman be executed for any crime, whereas a Sudra who even mentions the names and castes of the twice-born with contumely is to have an iron nail, ten fingers long, thrust red-hot into his mouth. Or again, 'with whatever limb a man of the lower caste injures a man of the three higher castes, even that limb should be cut off . . .' These forms of discrimination came to an end under British rule and not even the most orthodox Hindu today would wish to reintroduce them.

The second great evil of the caste system is untouchability, which in the extreme form which it assumed in the south was graphically described by James Forbes a century ago – 'The Pooleahs are not permitted to breathe the same air with the other castes nor to travel on the public road; if by accident they should be there and perceive a Brahman or Nair at a distance, they must instantly make a loud howling, to warn him from approaching until they have retired or climbed up the nearest tree. . . . Yet debased and oppressed as the Pooleahs are, there exists a caste, called Pariars, still more abject and wretched. If a Pooleah by an accident touches a Pariar, he must perform a variety of ceremonies and go through many ablutions before he can be cleansed from the impurity.'

Much has been done by enlightened Hindus since then to alleviate the disabilities of these outcastes, but in South India untouchability is still a grave social evil, which shows no signs of early disappearance. Even in North India it involves serious handicaps and Mahatma Gandhi's great efforts to break them down were often resisted by reactionary Hindus. The attempts of the various governments to secure the admission of untouchables to schools or temples have never proved more than partially successful and progressive Indians have found themselves baffled by the intransigence of their more conservative fellows in dealing with an evil which did not exist in Vedic times and which must be regarded as an excrescence on the caste system.

c

Brief attention must now be given to certain darker aspects of Hinduism. The conception of the gods as 'the Bright Ones', which the Aryans brought into India, was in complete contrast to the fear-haunted animism of the Dravidians and the aborigines, whose deities were frequently malevolent and blood-hungry. Although Hinduism in due course spread all over India, in the south it was often little more than a veneer. There, as stated in the *Imperial Gazetteer*, 'the great temples are of course dedicated to Aryan gods, but the people seldom visit them except on festival days. The religion of their daily life is that of their forefathers, namely, worship of local deities and of patron gods and goddesses, with propitiation of demons; praying to the former for temporal blessings and averting the anger of the latter by sacrifices.'

These primitive customs and superstitions vary so much from place to place as to make any general description of them impossible. They can perhaps be illustrated by the description of buffalo sacrifices in the south, written by that very competent observer O'Malley – 'Buffaloes are favourite victims in the Telugu-speaking districts in the north of Madras and are less frequently slain in the Tamil-speaking districts in the south. One curious part of the sacrifice is that, after the animal has been decapitated, its right foreleg is cut off and placed crosswise in its mouth. The places of sacrifice often become like shambles owing to hecatombs of animals. Festivals may last some days or a week or even a month, during the course of which scores of buffaloes and enormous numbers of sheep, goats and fowls may be slain.

'Blood may be offered to the godlings to drink; it may be smeared on the foreheads and breasts of the worshippers, on their houses and on their cattle; it may be sprinkled along the village boundaries and on the boundary stones. Blood is mixed with balls of rice which are thrown into the air for the spirits or demons to eat, and blood-soaked rice is strewn on the fields, houses and roads.'

The Brahmans of South India have done their best to have these revolting rites and the disgusting ceremonies that accompany them replaced by forms of worship more in keeping with the original spirit of Hinduism, but in many areas the primitive element has proved too strong. Even where blood sacrifices have disappeared, fear is still the keynote and the religion of the masses consists largely in the scaring away of evil spirits, the placating of petty godlings and the curious practice of devil dodging. Here again, general description is almost impossible and the nature of these superstitions can only be illustrated by reference to local, particular customs. In the south, for example, many villages still have their own guardian godlings, for whose use wooden or clay horses or elephants are provided. These guardians are regularly worshipped, in the hope that they will keep away all enemies, including the outside goddesses who bring smallpox and other diseases. In some areas the emphasis is on the widespread cult of mother-goddesses who were accorded a high place in the Brahmanical teaching, but who are regarded by the masses as spirits possessing great power and craving for blood.

The modern Western reader is apt to think of these superstitions as museum pieces of great anthropological interest, and to forget that to many millions of villagers they are the most terrible realities in life. The mother who will not call her child at night for fear of the night fiend, Jilaiya, who can suck the blood of anybody whose name he hears – or the villager who will not cross a particular field because of the ghost 'without a mouth and with feet turned backwards' that lives in the banyan tree – are not exceptions, but typical of Indian village life.

Primitive superstition has, in fact, to a great extent triumphed and Hinduism has had to compromise with pre-Aryan cults and come down to a lower spiritual level in order to achieve the conquest of all India.

The once simple and joyous religion of the Vedas thus wears today a triple aspect. It has fear for the masses, pessimism for the philosopher, and for the practical-minded, educated man, personal devotion to Vishnu or Siva. It ranges from the dark superstitions of the lower classes in South India to the spiritual beauty of the Bhagavad Gita. It gives to every man, in fact, what he is fitted to receive and, since the level of spiritual perception amongst the educated classes in India is high, Hinduism has been a formative influence of great power and beauty. It is unlikely that it will be replaced by a Western religion and if it lost its hold, the way would be open for the unchecked advance of materialism and Communism.

Chapter 2

Islam and Other Religions

LTHOUGH THE population of India still includes perhaps
forty-seven million Muslims, who enjoy a fair measure of
respect and security[1], since partition Islam has ceased to
be one of the governing forces in Indian life and politics. We
need not therefore study that religion in detail, but shall con-
fine ourselves to a brief review of the part it has played in
Indian history.

The effective influence of Islam on India began, not with the
Arab incursions into Sind in the eighth century, but with the
systematic invasions from the north-west, by men mainly of
the Turkish race, from early in the eleventh century onwards.
The invaders were fierce fanatics, rejoicing above all things in
the title of *Ghazi* or infidel slayer, and anxious in the early
stages only to slay and pillage and return to the hills with their
booty. Gradually the character of the invasions changed, and
the invaders sought to carve out kingdoms for themselves in
North-west India. The process was facilitated by the traditional inability of the Hindus to combine against a common
enemy, and by the end of the twelfth century a Muslim sultanate
was established in and around Delhi. For some centuries Turks,
Mongols, Persians and Afghans continued to pour down into
India, and before long all Northern India was under Muslim
rule, though extensive areas were left under the direct control of
the old Hindu chiefs, on condition of payment of tribute to the
Sultan. The Delhi sultanates were characterised by dynastic instability and in three hundred years no fewer than thirty-three
kings, belonging to five dynasties, occupied the throne. Only
three or four of them possessed any great capacity to rule and,
on the whole, the period was one of injustice and confusion.

[1] Though there have been serious communal disturbances this year.

36

In the sixteenth century a new group of Muslim invaders, belonging to a particular class of Mongols which had freely intermarried with Turks, Persians and other Muslim races, and possessing greater administrative capacity than most of their predecessors, founded what came to be known as the Mughal Empire. The newcomers brought with them not only the ability to rule, but also a genuine love of poetry and art, which in due course was to lead to the glories of Mughal architecture. Babur, the first of the great Mughals, thought little of India and its products and in his delightful memoirs thus comments – 'Hindustan is a country of few charms. Its people have no good looks; of social intercourse, paying and receiving visits there is none; of genius and capacity none; of manners none; in handicraft and work there is no form of symmetry, method or quality; there are no good horses, no good dogs, no grapes, musk-melons or first-rate fruits, no ice or cold water, no good bread or cooked food in the bazaars, no hot baths, no colleges, no candles, torches or candlesticks.' This may have been a jaundiced view, but it represented the general attitude of the Mughals towards the Hindus, whom they clearly regarded as an inferior people. If this attitude had persisted uniformly, it is doubtful if the Empire could have flourished, but in the middle of the sixteenth century there came to the throne a man of great genius and remarkable breadth of view.

The Emperor Akbar, a contemporary of Queen Elizabeth, set himself in every possible way to win the confidence of his Hindu subjects and gave outward demonstration of that determination by his abolition of the poll tax on non-Muslims, as well as by matrimonial alliances with the leading Hindu princes of Rajputana. At the same time he completely overhauled the administrative machinery of the State and established a just, though firm, rule over all North and much of South India. At the close of his reign, India was more closely consolidated than at any previous time. Unfortunately, Akbar's liberalism, together with some of the religious extravagances into which it led him, were extremely unpopular with the orthodox Muslim divines of India, and after his death they set themselves to secure a reversal of his policy. The Hindus were again oppressed, administration rapidly declined, provincial governments began to assert themselves and in spite of the outward glory and architectural magnificence of the reign of Shah Jahan, the foundations of the Empire were partiallly undermined before the Emperor Aurangzib came to the throne in the year A.D. 1658. Aurangzib was a narrow-minded Puritan, who treated his Hindu subjects with contempt at the very time when the great military confederacy of the Marathas was able to give active expression to Hindu resentment. The result of this policy, and of the unwise expansion of the bounds of empire, was disastrous, and within fifty years of the death of Aurangzib the once mighty, well-administered Mughal Empire had been reduced to a scene of chaos, where every powerful adventurer sought to carve out a kingdom for himself.

The treatment received by the Hindus during the seven hundred years of Muslim rule naturally varied, from time to time and place to place, with the character of the ruler. Kings whose temperament and position led them to be harsh were able to quote the strict theory of one school of Islamic thought, that a non-believer must be offered the choice of conversion or death; others preferred to accept payment of a poll tax; and at other times Hindus held high civil or military rank and enjoyed vast estates and great respect under Muslim rulers. Nevertheless, the balanced view would seem to be that during much of the Muslim period the Hindus suffered a good deal of oppression. The inducement to accept Islam must, therefore, have been considerable, and by the time the British began to rule, the three processes of conversion, immigration and mixed marriage had resulted in the existence of a very considerable Muslim population. The age-long cultural unity of India had thus been impaired, and it is important, therefore, to see how widely the outlook of Hindus and Muslims diverged.

This issue has at times been confused by writers who have emphasised either the influence of one particular school of Islamic philosophy, known as Sufism, on Indian mysticism, or the co-operation of Hindus and Muslims in the Mughal and later schools of art, or the partial adoption by wealthy Hindus in some areas of Muslim manners and dress. This emphasis is misleading and to form a true judgment we must forget the wholly exceptional man, whether mystic or artist, and think in terms either of the ordinary educated person or of the masses. The difference in outlook between the communities is fundamental and goes right down to such matters as the nature of the deity and the manner of worshipping. It has thus been described by the writer in *The British in India* – 'The Muslim believes in a Creator completely separated from his creation and in the survival of the individual after death. His attitude towards life is essentially positive and individualistic and it follows that both he and his creator must have a separate and permanent existence. Mohammed is indeed the Prophet of God, but he is not God – the gulf between the Deity and his creatures is unmistakable. Muslim worship is simple, indeed austere, and neither idols nor pictures are allowed. Until recent times, indeed, the use of photographs or pictures, even outside the religious sphere, was regarded as blasphemy against the Creator. There is much in Islam akin to the stern, austere and unyielding spirit of seventeenth-century Puritanism, and both religions alike are characterised by a democratic equality, based on an unyielding belief in the importance of the individual.

'Hinduism, on the other hand, is infinitely complicated, luxuriant in its forms and ideas and abounding in symbols. The creator and his creations are one and indivisible, as we have seen in an earlier chapter; there is no limit to the possible manifestations of the all-pervading spirit and a new god may therefore turn up at any time or place. The individual matters little, for he, after all, is but one link in an endless chain beginning and ending in a somewhat nebulous merging with the all-pervading spirit. As for equality, it is a concept necessarily foreign to Hinduism, with its highly stratified society. It is important to emphasise the fundamental difference between the psychological foundations of the two religions – Islam, clear-cut, individualistic, democratic, simple; Hinduism, abstruse, caring little for the individual, essentially undemocratic and extremely complicated.'

These contrasts in basic thought and belief were emphasised by the fact that Hindus and Muslims were forbidden by their religion to intermarry or even to eat together; that their customs at birth, marriage and death, and in respect of inheritance were widely different; and that even their names set them apart, inasmuch as Akbar Khan could never be mistaken for a Hindu, or Mukherjee for a Muslim. Tradition and literature divided them still further, since the Hindus looked to Sanskrit, and the Muslims to Arabic or Persian for their inspiration, and each in fact learned secretly to despise the other community. To the Muslims, the Hindus were idolators, while the Hindus, for their part, regarded with horror the Muslim practice of killing and eating the sacred cow.

The gulf between the communities was thus profound, and perhaps the most enduring effect on India of seven centuries of Muslim domination was the division of the stream of Indian life and culture into two independent channels, which were never again to become one.

Four other religions call for comment. The Sikhs, who number about six million, broke away from Hinduism early in the sixteenth century under the leadership of Guru Nanak, who had been profoundly influenced alike by the Sufi Muslim mystics and by the Vaishnavite revivalists amongst the Hindus. They were characterised by strict monotheism, disapproval of the caste system and a sternly puritanical approach to life and duty. The diatribes of Guru Nanak against the times are somewhat reminiscent of the thundering of the Old Testament prophets against sin and the enemies of Israel.

'The age,' declaimed Guru Nanak, 'is a knife. Kings are butchers. They dispense justice when their palms are filled . . . wealth and beauty which afforded men pleasure have now become their bane. . . . Decency and laws have vanished; falsehood stalks abroad. . . . The vocation of priest is gone and the devil reads the marriage vows. . . . Then came Babur to Hindustan. Death, disguised as a Mughal, made war on us. There was slaughter and lamentation. Did not thou, O Lord, feel the pain?'

The reference to the Mughals, who had just invaded India, was prophetic of the profound antagonism which was to grow up between the Sikhs and the Muslims.

The new community was closely knit, under the leadership of the ten successive Gurus, or Teachers, and the fifth Guru, Arjun, took effective steps towards organising the Sikhs, including the completion of the Adi Granth, or holy scripture.

According to Kushwant Singh, Arjun's last message to his son was 'Let him sit fully armed on his throne and maintain an army to the best of his ability.' Arjun himself was tortured and executed by the Mughal rulers in Lahore. By the time of his son's death, the Sikhs had become a formidable fighting force with a deep hatred of Islam. The tenth and last Guru, Govind Singh, whose father had been executed by the Emperor Aurangzib on account of his refusal to accept conversion to Islam, was a great and militant leader who instilled into the Sikhs a still more aggressive spirit. He preached vehemently against caste, made his followers of high and low caste by origin drink out of the same bowl, imposed on them certain uniform habits of dress and enjoined on them four rules of conduct, namely – 'not to cut the hair; to abstain from smoking tobacco and from alcoholic drink; not to eat kosher meat; and to refrain from carnal intercourse with Muslims'. The new fraternity was known as the Khalsa, or pure, and the Guru promised them that

> 'The Khalsa shall rule
> Their enemies will be scattered
> Only they that seek refuge shall be saved'.

The Sikh religion is of particular interest in that although, as Kushwant Singh puts it, in its general system of belief it is closer to Islam than to Hinduism, in practice, in ritual and above all in social affinities it never quite succeeded in freeing itself from Hindu influence. In spite of its theoretical condemnation of caste, Sikhs converted from Hinduism tended to retain their original caste distinctions and in many villages 'Sikhs of high caste refused to eat with Untouchable Sikhs and separate wells were provided for them'.

In other respects, too, such as the prohibition of the slaughtering of cows, the use of caste marks, the ceremonies at funerals and marriages and even in the employment in their temples of Hindu priests – since there are no Sikh priests – Sikhism bears all the marks of its Hindu origin. On the other hand, the Sikh teaching is strongly against the worship of idols, and rejects the Hindu theory of *avatars* or incarnations of God in human form.

The monotheism of the Sikhs is wholly distinct from the Upanishadic conception of immanent deity. Their idea of God is much akin to that of the Muslims and leads them to condemn the payment of divine honours to the Gurus or any other human being. Thus the tenth Guru wrote:

For though my thoughts were lost in prayer
At the feet of Almighty God,
I was ordained to establish a sect and lay down its rules.
But whosoever regards me as Lord
Shall be damned and destroyed.
I am – and of this let there be no doubt –
I am but the slave of God, as other men are,
A beholder of the wonders of creation.

God has no friends nor enemies.
He needs no hallelujahs nor cares about curses.
Being the first and timeless
How could He manifest Himself through those
Who are born and die?

An important outward characteristic of Sikhism is the fact that the Granth Sahib, or holy scripture, is the main object of Sikh reverence. 'It is opened with prayer and ceremonial each morning and similarly closed in the evening. Worshippers appear before it barefooted and with their head covered. They make obeisance by rubbing their forehead to the ground before it. Offerings of money or food are placed on the cloth draping the book.'

In the course of four hundred years the Sikhs have become a proud, aggressive, self-conscious people, aware of the value of their own way of life and determined to protect it with their lifes against all enemies. They were perhaps at their zenith when this martial spirit was able to express itself in the great kingdom built up by Ranjit Singh in the Punjab early in the nineteenth century. Under British rule they were often rest-less and, as we shall see in a later chapter, the bitter antagonism between the Sikhs and the Muslims led to a terrible tragedy after the transfer of power.

Although the Christians in India are as numerous as the

Sikhs, they call only for a brief mention here. The social work done by Christian missionaries in India has earned the admiration of all thoughtful observers, but the great majority of their converts have been amongst the lower classes and the despised outcasts. A small number of Christians occupy high positions in political or official life, but the Christian church in India cannot be described as one of the forces moulding Indian life and policy and it need not therefore be discussed in this book.

It is not possible in a few words to describe the religion of the Jains, who broke away from the main Hindu fold at about the same time as the Buddhists, or to explain the somewhat subtle metaphysical differences between their beliefs and those of the Hindus. It must suffice to say that they number about one and a half millions, that they live chiefly in the west of India, that they go far beyond the average Hindu in their veneration for the sanctity of even the lowest forms of life, and that their main importance arises from the fact that they include within their number the great commercial and financial community known as the *marwaris*.

The Parsees came to India from Persia over twelve hundred years ago in search of religious freedom and when the Hindu ruler of the locality north of Bombay, where they first settled, questioned them about their religion, he received the following reply:

'O Prince of excellent fortune!
We are the poor descendents of Jemshid;
We reverence fire and water,
Also the cow, the sun and the moon.
Whatever God has created in the world
We bow to it.'

Although their philosophy, beliefs and practices are widely different from those of the Hindus, they have identified themselves remarkably with Indian life. They include in their community many of the most enterprising business men of India and they have a high reputation for integrity and for being good Indian citizens. Their numbers do not much exceed one hundred thousand, and as their religion exercises no direct influence on Indian thought, a digression to discuss it here would not be justified.

There are still in India many millions of primitive peoples, dwelling generally in the hills and forests, whose religion is classified in official documents as animism. Their customs and beliefs vary greatly from tribe or place to place and cannot be summarily described. Hinduism and Christianity have made a great deal of headway amongst them in recent years, and their way of life is probably doomed. They still provide the Government with many social and economic problems, but they have little share in shaping India's destiny to-day.

Chapter 3

The Rise of British Power in India

I N SPITE OF the aloofness with which the British rulers of
India have often been charged, the most important outcome of their rule was that unique fusion of Western and
Eastern thought and practice which constitutes modern India.
In order to understand the nature and extent of the British
element in that amalgam, we must first consider briefly how it
came into being.

During the early Middle Ages there was practically no direct
contact between Europe and India, since the trade in spices,
precious stones, silks and ivory was in the hands of the Semitic
races who lived along the three main trade routes through the
Middle East. The volume of that trade was considerable and it
contributed a great deal not only to the wealth of Venice and
the other cities engaged in it, but to the whole economy of
Europe. When the advance of the Turks in the fourteenth and
fifteenth centuries blocked all three trade routes, the loss was
severe and it was to be expected that Europe would search
diligently for alternative ways of access to the wealth of
India.

The lead in that search was taken by Portugal, where the
nascent European spirit of exploration and adventure was
abundantly manifest in Prince Henry the Navigator, who set
himself systematically, over a long period of years, to explore
the ocean routes down the west coast of Africa. Portuguese
enterprise received a further stimulus from the fact that the
Pope, as the accepted authority on international affairs, assigned
to Portugal all lands then known, or thereafter to be discovered,
in the East. In 1498 Vasco da Gama landed at Calicut on the
Malabar coast, and the King of Portugal assumed the magnificent title of 'Lord of the Conquest, Navigation and Commerce
of Ethiopia, Arabia, Persia and India'. In the second half of

45

the sixteenth century the Reformation gave the commercially-minded Protestant nations of Western Europe a good reason for defying the Papal allocation of the Eastern lands and left them free to compete with Portugal for the profitable, though hazardous, Indian trade. The Dutch were the first in the field, followed quickly by the English and, on a smaller scale, the Danes. The French had indeed made isolated voyages to India long before the first English ship arrived there, but it was not until the middle of the seventeenth century that the foundations of French trade were laid by Colbert.

The four great European competitors for the Indian trade differed from one another greatly in their approach and backing. Portuguese Eastern ventures were financed by the Crown, often in the face of opposition from business men and the public, and were as much concerned with the propagation of the Faith as with trade. The Portuguese displayed an aggressive and intolerant spirit, which combined with their European complications to bring about their decline in the East. The earliest Dutch ventures to the East were due to private initiative, but the government soon stepped in and the resulting consortium of State and business interests pursued a narrow policy of attempting to exclude all other nations from the Eastern trade. This was not practicable and compelled them to maintain large and expensive overseas garrisons. For reasons outside the scope of this book, the Dutch soon turned their main attention to the Far East and in the eighteenth century they ceased to be serious rivals to the English in India.

The French East India Company owed its origin mainly to Louis XIV and his Minister Colbert, and had little backing from either the aristocracy or the French business world. Even when it was reorganised in the eighteenth century, it was little more than a second-rate Department of State, in constant receipt of loans and subsidies from the French Treasury.

The East India Company, which came into being in A.D. 1600, was wholly different in character. It was an association of business men accurately described as 'The Governor and Company of Merchants of London trading into the East Indies'. It had of necessity to be chartered by the Crown, which gave it a monopoly of the Eastern trade, but the State took no other part in its formation and it owed its existence to one hundred and one 'ironmongers, clothiers, and other substantial people of that kind', headed by the Lord Mayor, who between them subscribed £30,000 and began to equip fleets. In the first phase, each adventure to the East was separately subscribed for and the profits were divided amongst the shareholders in proportion to their subscriptions, but after a few years it went on to a permanent joint stock basis. During the next one hundred and seventy years, the company was frequently mulcted by the Crown, but otherwise it remained a body of business men with whose affairs the Home Government seldom sought to interfere.

When Europeans first established trading centres, known as 'factories',[1] in India, the power of the Mughal Emperors was at its zenith The English were quicker than their rivals to understand this and regarded themselves simply as foreign traders, dependent on the goodwill of the Emperor. Kaye, the historian of the East India Company, tells us that the London merchants, above all things, hated an increase of 'dead stock'. 'The multiplication of factories was odious to them; and the fort was an abomination. They looked only for a brisk trade and a good dividend.' This pacific and wholly commercial attitude was well suited to Indian conditions in the seventeenth century, but ceased to be maintainable when the Mughal Empire broke down into chaos in the following century. For a time it looked as though the Marathas might become the ruling power, but their own dissensions and their catastrophic defeat by Ahmed Shah in 1761 destroyed this possibility. Thenceforth, the country rapidly dissolved into anarchy, with Muslim nobles and other adventurers carving out kingdoms for themselves wherever they could. The friendship of the Mughal Emperor was now of little value and the English and French East India Companies, far in advance of the country powers in military science and the use of artillery, began to be conscious of their own strength. Recurring wars between England and France stimulated local rivalries in India, and the English and French Companies took sides in local domestic wars in South India. Half a century of continuous struggle led to the complete triumph of the East India Company, and by the last quarter of the eighteenth century France had ceased to count in Indian

[1] i.e. warehouses or buying depots.

politics. The South Indian struggle had not, however, taken the English far on the road to empire, nor was that the aim of the very commercially minded directors of the East India Company. The company's territorial jurisdiction in South India at that time covered only a small area round Madras, granted to it by the Nawab of the Carnatic, together with the Northern Circars[1] which the company held on payment of tribute. The directors forbade their servants – who were in an aggressive mood – to seek any expansion of this territory and stated emphatically that it was not for the company to take the part of umpires of Hindustan.

Developments in the north soon made these pacific sentiments meaningless. The company had established important factories at Kasimbasar, Patna, Dacca and elsewhere, besides their headquarters settlement in Calcutta, and they were in fact very much at the mercy of the Nawab of Bengal. The refusal of local officials to implement fiscal arrangements made between the Mughal Emperor and the company, together with oppression by the Nawab and the general state of chaos in Bengal, created a difficult situation for the company's servants. It is, however, doubtful if the directors would have countenanced any large-scale aggressive action if Nawab Siraj-ud-daula had not himself seized Kasimbazar and attacked and captured Calcutta. Thereafter, events moved rapidly, and the battles of Plassey in 1757 and Buxar in 1764 made the English masters of Bengal, though the company did not fully take over administration until it 'stood forth as Dewan[2] in 1772'.

The tortuous and sometimes dishonest policy of the company in its dealings with the Nawab; the shameful exploitation of Bengal by the company's servants during a decade or so; and the not very creditable proceedings of Warren Hastings with regard to Benares and Oudh, are well known. Hastings's greatest achievements were the establishment of the company as the strongest power in India, though its territory was still very limited, and the considerable reforms which he effected in the company's administration.

Parliament now began to take its responsibilities to India seriously and the British Government assumed consider-

[1] Circars – districts along the Bay of Bengal between Orissa and Madras.
[2] The Dewan was the head of the Provincial Revenue Administration.

able powers of control over the company's political and administrative activities. The appointment of Cornwallis as Governor-General in 1786 ushered in an era of integrity in the administration of India, and although the doctrine of trusteeship was not at that time explicitly stated, its principles began to animate the most important of the British rulers of India.

While the East India Company was in supreme charge of Indian affairs, it could fairly be said that the directors always put a brake on territorial expansion, though the men on the spot might sometimes hanker after extended power or feel that it was necessary. Now that the Home Government was in effective charge, no such uniform tendency was observed. There were times when non-involvement was the official policy, and there were times, as for example during the Wellesley régime, when imperialism was rampant, and the addition of fresh territories to the company's jurisdiction was considered good in itself. It is interesting to note that even Cornwallis, pacific by nature, and under particular orders to avoid wars and entanglements, was ultimately forced to annex a considerable portion of Tipu Sultan's territory and to inaugurate the second phase of British expansion in India. There was indeed a vacuum in the Indian political system and it was inevitable that the British should fill it. The pace of advance might vary from time to time, but the restraining influence formerly exercised by the directors of the East India Company no longer operated, and the jurisdiction of the British Government in India was continually enlarged. The process reached its logical conclusion in the time of Dalhousie, who frankly regarded any extension of British rule as desirable in itself. India then assumed the political pattern which was, in the main, to endure until the final transfer of power. About two-thirds of the country was included in provinces directly ruled by the British, while the remaining third consisted of native States in which the princes continued to rule, subject to the exercise of paramountcy by the Viceroy and to the various treaties between the States and the British Crown. On the whole there was little interference with the internal affairs of the States, and it is perhaps a fair criticism of British paramountcy that it maintained intact, for nearly a century, a system of autocratic rule

D

which was gradually becoming more and more of an anachronism. In matters of great importance, however, the power of intervention by the Crown was always there and it is true to say that, after the brief interruption of the mutiny in some areas, the British Government was the supreme ruler of all India.

Chapter 4

The Impact of the British (1)
Law and Administration

HE FOUR HUNDRED years of the Roman occupation of
Britain left so little permanent effect that a modern historian was able to assert that 'from the Romans who
once ruled Britain, we Britons have inherited practically
nothing'. British rule over most of India lasted not for four
hundred, but for less than one hundred and fifty years. It
nevertheless seems improbable that an Indian historian,
fifteen hundred years from now, will brush aside the British
period as having left no mark on India. He is perhaps more
likely to say that the advanced civilisation of India before the
advent of the Western traders, together with the high degree
of centralised, governmental efficiency made possible under
British rule by modern communications, and the conscious
direction of British policy in India towards self-government,
made it certain that British rule would have an enduring effect
on every aspect of Indian life. Unlike Rome, Britain left the
dependent territories of set purpose, because her mission was
fulfilled, and in doing so ensured a continuity of policy and
administration.

It is perhaps in the sphere of law and administration that the
influence of Britain on India has been most spectacular. There
has, indeed, been a tendency to give undue credit to Britain
for the restoration of law and order – a task which must be
regarded by any stable government as elementary – and to over-
look certain by-products of that process which distinguished
British rule from earlier governmental systems in India.
Amongst those by-products was the new concept conveniently
described as the rule of law. This doctrine, which binds the
Government as much as the subject to justify its actions in the

Courts, was a typically British contribution to the Indian
polity, and was in fact a complete negation of the absolutism
which characterised all earlier periods of Indian history. It is
true that in Hindu and Muslim India the people had customary rights, and the ruler was under certain traditional
obligations and limitations. There was, however, no forum in
which the subject could plead his rights against the ruler and
he had no means of enforcing them except by rebellion. For a
short period the East India Company tried to place itself similarly above the law, by claiming that its acts and those of its
officers should be outside the jurisdiction of the Supreme
Court. Fortunately, the Home Government and the British
Parliament would have none of this doctrine of *droit adminis-
tratif*, and before the end of the eighteenth century 'the rule of
law' was firmly established in India. Educated Indians soon
came to regard it as the sheet anchor of their liberties, and as
the present writer has stated elsewhere – 'This principle of the
"rule of law" entered so deeply into the minds and hearts of
educated Indians that the occasional departures from it, under
public security regulations in times of emergency, provoked
quite genuine outbursts of indignation and horror. Indians,
whose ancestors would have accepted arbitrary execution by
earlier despots as part of the natural order of things, denounced
internment and externment orders against terrorists in the
twentieth century as gross tyranny and thus paid unconscious
tribute to the success of the British in introducing a new concept of human rights.'

The rule of law, together with the liberal tendency of British
thought in the nineteenth century, led to the enjoyment by
Indians of a remarkable degree of personal liberty. Even in
the heyday of British bureaucracy, freedom of speech to abuse
the Government or to ventilate a grievance was limited only by
the obligation to avoid incitement to violence. The scope of
this freedom is most easily understood by a study of the proceedings of the Indian National Congress and may well be
illustrated by the following extracts from a speech of Lala
Murlidhar in the 1891 session of that body – 'You, you, it seems
are content to join with these accursed monsters in fattening on
the heart's blood of your brethren.' (Cries of No. No.) 'I say
"Yes": look round: what are all these chandeliers and lamps

and European-made chairs and tables, and smart clothes and hats, and English coats and bonnets and frocks, and silver-mounted canes, and all the luxurious fittings of your houses, but trophies of India's misery, mementoes of India's starvation! Every rupee you have spent on Europe-made articles is a rupee of which you have robbed your poorer brethren, honest handicraftsmen who can now no longer earn a living. Of course, I know that it was pure philanthropy which flooded India with English-made goods, and surely, if slowly, killed our every indigenous industry – pure philanthropy which, to facilitate this, repealed the import duties and flung away three crores a year of revenue which the rich paid, and to balance this wicked sacrifice raised the Salt Tax, which the poor pay; which is now pressing factory regulations on us to kill, if possible, the one tiny new industrial departure India could boast of. Oh, yes, it is all philanthropy, but the result is that from this cause, amongst others, your brethren are starving. Free trade, fair play between nations, how I hate the sham! What fair play in trade can there be between impoverished India and the bloated, capitalist England? As well talk of a fair fight between an infant and a strong man – a rabbit and a boa-constrictor. No doubt it is all in accordance with high economic science, but, my friends, remembers this – this, too, is starving your brethren.'

The speech is of no particular interest, except for the fact that it was made, with impunity, by a member of what was then a subject race, against powerful rulers who deliberately gave him the freedom to make it and who had indeed encouraged the formation of the Indian National Congress as a platform where such complaints could be voiced.

A second concept introduced by the new rulers of India was that of equality before the law. This idea was wholly at variance with Hindu thought and the insistence of the British Courts on dealing equally with a Brahman and an outcaste was at first greatly resented by Hindus. As we have seen, Manu, the greatest of the early Indian law-givers, had based his system of criminal law largely on the prescription of punishments which varied according to the caste of the offender. Even in civil law, caste played its part and in regard to the maximum rates of interest which might be charged to a borrower, it was

laid down that 'the higher the caste the less the rate'. The con-
tradiction between the Hindu and British idea was thus complete, but gradually the new concept gained acceptance and
not even the most die-hard, orthodox Hindu today would
plead for a return to the old inequality before the law.

As soon as Britain began to take her responsibility for India
seriously, it was obvious that the East India Company must
rebuild the administrative and judicial machine. The fairly
efficient organisation of the early Mughal Emperors had long
since broken down; the *zemindars*[1] seldom carried out their
obligations to maintain law and order; and the village watch-
men were, as often as not, in league with the chief local crimi-
nals. In the last decade of the eighteenth century Cornwallis
set himself to purify and reorganise the administration, and
filled all key posts with men from Britain. A little later Wellesley took in hand the training of young Civil Servants, and in
1806 the East India Company founded the Haileybury College
'to provide a supply of persons duly qualified to discharge the
various and important duties required for the Civil Service of
the company'. Gradually the Indian Civil Service took shape
and acquired those traditions of integrity and intellectual
attainment which even its enemies acknowledged. In the
second half of the century other more specialised services were
established and the Public Works Department, the Indian
Police, the Indian Forest Service and the Indian Medical
Service undertook the process of converting India into a
modern State.

This process of modernisation was well described by the
Viceroy, Lord Northbrook, on the occasion of the visit of the
Prince of Wales to India – 'There is one thing above all others,'
said the Viceroy, 'that this British Empire in India does mean.
It means this. It means that all its subjects shall live at peace
with one another; that every one of them shall be free to grow
rich in his own way, provided his way be not a criminal way;
that every one of them shall be free to hold and follow his own
religious belief without assailing the religious beliefs of other
people, and to live unmolested by his neighbour. At first sight,
that may seem a very plain and simple policy, and very easy to

---

[1] Literally, landholders – but better interpreted as those responsible for
the payment of the revenue to the Emperor.

be applied. But when you come to apply it to an empire multitudinous in its traditions, as well as in its inhabitants, almost infinite in the variety of races which populate it and of creeds which have shaped their character, you find that it involves administrative problems unsolved by Caesar, unsolved by Charlemagne, unsolved by Akbar. It seems a very simple thing to say that we shall keep the peace of the empire; but if we are to keep the peace of it, we must have laws to settle quarrels which would otherwise disturb its peace; and if we are to have such laws, we must frame them into a system at once comprehensive and intelligible. Again, if we are to enforce any such system of law, we must have judges to administer it, and police to carry out the orders of the judges, and then we must have troops to protect the judges, the police, the people and all concerned. Well then, when you come to introduce this elaborate system of administration into a vast continent . . . you find that the work in which you are engaged is nothing less than this, that you are modifying, unavoidably modifying – not harshly, not suddenly, but slowly, gently and with sympathy, but still modifying – the whole collective social life and character of the population of the Empire.'

As Indian political consciousness grew, the almost exclusively British character of the Imperial Services and their customary aloofness from educated Indians led to bitter criticism. The directors of the East India Company had anticipated this complaint, and in their dispatch forwarding the Charter Act of 1833, thus expressed themselves – 'Opportunities of official advancement can little benefit the bulk of the people under any Government . . . it is not by holding out incentives to official ambition but by repressing crime, by securing and guarding property, by creating confidence, by ensuring to industry the fruit of its labour, by protecting men in the undisturbed enjoyment of their rights and in the unfettered exercise of their faculties, that Governments best minister to the public wealth and happiness. In effect, the free access to office is chiefly valuable when it is part of general freedom'.

This explanation may be regarded as too facile, in as much as it overlooks the depressing effect on the national character of the exclusion of the best men in a country from any important share in the administration. Nevertheless, it must be remembered that Britain had set herself to rehabilitate India and to introduce Western standards of administration. It is doubtful if that result could have been achieved, except through services which, in the higher ranks, remained exclusively British until the new ideas had permeated educated Indian society. When that stage was reached, Indians were admitted at a rate sufficiently slow to ensure that they would be moulded in the right tradition. The slowness of this development must have been galling to educated Indians, but perhaps it may be considered justified by the high standard of the Indian administrative services today. The senior members of those services are proud of their Indian Civil Service origin and carry out their duties with an efficiency and an integrity which Whitehall could scarcely excel.

Chapter 5

The Impact of the British
(2) Education

IN THE EIGHTEENTH century India was intellectually stagnant. She had not been touched by the new scientific spirit
which was so rapidly transforming the West, while in those
realms of philosophy and mathematics where she was once
pre-eminent the virtue seemed to have gone out of her. Her
ablest philosophers had become content to be mere commenta-
tors; her people knew nothing of their own history; and even
Sanskrit learning was at such a low ebb that in Calcutta there
were comparatively few Brahmans who understood the sacred
texts. The tradition of learning lingered only in the village *tols*,
where the *guru* or preceptor would gather round him a group
of resident disciples and instruct them in Sanskrit studies.
Many of these *gurus* were true scholars by nature, but they
knew nothing of geography, world history, or science. Their
outlook was necessarily narrow and their curriculum limited.

D. S. Sarma, in his account of the Renaissance of Hinduism,
rightly states that for a hundred years from the middle of the
eighteenth century nothing of first rate importance was produced in any Indian language. In 1811 Lord Minto wrote of
the intellectual backwardness of the time and feared that 'the
revival of letters may shortly become hopeless from a want of
books or of people capable of explaining them'. Except for the
hill schools of painting, the arts were in a similar state of
decline and lacked both patronage and appreciation.

Several new factors now combined to produce an awakening.
In the first place a small band of British scholars began to
devote themselves to research in Indian history and philology,
with spectacular results. Sir William Jones, by his identification of the Emperor Chandragupta with the Sandrokottus of

57

the Greek historians, established the first fixed point in Indian chronology. A generation later, James Prinsep, Mint Master of Calcutta, after seven years of patient examination of bilingual inscriptions on coins collected for him in Afghanistan by his friend, Henry Masser, found the key to the Brahmi script. At long last the Asoka pillar inscriptions could be deciphered and a vast treasure house of Buddhist literature was opened to the world. These and other great discoveries by European scholars were bound in due course to stimulate Indian scholarship, but education had first to be revivified in India. Very early in his term of office, Warren Hastings set himself to promote an intellectual revival amongst both Muslims and Hindus. He founded a Mohammedan College in Calcutta for the teaching of Islamic subjects, and he lent his full support to that great Orientalist, Sir William Jones, in the establishment of the Bengal Asiatic Society, which was to prove a true home of Sanskrit learning. Jonathan Duncan, who founded the Hindu College at Benares, was but one of many officials who joined this new movement.

At this stage a second factor began to operate. William Carey, a Baptist missionary, settled at Serampore, in Danish territory, with a small band of helpers and established schools for Indian boys. Carey was a natural linguist and the Serampore missionaries soon began to issue translations of the Bible in several Indian languages, and to write pamphlets in a vigorous style of Bengali which had no little influence on the development of that language and literature. The Company's servants were, on the whole, distrustful of these missionaries, who would, they thought, disturb the people, but Carey won the respect of Wellesley and, indeed, became lecturer in Bengali in Wellesley's new college for the Company's servants. The violent and unrestrained attacks of the Serampore missionaries on the beliefs of the Hindus created great resentment and led to a temporary ban on missionary propaganda in Calcutta, but the missionary publications nevertheless did a great deal to stimulate thought and contributed to the renaissance which was at hand. In Madras, too, the missionaries were as active as in Bengal, although there were amongst them no names as outstanding as those of Carey and Marshman of Serampore.

At this stage help came from a third quarter. David Hare, a

watchmaker who settled in Calcutta in 1800, was a rationalist, endowed with all the devotion of a missionary. His work is best described by the epitaph on his tombstone in Calcutta – 'He adopted for his own the country of his sojourn and cheerfully devoted the remainder of his life with unwearying zeal and benevolence to one pervading and darling object, in which he spared no personal trouble, money or influence, viz., the education and moral improvement of the natives of Bengal'. He soon came to the conclusion that the narrow round of Sanskritic studies was insufficient and that Bengalis must be taught Western literature and science. He pursued this aim steadily until, some years later, a Hindu college was established for this purpose.

In 1813 Parliament directed that one lakh[1] of rupees should be spent annually by the East India Company on the improvement of education in India, and a Committee of Public Instruction was set up to administer the grant. The sum may seem paltry, but it must be remembered that at that time, even in England, education was not the responsibility of the State. Plans for a Sanskrit college in Calcutta were almost complete when Raja Rammohan Roy, the outstanding Bengali scholar and thinker of his time, protested in the most vigorous terms that the grant should have been spent on the teaching of Western science. 'We were filled with sanguine hopes,' he wrote, 'that this sum would be laid out in employing European gentlemen of talents and education to instruct the natives of India in mathematics, natural philosophy, chemistry, anatomy and other useful sciences. . . . We now find that the Government are establishing a Sanskrit school under Hindu pandits to impart such knowledge as is already current in India. . . . The Sanskrit language, so difficult that almost a lifetime is necessary for its perfect acquisition, is well known to have been for ages a lamentable check on the diffusion of knowledge; and the learning concealed under this almost impervious veil is far from sufficient to reward the labour of acquiring it.' Rammohan Roy was not the only Bengali who thought on these lines. A number of well-to-do Indians had learned English and many more were clamouring for the opportunity to do so. 'Upwards of 31,000 English books were sold by the School

[1] One lakh = 100,000.

Book Society in the course of two years, while the Committee did not dispose of enough Arabic and Sanskrit volumes in three years to pay the expense of keeping them for two months.'

The Committee of Public Instruction was sharply divided on this new issue. One party favoured 'letting the natives pursue their present course of instruction and endeavouring to engraft European science thereon'. The other party would devote all the available money to education through the medium of English, in the belief that though the numbers affected would be few to begin with, the knowledge would gradually filter through the whole of society. This school became known as the Filtration School. Outside the Committee true friends of India differed keenly on this question. Elphinstone and Malcolm would have imparted Western knowledge in the vernaculars, leaving English to be studied as a classical language by those disposed to pursue it. Bentinck, on the other hand, when Governor-General, strongly supported the 'filtration' theory. Eventually Macaulay's vehement rhetoric, though based on no knowledge of Indian languages, carried the day against the Orientalists, and in 1835 it was decided that 'the great object of the British Government ought to be the promotion of English literature and science among the natives of India and that all funds appropriated to education would best be employed in English Education alone'. Macaulay's frank aim was to create a class of persons who would be 'Indian in blood and colour but English in tastes, in opinion, in morals and in intellect'. Few of us today would regard such a complete denationalisation as desirable, but there can be little doubt that the decision taken in 1835 was one of the turning points of Indian history. It opened the floodgates to European thought and literature and subjected the best brains of India, from their childhood onwards, to the powerful influence of English liberal and scientific thought.

The political results of this influence will be discussed later. Its intellectual effects were profound, and it is no exaggeration to say that India awoke after a long sleep and began to prepare for the greatest transformation in her history. Lest an Englishman writing on this matter should be suspected of exaggeration, let us turn to two Indian writers for their estimate of the change. D. S. Sarma in *The Renaissance of Hinduism* writes thus: 'Already there were new forces working silently towards a great Renaissance which came into full vigour in the early years of the present century. The most important of these forces is, of course, the spread of English education, which broke the intellectual isolation of the Indian mind and brought it into contact with Western science, literature and history. The result of this was a great mental expansion similar to that which the European nations experienced at the revival of Classical Learning in the fifteenth and sixteenth centuries. A new world of ideas revealed itself to the wondering gaze of our young students in schools and colleges. In place of the extravagant mythical geography, legendary history and pseudo-science with which they had been acquainted, came sober and correct ideas about the configuration of the earth, the rise and fall of nations and the unalterable laws of Nature.'

K. M. Panikkar in *A Survey of Indian History* describes the decision in favour of English education as the most beneficent, revolutionary decision taken by the Government of India and goes on to say that 'some idea of the importance of the decision which was forced on the British Government may be gauged by considering what the results of the alternative policy would have been. The particularisms based on vernaculars would have grown so greatly as to break up even the idea of an Indian unity. Much of the New Learning on which India's Great Recovery has been based would not have been available to us. No doubt the scientific development of the West would have reached us second-hand, but participation in the scientific work of the world would have been but a distant ideal. By going in for education in English, India joined a world community. Besides, what was the alternative? Even the most advanced Indian languages of the time, excepting Sanskrit and Persian, had not reached the level of literary standard for secondary education. Education up to university standards would have been impossible without decades of preparation, which would have required an army of men trained in English and familiar with the new learning of the West. This, after all, is what Macaulay's system has done. It has developed the Indian languages to standards in which a university education is now becoming possible. But without the universities teaching in

English and producing the army of workers, such a development would hardly have been possible. The great colleges, universities and schools of India, which have attained a position of some eminence in the world of learning, are the direct result of Macaulay's system.'

Whatever else of good or ill Britain may have achieved in India, she may justly claim to have brought about the great Indian Renaissance.

Chapter 6

The Impact of the British
(3) The Spiritual Impact

A T THE BEGINNING of the nineteenth century, the state of religion in North India was as debased as that of learning. Contemporary Indian writers record the corruption and degeneracy of the priesthood, their ignorance of the spiritual teachings of Hinduism, their obsession with disputes over points of ceremonial, their addiction to the sensual practices introduced into Hinduism some centuries earlier by the Tantrics,[1] and the prevalence of animal sacrifice. Even reforming sects such as the Vaishnavas had become infected with the general corruption, and the great mass of the people were left in utter spiritual darkness. It was perhaps fortunate that the situation was at its worst in Bengal where British influence was now becoming paramount. The impact on Bengal society – and to a lesser extent on that of Madras – of Western education and of Christianity in one of its dynamic phases was bound to be shattering. Thoughtful men compared their own customs with what they read of other countries and revolted against *sati*,[2] polygamy, child marriage and the extreme forms of untouchability. They were led to an exaggerated respect for Western institutions and an undue disparagement of their own religion.

These tendencies led young men in one of two directions, according to their temperament. Some rebelled against religion altogether, and, indeed, against all authority, while others turned to Christianity. The story of the rebels is well illustrated

[1] Tantrics – a sect addicted to magic ritual and the use of spells.

[2] *Sati* – the self-immolation of a widow on the funeral pyre of her husband.

by events in the Hindu college at Calcutta, where a Portuguese-Indian, Derozio, exercised an extraordinary influence over the students and imbued them with a fervent desire to revolution-ise society. Derozio himself, although a free thinker, never ceased to lay stress on moral values, but, according to the historian of the Brahmo Samaj, to Derozio's students 'indepen-dence mean open defiance of the authority of their elders and moral courage meant contemptuous reviling of the ancient faith, together with the undisguised profession of infidelity'. As might be expected, the effect on the behaviour and morals of this section of Bengali youths, and those infected by them, was disastrous.

Others turned to Christianity and fell particularly under the influence of Carey and the Serampore missionaries. Here, though they learned much of spiritual value, they were con-fronted with earnest narrow-mindedness and intolerance, and the missionaries might have had far more enduring success if they had been a little more restrained in their attacks on all aspects of Hinduism. As Lord Minto reported, they filled pages with 'hell fire and hell fire and still hotter fire, denounced against a whole race of men for believing in the religion which they were taught by their fathers and mothers'.

Amongst those who had close contact with the missionaries was Raja Rammohan Roy. It is not easy to delineate the charac-ter of this great Bengali. A man of versatile ability, profoundly learned in both Indian and European languages, he was above all a social and religious reformer and can justly be regarded as the outstanding Indian of his generation. He was deeply moved by the teachings of Jesus, but felt unable to accept the historical and doctrinal assumptions of orthodox Christianity. At the same time he was fundamentally opposed to what he regarded as the idolatry which had crept into Hinduism, and in due course he founded a church known as the *Brahmo Samaj* which can best be described as a synthesis of some of the main elements in Hinduism and Christianity – an attempt at pure theism without any adequate philosophical basis. Like most artificial constructions in religion or philosophy, it was unsatisfactory and had neither a lasting emotional hold nor a philosophic appeal. Nevertheless, it was a powerful influence in Bengal for several generations, as was its counterpart in Bombay, the

Prarthana Samaj. It perhaps met for a time the spiritual needs of those who, as a result of the impact of Western thought, could neither be Hindus nor Christians, and it was indeed the natural outcome of the first confusing effect of Western thought on Indian minds.

In the middle of the nineteenth century a reaction set in, and thoughtful men began to wonder if they had strayed too far from the traditions of their ancestors. Swami Dayananda Saraswati, the chief apostle of this new school of thought, founded a body known as the *Arya Samaj*, which was violently anti-Muslim and the keynote of which was 'back to the Vedas'. In those scriptures, he taught, the germ of all knowledge was to be found, and he condemned polytheism and idolatry as excrescences not to be found in the Vedic teaching. Dayananda, in fact, presented his educated fellow countrymen with a form of Hinduism of which they could approve. Dr. Griswold, in a most interesting passage, thus describes the philosophy of Dayananda: 'The watchword of Luther was "back to the Bible"; the watchword of Pandit Dayananda was "back to the Vedas"; with this religious watchword another watchword was implicitly, if not explicitly, combined, namely "India for the Indians". . . . Indian religion was to be reformed and purified by a return to the Vedas and foreign religions such as Islam and Christianity were to be extirpated . . . a return to the pure teachings of the Vedas would gradually fit the people of India for self-rule, and independence would ultimately come to them.'

This was indeed a far cry from the teaching of Rammohan Roy fifty years earlier, but the religious reaction against surrender to Western and Christian influence was to go still further. In the last quarter of the nineteenth century, spiritual leadership again switched back to Bengal, and Ramakrishna Paramahansa, with his disciple Swami Vivekananda, preached the purest form of Hindusim, freed from the Western influence which had been paramount in the *Brahmo Samaj* and had not wholly disappeared in the time of the *Arya Samaj*. Ramakrishna was a true mystic who cared little for practical politics, but Vivekananda soon linked the devotionalism of his master with patriotism and the desire for independence. From the end of the century onwards, militant Hinduism and the

E

demand for self-government were closely intertwined, and there were indeed two distinct elements in the party which struggled for independence – one consisting of orthodox and militant Hindus and the other of Westernised intellectuals who cared little about any form of religion, but were determined to govern themselves.

These developments were mainly confined to the north, where the conflict between Hindu and Islamic ideas had confused men's minds and brought Hinduism to a low level. The south was little affected by Muslim culture and thought. There the traditional forms were enforced rigorously by the Brahmanical hierarchy and 'the south was able to retain a mature and poised mind, able to assess the fundamentals of spiritual and human problems with rationality and without frustration.' In the south, therefore, the impact of the West was less shattering than in the north, and neither the religious reforms of the early nineteenth century nor the reaction against them had any marked effect south of the Narbada.

It was thus primarily in Northern India that Hinduism, stagnant as it was at the beginning of the nineteenth century, was purified and revivified by its contact with Western thought, while simultaneously Western influence created a class of Indians who were neither Hindus nor British in their outlook – a class of which Nehru was perhaps the outstanding example of modern times.

Chapter 7

The Impact of the British
(4) The Growth of Nationalism

AMONGST THE MOST important results of British rule
in India were the emergence of an Indian nationality
and the growth of a spirit of nationalism so strong that
it led inevitably to independence. Before the modern period,
that sense of separateness and solidarity which is the only
criterion of nationality did not exist, nor were there present all
the elements from which it might have been built. Diversities
of race and language had encouraged the existence of large
numbers of separate and hostile states; religion, since the
Muslim invasions, had been a dividing factor and the cultural
unity formerly provided by Hinduism had been destroyed;
social traditions were enshrined in the caste system, which was
a strong stabilising element but was nevertheless too narrow
to lead to the growth of nationality; while that 'identity of
political antecedents', which Mill regarded as the most important basis of nationality, was wholly lacking.

In the nineteenth century two new factors began to weld the
people of India together. The first was the relentless pressure
of a uniform system of law and administration which, by im-
posing on the Bengali, the Madrassi and the Punjabi a uniform
code of behaviour in certain important matters, gave them in
the process a common substratum of thought. This process was
made easier by the vast network of roads and railways, by which
the towns of India were linked under the rule of the Crown.

The second important factor was the decision, in 1835, to
provide English rather than vernacular education. From that
time onwards, the best brains of India drank deeply at the well-
springs of British liberal thought. They learned from Edmund
Burke and John Stuart Mill the meaning of liberty; they

67

shared the sympathy of England with the struggles of Mazzini and Cavour; they read of the French Revolution and the hated salt-tax; and they read, too, of the wrongs of Ireland. Their political consciousness was aroused and they soon began to apply their newly-acquired ideas of the rights of individuals and of peoples to their own country. Nationalism had, in fact, been born and its potent forces began to bind the Western-educated classes more closely together, so that nationality became more of a fact than of a fiction. There was nothing un-expected about these developments. Elphinstone had written with prophetic insight as early as 1819 – 'the most desirable death for us to die of should be the improvement of the natives reaching such a pitch as would render it impossible for a foreign nation to retain the government; but this seems at an inmeasurable distance. . . . A time of separation must come; and it is for our interest to have an early separation from a civilised people rather than a rupture with a barbarous nation, in which it is probable that all our settlers and even our commerce would perish, along with all the institutions we had introduced into the country.' Munro and Macaulay had written in a similar strain, and, indeed, until the Mutiny bred a spirit of in-tolerance, most of the great British rulers of India had visualised the growth of nationalism and the ultimate grant of self-government.

The development of national consciousness was greatly stimulated by the growth of an active and independent Press, both in English and in the vernacular. In view of the suspi-cion with which the government in England regarded jour-nalists and their ways in the eighteenth century, it is not surprising that many of the servants of the East India Com-pany looked unfavourably on the Press in India. Their position as rulers of an alien people, only remotely responsible to the British Parliament, engendered in them an authoritarian habit of mind which led them to equate criticism with disloyalty. In the early part of the nineteenth century, even though the editors of newspapers in India were mainly British, they had to fight hard for reasonable freedom, but in 1835 Metcalfe, the Acting Governor-General, repealed the Press Licensing Regulations on the ground that 'if India could be preserved as a part of the British Empire only by keeping its inhabitants in a state of ignorance, our domination would be a curse to the country and ought to cease'. From that time, the Press enjoyed a remarkable degree of freedom and Indian-owned newspapers multiplied rapidly. The existence of the Press as a forum where educated Indians could, with impunity, express their views on such matters as the relations between Britain and India did much to encourage the spread of political ideas. There were times, particularly in the last stages of the progress towards independence, when the Indian sections of the Press showed a good deal of irresponsibility, but, broadly speaking, in the century between the repeal of the Press Licensing Regulations and the final transfer of power, the Press was a most important medium of political education and greatly stimulated the growth of true nationalism.

Under the influence of these factors, in the third quarter of the nineteenth century such men as Dadabhai Naoroji, the Grand Old Man of India, W. C. Bonnerjea, Surendranath Banerjea, Pherozeshah Mehta and D. E. Wacha began to give a definite shape to political thought in India. They needed, however, an organisation more effective and widespread than the British-India Association, which had been founded in the 'sixties, or the Bombay Association. The need was all the more urgent in view of the deterioration of relations between Englishmen and Indians. The Mutiny had naturally engendered bitterness on both sides, and when that feeling faded it was succeeded by suspicion and constraint. Indians began to be resentful of their virtual exclusion from higher offices, while British officials, at the heyday of their power, developed the aloofness characteristic of most bureaucracies and grew out of touch with educated Indians. A stage was reached when the Government of India was seldom aware of currents of thought and feeling until real resentment had been aroused.

These troubles were at their height in the early 'eighties when the Vernacular Press Act, the Arms Act and the controversy over the Ilbert Bill – which would have made Europeans liable to trial by Indian Magistrates – had strongly inflamed opinion. At this time, Allan Octavian Hume, a retired member of the Indian Civil Service, endowed with a sensitive imagination and an unorthodox mind, became convinced that the cure for the unrest lay in the foundation of a genuine nationalist movement. With the encouragement of the Viceroy, Lord Dufferin, he issued an appeal asking for fifty graduates to volunteer as its founders. The terms of his appeal are so moving as to justify extensive quotation:

'Whether in the individual or the nation,' he wrote, 'all vital progress must spring from within and it is to you, her most cultured and enlightencd minds, her most favoured sons, that your country must look for the initiative. In vain may aliens, like myself, love India and her children, as well as the most loving of these; in vain may they, for her and their good, give time and trouble, money and thought; in vain may they struggle and sacrifice; they may assist with advice and suggestions; they may place their experience, abilities and knowledge at the disposal of the workers, but they lack the essential of nationality, and the real work must ever be done by the people of the country themselves. . . . As I said before, you are the salt of the land. And if amongst even you, the *élite*, fifty men cannot bc found with sufficient power of self-sacrifice, sufficient love and pride in their country, sufficient genuine and unselfish heart-felt patriotism to take the initiative, and, if needs be, devote the rest of their life to the cause – then there is no hope for India. Her sons must and will, remain mere humble and helpless instruments in the hands of foreign rulers, for if "they would be free, *themselves* must strike the blow". And if even the leaders of thought are all either such poor creatures, or so selfishly wedded to personal concerns, that they dare not or will not strike a blow for their country's sake, then justly and rightly are they kept down and trampled on, for they deserve nothing better. Every nation secures precisely as good a government as it merits. If you, the picked men, the most highly educated of the nation, cannot, scorning personal ease and selfish objects, make a resolute struggle to secure greater freedom for yourselves and your country, a more impartial administration, a larger share in the management of your own affairs, then we, your friends, are wrong, and our adversaries right; then, at present at any rate, all hopes of progress are at an end, and India truly neither lacks nor deserves any better government than she now enjoys.'

The appeal met with a ready response and at Bombay in 1885 the Indian National Congress was inaugurated. It is not necessary for our purposes to recount the history of the Congress. We need only refer to the main phases in its development in so far as they contributed to the growth of nationalism. For reasons which will be discussed later, the Muslims as a whole kept aloof from the Congress, but as far as Hindus were concerned, it soon became the focal point of nationalist feeling. For the first twenty years it pursued a moderate course and showed exemplary patience over the long delay on the part of the British Government in meeting the demands for an expansion of the Legislative Council on an elective basis and for the increased employment of Indians in superior Government posts.

Before the end of this phase, there had been a remarkable resurgence of Hinduism in a militant form under the leadership of Bal Gangadhar Tilak, who 'set himself to fight every kind of social reform that might interfere with the ancient ways of orthodox Hinduism'. The Age of Consent Bill, which forbade consummation of a marriage until the wife was twelve years old, was violently denounced by Tilak, as well as by the Hindu Press of Bengal. Young Indians were organised into gymnastic societies, where they were trained for the fight with the British which they were taught to expect. The memory of the great Maratha hero, Shivaji, was invoked against the interfering foreigners – as well as against the Muslims – and a cult of revolutionary violence was firmly established. The growth of a similar cult in Bengal was stimulated by the Curzon Partition of Bengal in 1905. That partition had much to commend it on logical grounds, but Bengali Hindus regarded, it, perhaps without justification, as a deliberate attempt to destroy their influence and so weaken the nationalist movement of which they then considered themselves the leaders. The emotional, Bengali temperament was easily influenced by the extremist propaganda to which certain sections of the Press lent themselves without restraint. The atmosphere created can best be illustrated by the following extract from a Bengali newspaper during the anti-partition agitation. 'A handful of alien robbers is ruining the crores of the people of India by robbing the wealth of India. Through the hard grinding of their servitude, the ribs of this countless people are broken to pieces. Endless endeavours are being made in order that this great nation by losing, as an inevitable result of this subjection, its moral, intellectual and physical power, its wealth, its self-reliance, and all other qualities, may be turned into the condition of the beasts of burden or be wholly extinguished. . . . Will the Bengali worshippers of *Shakti* shrink from the shedding of blood? The number of Englishmen in this country is not above one lac and a half, and what is the number of English officials in each district? If you are firm in your resolution, you can in a single day bring English rule to an end. Lay down your life, but first take a life. The worship of the goddess will not be consummated if you sacrifice your lives at the shrine of independence without shedding blood.'

We are not concerned with the history of the terrorist movement, but only with the fact that the anti-partition feeling in Bengal and the Tilak's Anti-Cow-Killing Society in Bombay gave the Nationalist Movement a new twist. Henceforth, its supporters consisted of two wings – on the one hand, Westernised intellectuals, and on the other hand orthodox and militant Hindus. Both wings were a product of the impact of the British, the former by the process of education, and the latter by a violent reaction against the excessive depreciation of the ancient religion in which Hindus of the previous generation had indulged. The important fact, for the purpose of this chapter, is that the emergence of a militant Hindu wing of the Nationalist Movement greatly extended the appeal of that movement and brought within its scope many who might not otherwise have been influenced by it. For some years the militant section was not strong in the Congress Party itself but the Congress leaders often found themselves in a dilemma. They might disapprove of the attitude of the extremists, but they could hardly condemn it without incurring the charge of lack of patriotism, or of not being good Hindus. As must always happen in such a case, the extremists grew in strength as the years passed. Educated Indians failed to understand the British belief in gradualness, and began to distrust the ultimate intentions of the British Government and to resent what they considered the slowness of the steps towards self-government.

Although these developments stimulated the growth of the very nationalism of which they were the product, it seems clear that up to 1914, or a little later, the overwhelming majority of Indian villagers were largely indifferent to politics and cared little about the colour of their rulers. The effect of the First World War on India was profound. It brought some knowledge of the outside world into many Indian homes for the first time and men began to ask themselves whether, if they were fit to die for this freedom of which they had just come to hear, they were not also fit to govern themselves. A new ferment had been set up, and when Edwin Montagu laid himself out to disturb the pathetic contentment of the masses, he was merely canalising an existing stream.

It was at this stage that the leadership of political India was assumed by the greatest man in modern Indian history, Mohandas Karamchand Gandhi. We cannot here describe how he came to dominate the minds and hearts of Hindus for three decades, or explain the almost unparalleled devotion of the masses to the Mahatma, or Bapuji as he came to be affectionately called. It is perhaps impossible for anybody who did not live in India and in close contact with Indians at that time to realise the Mahatma's astonishing ascendancy. He quickened patriotic sentiment in the hearts of the middle classes and, above all, he took Indian nationalism to the masses. What had been almost totally an affair of the educated few, became the concern of every Indian, rich or poor, learned or ignorant, lawyer, shopkeeper or agriculturist. Gandhi taught India a new self-respect, which could be content with nothing less than self-government, and he inspired his countrymen with a readiness to suffer in the cause of their country. There are many aspects of his teaching with which one must disagree. One may condemn civil disobedience on the ground that it was bound in practice to lead to terrorism; one may regard his encouragement of the boycott of foreign cloth as economically unsound and reactionary. These are matters about which there is endless scope for argument, but the more important point is that the movement inspired by Gandhi gave the common people a practical share in political activity. It enabled the villager or the humble townsman to feel that he, too, was helping his country to achieve that self-government in which the Mahatma had taught him to believe. Gandhi, who had himself learned from Britain the meaning of justice and freedom, imparted those ideas to his fellow countrymen with such success that Indian nationality became a reality and Indian nationalism a unanimous expression of the feeling of Indians. The change took place with remarkable rapidity. When the writer first went to India in 1922, it is doubtful if more than a small percentage of Indian villagers had any conception wider than that of their own position as inhabitants of particular villages, or members of particular castes. By the Second World War the position had changed beyond recognition, and even the Muslims, or the minority of Hindus who opposed the Congress, were nevertheless determined that their country should govern itself. Indian nationality had become a reality and nationalism was paramount.

It must, however, be remembered that the concept of nationalism in Asia differs considerably from that which prevails in England and France. In those countries, a strong, centralised monarchy was able to create, out of linguistic, cultural and religious unity, a closely knit form of nationalism, which could not apply in the large continental types of society seen in the U.S.S.R., the U.S.A., India and China. It has been remarked by an acute Indian observer that in such societies 'the ideal is not of one people, but of different peoples behaving and acting together as one people – and such an ideal must to no small extent depend on having accomplished things together and shared common glories in the past. This ideal could not have been achieved merely as the result of the external unifying factors provided by the British. It demanded an effort from the Indian people themselves and it was by recovering their own prestige as a people, by trying to recapture the continuity of their past and by rekindling the almost extinct sense of patriotism, that Indians themselves created the new nationalism that inspires them today.'

Chapter 8

The Impact of the British
(5) Economic Development

THE MAIN IMPACT of the British on India was felt at a time when the Industrial Revolution was in full swing and the forces which had been released by it in England began to operate also, though with less intensity, on the primarily agricultural economy of India. Their first effect was the breakdown of the old self-sufficiency of rural India. Before the coming of the British, 'in each village there were cultivators who grew practically all that the cultivators required in the way of food or materials for clothes; artisans who prepared the ploughs, utensils and furniture in return for a share of the village produce; barbers and other village servants who received their traditional share of grain; *banias* who advanced seed or grain to cultivators in time of need; and priests who attended to the religious and cultural needs of the community and whose maintenance was a common responsibility'. Transactions with the outside world were, in general, limited to payment of revenue in kind, or to barter with adjacent villages.

The advent of the British soon disrupted this closed economy; first, because they were energetic traders, determined to sell their own commodities in exchange for the produce of the villages; and, secondly, because, as great builders of roads and bridges, they made extensive internal trade possible. In the Mughal times a few great imperial highways had linked the great cities together, but in the rest of the country roads suitable for carts were few and far between, and it is reported that in Oudh, as late as 1862, even cart tracks were non-existent.

The effect of the opening up of communications by the East India Company was spectacular, but in the early phases not wholly beneficial. Few Asian countries in the eighteenth century wanted British goods and in spite of the theories of contemporary economists in England, exports from Asia were paid for either in bullion or, as was largely the case in India, out of the surplus from the territorial revenues which accrued to the East India Company. The 'drain' of which Indian politicians have written so much was a grave reality in the last half of the eighteenth century. In the nineteenth century, when Manchester became able to provide cheap textiles and a great variety of consumer goods from England were imported, the situation was completely changed. European goods were now made available to the better class of villagers; cheap mill-made products greatly extended the use of cloth by the poorer classes; brass vessels began to take the place of earthenware; and the cultivator was able to export his produce to deficit areas, to pay for his newly-created wants. The change inevitably brought suffering and in some cases ruin to weavers and others who could not compete with foreign mill-made goods, but it increased the amenities of life for the community as a whole and converted a static into a dynamic economy.

The next step in economic progress was the growth of large-scale organised industry. It is not possible here to describe either the strange blend of enterprise, efficiency and tyranny that led to the establishment of indigo plantations; or the romance of the opening up of tea gardens in the trackless, malarial jungles of Assam; or the rapid growth of the jute industry in the last quarter of the nineteenth century; or the combination of administrators, financiers and engineers to give India one of the greatest railway systems in the world. All these enterprises were the direct result of the release in India of British energy and British capital, and, although at no time debarred from participation, Indians played singularly little part in these early developments.

Two difficulties were soon experienced. One was the reluctance of Indians to invest in joint stock companies or in industry at all, as illustrated by the fact that in 1868, of 49,688 shareholders in Indian railways, only 817 were living in India and less than half of those were Indians. The second difficulty was the serious shortage of managerial *expertise* to meet the needs of expanding industry. A solution to these problems was found in the Managing Agency system, and the way in which this worked has been thus described by the writer in *The British Impact on India;* 'A British partnership or firm would float a company to run a new project and would itself put up most of the capital. When the new concern had paid a profit for some years, Indian investors would be attracted. The British would then sell part of their interest, though generally retaining a sufficient share to give them practical predominance and at the same time they would secure a Managing Agency agreement. The agreement might be either perpetual or for a long term and would give effective control to the managing agent. With the capital released by this transaction, the managing agent would then take up another new project. In the meantime the British promoters would have borne the early risk, which at that time Indian investors were not willing to take.

'After several transactions of this kind, the British partnership or firm would find itself managing a number of independent companies and would thus develop considerable managerial *expertise*.'

The Managing Agency system has been much criticised in recent years as involving undue concentration of economic power in a few hands and laying the way open for abuses where the agents are unscrupulous, but it provided exactly the galvanic impulse required by India in the middle of the nineteenth century. New industries sprang up with remarkable rapidity and gradually a few Indians began to be infected with the manufacturing enthusiasm which characterised the British at that time. The cotton textile industry in Bombay, established with Indian capital and British technicians, and the great iron and steel industry brought into being by the genius and vision of Jamsetjee Tata were the earliest results of the new spirit, and from then onwards Indian-owned industries have made vast strides.

Industrial development in India has not been without its unhappy aspects. The old cottage industries which played such a large part in village life have been seriously impaired, and modern attempts to rehabilitate them have not been very successful. Nor can there be any cause for satisfaction in the transfer of millions of Indians from the villages, where even poverty was not soul-destroying, to the slums of Calcutta, Bombay or Cawnpore. No European, estimating the impact of Britain on India, is entitled to ignore the unspeakable degradation of the life of the poor in the great modern Indian cities, and in India, as in Europe, the thoughtful observer must often wonder if the price paid for progress has been too high.

One important by-product of all these changes has been the emergence of an educated and influential middle class. The towns of medieval India grew up round the palace of a king or a great nobleman and existed solely to satisfy the needs of the Court. There was in them no class comparable to the men of commerce, the industrialists, the bankers, the lawyers, the doctors and the other professional men who count for so much in Bombay and Calcutta today. These are the men who have made modern India, and the rise of the upper middle class may be regarded as one of the most important results of British influence in India.

Fairness compels us to record that the result was largely unintended. When the nationalist movement grew, the middle classes were in the forefront of the struggle for independence and were, in fact, the potential supplanters of the British official hierarchy. British officials tended, therefore, to write them off as agitators and to compare them unfavourably with the undemanding peasants. The middle classes were nevertheless created and conditioned by English education and might, with justice, be regarded as the creation of Macaulay and his colleagues of the Filtration School.

An important factor in economic progress under British rule was the development of public health services. The campaign against the most malignant tropical diseases, the struggle to reduce infantile mortality, the development of vast irrigation projects, and the gradual evolution, after many failures, of a technique for fighting famine are too well known to require description here. Their combined result was a rate of growth of population so high that even the increased productive capacity of industry and agriculture could scarcely keep pace with it.

It is, unfortunately, impossible to sum up in exact quantitative terms the effect of these various factors in such a way as to compare the standard of living of the twentieth-century Indian with that of his predecessor in Mughal times. We can only say tentatively that the British economic impact on India has probably made life a little more comfortable for the average man and that India had certain progressive tendencies in 1947 which augured well for economic development.

Chapter 9

Towards Independence

I T IS NOT NECESSARY, for the purpose of understanding modern India, to study in detail the stages by which India moved towards independence, but there are four aspects of that progress which require our attention, since they govern conditions in India today. First, the fact that, notwithstanding the struggle between the British Government and the Congress over three decades, the final transfer of power was a voluntary act, in no way extorted by force, has had a profound effect on relations between Britain and independent India. Secondly, the gradualness of the progress towards self-government gave time for parliamentary institutions to take root, and for Indians to be trained in higher administration. Thirdly, the parliamentary character of the self-governing institutions introduced by Britain made partition unavoidable; while, finally, the long-drawn-out transition led to the consolidation of the Congress into the powerful party, firmly committed to a planned semi-socialist economy, which rules India today.

It is a significant fact that the first, short step towards far-distant self-government was taken when Britain was in a position of absolute and unquestioned authority. The Mutiny had been completely crushed and not even an incipient nationalist movement had yet come into being. Wise administrators nevertheless recognised that the British rulers were dangerously out of contact with their Indian subjects, and Bartle Frere wrote of 'the perilous experiment of continuing to legislate for millions of people, with few means of knowing, except by rebellion, whether the laws suit them or not'. To remedy this lack of contact, in 1861 the Legislative Council was for the first time expanded to include a small number of non-officials nominated by the Governor-General and similar Councils were established in the Provinces. Although the Governor-

General's choice was not limited by statute, in practice the majority of non-officials nominated by him were, right from the start, Indians. Their number was, however, small and the educative effect of the 1861 Act was less than that of the steps taken in the eighth and ninth decades of the century to establish local self-governing bodies. Committees, composed of both Indians and Europeans, were set up in some Provinces to deal with health, education and similar matters, and with the purpose of affording opportunities for participation in self-government, as well as of associating Europeans and Indians in joint action. A little later, regular municipalities and local boards were created on an elective basis, and Lord Ripon frankly thought of them 'not primarily with the view to improvement of administration . . . but as a measure of political and popular education'. In some respects the early results of this development were disappointing: Indians of standing tended to hold aloof from these bodies and District Magistrates so dominated them that they were regarded almost as departments of government. When this phase passed some decades later, and non-officials replaced the District Magistrates as Chairmen, there was a marked deterioration in the standard of administration and many observers regarded the system as a failure. A sounder view of these later years would perhaps be that local self-government provided the educated classes with a valuable experience of the working of the representative principle, as well as of the technique of committee work and law-making.

When the next constitutional change took place in 1892, the Indian National Congress had existed for seven years. Its moderate attitude, and the experience of politics gained through it by a limited class of Indians, justified an advance. The scope of the Provincial Councils was expanded and, although it was still considered premature to apply the elective principle to them, certain commercial associations, municipalities, universities and other bodies were given the right to put forward names which the Government would accept if it thought fit. In practice, the suggested names were almost always accepted. The new Councils on the whole worked well, and although the new Hindu militancy associated with Tilak in Bombay, and with the anti-partition agitation in Bengal,

F

had created a good deal of unrest and some violence, it was considered possible to embark on a further advance in 1909.

The Morley-Minto reforms of that year abolished the official majorities in some of the Provincial Legislatures and introduced a system of election, though the constituencies were not general, but consisted of municipalities, district boards, Chambers of Commerce, landholders and other special interests. John Morley denied that these reforms were intended to lead to the establishment of the Parliamentary system in India, and declared that, if that had been the aim, he would have had nothing to do with them. It is difficult to know what he meant and it is abundantly clear that the reforms did, in fact, amount to a decisive choice of the Parliamentary system as the foundation of future self-government.

By the time of the next constitutional advance in 1919, the political atmosphere had become charged with electricity. Resentment at the overwhelmingly British character of the superior services was keen, and Britain was charged with having been consistently false to the declaration, first enunciated in the 1833 Charter, and frequently repeated, that 'no subject of Her Majesty should by reason only of his religion, place of birth, descent, colour or any of them be disabled from holding any place, office or employment under the company'. The demand for still more liberal institutions had gathered strength rapidly under the educative influence of the Morley-Minto reforms and was further stimulated by the consciousness of the magnificent part which India had played in the First World War. Additional weight was given to this demand by the pact – destined, unfortunately, to prove very temporary – entered into between the Hindus and Muslims at Lucknow in 1916. Edwin Montagu, Secretary of State for India, was in tune with the spirit of the times in India and truly represented the most progressive thought of war-time England, when, on August 20th, 1917, he made the most momentous announcement in Indian history: 'The policy of His Majesty's Government, with which the Government of India is in complete accord, is that of the increasing association of Indians in every branch of the administration and the gradual development of self-governing institutions with a view to the progressive realisation of responsible government in India as an integral part of the British Empire.'

The announcement in effect repudiated Morley's attitude and made it clear that the goal for India was parliamentary self-government, and the resulting Government of India Act of 1919 set India firmly on the path to that goal. The Act distinguished between Central and Provincial subjects and so laid the foundations of future federation. Within the Provincial sphere it established the system of dyarchy, under which elected Ministers had charge of certain departments, while officials remained in control of others. A few years earlier, such an advance would have been hailed with delight, but the atmosphere had been poisoned, first by the agitation against the Rowlatt Acts which it had been necessary to enact in order to deal with terrorism, and, secondly, by the Punjab Rebellion, the events of the Jallianwala Bagh,[1] and General Dyer's infamous 'crawling order'. The Reforms were accordingly denounced by important sections of the Congress as hopelessly inadequate. After a good deal of vacillation, Gandhi threw in his lot with the extremists and the Non-Co-operation Movement was launched.

We are not concerned with the history of that sterile movement, nor with the terrorist activity which naturally grew out of it. It is doubtful if non-co-operation or its successor, civil disobedience, advanced self-government by a single day. On the other hand, it engendered a racial bitterness, which has fortunately disappeared since the transfer of power, and a disregard of law and order which has left an enduring mark on the youth of India. It also prevented the growth of that sense of joint responsibility between elected Ministers and official members of the Provincial Councils which it had been hoped would lead insensibly to true Cabinet government. Nevertheless, dyarchy gave Indian public men valuable administrative and parliamentary experience and taught the public the use of the ballot box. In the writer's judgement it was an essential preliminary to full parliamentary self-government.

The Government of India Act of 1935, which followed the Simon Commission, the Round Table Conferences, and the

[1] Jallianwala Bagh – where troops under General Dyer fired to disperse a mob of 5,000, and 379 persons were killed.

Joint Select Committee of 1933, carried the progress towards self-government a long stage further. The Provinces were made autonomous in many important respects, while elected Ministers obtained full control over Provincial affairs, subject only to certain reserve powers vested in the Governor. Officials disappeared altogether from the Provincial Legislatures. At the outset the Congress treated the new Constitution with great suspicion and contended that the Governor's special powers would render Ministers unable to discharge their responsibilities. These fears were soon overcome and, on taking office, Ministers discovered not only that they possessed the substance of power, but also that British officials were their strongest defenders.

The 1935 Act set the final seal on parliamentary government as the pattern which would in due course be adopted by a self-governing India. It is useless to discuss the suitablity or otherwise of that form of government for the conditions and background of India. Educated Hindus, brought up on the English classics of the nineteenth century, had become deeply impregnated with the belief in parliamentary institutions and regarded all other systems of government as vastly inferior. The establishment of parliamentary government in India seemed to be the logical consequence of British work and influence – the end-product which gave meaning to all that had gone before.

The 1935 Act also contemplated the establishment of an all-India Federation, with something very near responsible government at the centre, but this was to be conditional on the accession of half of the Indian States. It will be remembered that it was largely an historical accident whether any particular area was brought under direct British rule and incorporated in a province of British India, or was left under the rule of an hereditary rajah or nawab. During some phases British policy had avoided extensions of direct rule wherever possible, while in other periods, notably during the time of Dalhousie, every opportunity had been taken to pension off Indian princes and absorb their territories in British India. By 1935, the resulting map of India was like a patchwork quilt, with 562 Indian States scattered amongst the eleven Provinces and five Chief Commissionerships of British India. These States varied greatly in importance and degree of independence. Some were little more than the domains of feudal landlords, while others were great semi-independent kingdoms, whose rulers were very jealous of any encroachment on their prerogatives. Many of the States had treaties governing the relations between them and the British Government, whilst all were controlled in those relations by the doctrine of paramountcy. That doctrine was never defined, save perhaps in the cryptic phrase 'paramountcy must remain paramount'. The combined effect of treaties and paramountcy was that defence and external affairs were in the hands of the Crown, while for other purposes most of the States were virtually independent, except for the possibility of intervention by the Viceroy in the event of gross misrule. The political department, whose officers represented the Viceroy in the States, tended as a rule to resist interference with the rights of the rulers, and it could fairly be said that the Viceroy left the Indian States to govern themselves well or badly, unless intervention became quite unavoidable. There is room for difference of opinion as to the wisdom or otherwise of this policy. Its defenders argue that it made for stability and was merely an honest fulfilment of Britain's original engagements with the princes, while critics maintain that many of the smaller States were run solely for the benefit of their rulers and that they had become an anachronism which would have been swept away but for British protection.

The link between British India and the Indian States was provided by the Viceroy, who, as Governor-General, was the head of the administration of British India, while as Viceroy he represented the Crown in relation to the States. As India approached self-government, it was clear that this link would be severed when the Governor-General became the purely constitutional head of the State in British India. There would thus be a complete gulf between the two parts of India and there might even be radical divergence of policy in important matters. Federation was conceived partly as a method of bridging this gulf and the intention of the Government of India Act, 1935, was to weld the Provinces of British India and the States into a great federation.

There were many practical difficulties in the way of such a

process. Although at least some of the States were very well administered and in advance of British India in education and other matters, the democratic ideas with which the politicians of British India were then obsessed had made little headway in the States. The difficulty of establishing a federal legislature, two-thirds of the members of which would be elected by democratic processes from British India, while the remaining third would be nominated by autocratic rulers, was obvious. The real difficulty, however, arose not so much from the nature of the problem itself, as from the lack of wisdom on the part of the princes and the Indian National Congress alike.

The accession of a State to the Federation was to be governed by an instrument of accession, which would specify the subjects in respect of which power was to be transferred from the State to the Federal Centre. Lord Linlithgow, a great Viceroy, who realised that federation was the best hope of India, strove valiantly between 1937 and 1939 to persuade the princes to accede, and there is little doubt that at that time they could have made a satisfactory bargain as to the limitations on the authority of the Federal Centre. They failed to understand that they could never hope for a recurrence of such favourable terms and threw away their last chance of effective survival. In this attitude they were to a considerable extent encouraged by the political unwisdom of the Congress Party in 1937 in embarking on a policy which Coupland has described as 'undisguised hostility to the States Governments and of open encouragement of agitation within and without the States against them'. Just as the Congress mass campaign against the Muslims at this time was one of the ultimate causes of the demand for partition, in the same way the militant Congress campaign in the States resulted in a definite hardening of the attitude of the princes, who not unnaturally feared inclusion in a federation in which the Congress, in its new militant mood, would be the predominant factor. It is no exaggeration to say that, by its unhappy timing of these campaigns, the Congress helped to kill the federal scheme and perhaps destroyed the last chance of preserving a united India. Nevertheless, this unwisdom on the part of the Congress cannot excuse the obstinacy and blindness of the princes in 1937. It is by no means certain that they could in any case have survived as

islands of autocracy in a sea of popular government, but by
their refusal to join the Federation then, they made their own
destruction inevitable.

In order to understand the final steps leading to the transfer
of power, we must go back a little and consider briefly the
position of the Muslims during the formative years of modern
Indian political thought. The Muslims felt that it was they,
rather than the Hindus, who had lost as a result of the replacement of the Mughal Empire by British rule. Under the Mughals, although Hindus were often employed in high office, the
ultimate power was generally in Muslim hands, and as Qazis,[1]
zemindars or courtiers, Muslims occupied a privileged position. The substitution of English for Islamic law, and the
abolition of Persian as the official language, were greatly
resented by the Muslims, who failed to imitate the more
flexible-minded Hindus in taking to the new system. The
Hindus rapidly filled all important posts open to Indians and
the Muslims were left sullen and helpless. Hinduism and Islam
both underwent militant revivals in the latter half of the nineteenth century and the sullenness of the Muslims was fanned
into open hostility, fully reciprocated by the Hindus, which led
to numerous, serious, communal riots before the century was
over.

When Western-educated Hindus began to talk of democratic
forms of government, the Muslims became profoundly apprehensive. They were conscious that the Hindus outnumbered
them by three to one, and that their own intellectual backwardness would make their position even weaker than mere
numerical considerations might suggest. It seemed to them that
they could never hope to count in the government of a self-
governing India and that they could not even form an effective
opposition. In 1883 the great Muslim leader, Sayyid Ahmad
Khan, thus gave utterance to these fears: 'The system of representation by election means the representation of the views
and interests of the majority of the population. . . . In a country
like India, where class distinctions still flourish and where
there is no fusion of the various races, where religious differences are still violent, where education in the modern sense
has not made an equal or proportionate progress amongst all

[1] Judges.

sections of the population, I am convinced that the introduction of the principle of election pure and simple, for the representation of various interests on local boards and district councils, would be attended with evils of greater significance than purely economic considerations. . . . The larger community would totally over-ride the interests of the smaller community.'

When the Indian National Congress was founded in 1885 Sayyid Ahmad Khan advised Muslims to have nothing to do with it and founded a Muslim body to oppose its political aims and ideals. At the same time, he strongly urged Muslims to take to Western education and did much to provide them with the necessary facilities. Muslim fears were strengthened when the Indian Councils Act of 1892 increased the non-official membership of the Councils, since that seemed to be a step on the road to government by a majority. In 1905 the violent Hindu agitation against the partition of Bengal dismayed the Muslims, confirmed them in the belief that their interests were separate from those of the Hindus, and led to the foundation of the Muslim League in 1906. Moslem fears were confirmed when the partition was annulled in 1911.

During the next decade the Muslim leaders gave much thought to devising methods for their protection as a backward minority community. 'Weightage', or the allocation to them of more seats in the Legislatures than they could claim on a purely numerical basis, was one of the suggested methods. It would, however, avail them little if the Muslim members were to be elected by general territorial constituencies in which Hindus would also vote. They therefore began to put stress on the demand for separate electorates in which Muslims alone would vote for the Muslims members. This principle had, indeed, been accepted in the field of self-government as far back as the 'eighties, when the various Municipal Acts provided for the separate representation of Hindus, Muslims and Europeans. When the Morley-Minto reforms were under discussion, the Muslims resisted all the attempts of John Morley to persuade them to abandon this claim. The Viceroy, Lord Minto, took a more realistic view than Morley and recognised that 'any electoral representation in India would be doomed to mischievous failure which aimed at granting a personal enfranchisement regardless of the beliefs and traditions of the communities composing the populations'. Separate electorates were included in the new constitutional scheme, and the Muslims never afterwards showed the slightest sign of being ready to abandon them. The Hindus, on the other hand, being the majority community, could afford to stand on abstract, democratic principles and denounced communal electorates bitterly until 1916.

At that time, war between Britain and Turkey had created anti-British feeling amongst the Muslims in India and thrown them temporarily into the arms of the Hindus. The Lucknow Pact of 1916 provided that the Muslims would join the Hindus in demanding self-government, while the Hindus, for their part, agreed that the Muslims should have 'weightage' and separate electorates. At the end of the war, the Indian Muslims failed to persuade the British Government to adopt a lenient attitude towards Turkey and, in anger at their failure, launched the *Khilafat* movement. Gandhi skilfully exploited this movement and the somewhat unnatural alliance formed at Lucknow continued for several years.

In the middle 'twenties the alliance broke down and fierce antagonism flared up between Hindus and Muslims, partly as a result of growing Muslim fears of Hindu domination and partly on account of two highly militant campaigns known as the *Suddhi* and *Sangathan* movements conducted by the Hindu *Mahasabha*, or right-wing Hindu party. The *Sangathan* movement was the complete antithesis of Gandhi's non-violence, in as much as its most spectacular aspect was the training of Hindu boys in lathi play and gymnastics in order to fit them for the coming struggle. The *Suddhi* movement was concerned with the reconversion of Hindus who had become Muslims or Christians. These two movements seriously alarmed the Muslims and permanently widened the breach between the two communities. In 1927 a committee set up by Congress, under the chairmanship of Motilal Nehru, to make constitutional proposals, repudiated the Lucknow Agreement regarding 'weightage' and separate electorates, and left the Muslims more than ever convinced that the Hindus were determined to secure power.

The following decade was an unhappy one, marked not only by civil disobedience, and its inevitable offspring terrorism, but also by serious communal tension, which in many places led to rioting on a considerable scale. An interesting illustration of the way in which the demand for independence led to communal trouble is provided by events in the East Bengal city of Dacca. In that city, the wealthy shopkeepers and moneylenders were almost exclusively Hindus, while the small stallholders, cab drivers and other lowly persons were mainly Muslims. Again and again these Muslims were forced by the powerful Hindus – to whom they were frequently in debt – to observe *hartal*, that is to close down business, as a protest against some action taken by the Government against subversive or violent movements connected with the Congress. The Muslim masses began to feel that they were hopelessly in the grip of the Hindus, and in 1930, resentment of this position and of their constant harassment by the Hindus, led to communal rioting on a considerable scale. Similar developments occurred in many parts of the country and in those areas where the Muslims, by their superior physical prowess and courage, terrorised the more highly educated, but timorous Hindus, the constantly maligned British official spent much of his time protecting those very Congressmen who were his chief critics.

At this time the question as to what the relations between the Federal Centre and the Provinces should be after the next constitutional change took place, was in the forefront of the minds of educated men. The Muslims were in a strong position in certain Provinces, but were fearful of the overwhelming Hindu majority in the All-India Legislature. They demanded, therefore, that the Federal Centre should be limited in scope and power and that the Provinces should be the predominant element in the Federation. Hindus, on the other hand, genuinely believed in the unity of India and were at the same time conscious of their own strength. They accordingly insisted on a strong Federal Centre. The Government of India Act, 1935, was perhaps a workable compromise between the two views, and though the Muslims were not happy about it, they would at that time have accepted it as a whole. Unfortunately, as we have seen, the Princes held back and the Federal part of the Act never came into force. The remainder of the Act was put into operation and in 1937 Provincial autonomy was established.

It had been hoped that, in the mainly Hindu Provinces, Muslims would be included in the Provincial Cabinets. The Congress, however, declined to include in their Cabinets any Muslims who would not subscribe to the Congress creed, and at the same time they launched an intensive campaign to recruit Muslims to the Congress Party. They were fully entitled to do this, but the timing of their action was unfortunate and it inspired genuine apprehension in the minds even of reasonable Muslims. During the next two years the Muslims alleged that they had suffered injustice and oppression in the Hindu-majority Provinces, and at one stage their leader, M. A. Jinnah, demanded a Royal Commission to inquire into the oppression of the Muslims. No such inquiry was ever held and it is impossible to judge as to whether the complaint was justified or not. The important practical point is that Muslims genuinely believed it. It may be that many Hindus in Muslim-majority Provinces had similar complaints, but their All-India strength made them less apprehensive. The upshot of all these transactions was to leave the Muslims convinced that their position under Hindu rule would be hopeless, and it was from the conviction that the Hindus would be all-powerful in any Central Government of undivided India that the demand for partition sprang.

Some years before the Muslims generally had begun to think of the partition of India, the idea of Pakistan was promulgated by four pamphleteers, of whom Rahmat Ali was the best known. In 1933 they issued a pamphlet asserting that the Muslims in India were a distinct nation from the Hindus, and demanding a separate State consisting of the Punjab, the North-west Frontier Province (Afghanistan), Kashmir, Sind and Baluchistan. 'The initial letters of those States were formed into the word Pakistan and it was then fortunately discovered that in Arabic this would mean the land of the pure.' Few at that time took the suggestion seriously, but as the years passed the idea of partition began to appeal more strongly to the Muslims, particuarly in the Provinces where they were in the minority. In 1939 Sir Sikandar Hyat Khan, the Premier of the Punjab, followed up this line of thought by putting forward a proposal for a loose federation of zones, which would, in fact, give a considerable measure of autonomy to the main Muslim areas. This proposal, however, was overtaken by events and Muslim fears soon passed beyond the stage when they could be allayed by half-measures.

In 1940 the demand for partition was formally made. The present writer has described elsewhere a dinner party just before the demand for Pakistan was officially formulated by the Muslim League. 'Mr. Jinnah declared that at the stage of imperial rule where self-government was not in sight the British were the finest administrators known to history, but that when politics and national feeling had begun to count they completely failed to understand the mentality of subject races. "You talk," he said, "of the unity of India, but you ought to know that it is a chimera, existing nowhere except in your own minds and in the external unity which you wisely forced on the country. You go on to talk of parliamentary democracy and you fail to realise that the assumptions on which it depends have no application at all to Indian conditions." He went on to develop, cogently and impressively, his two-nation theory and to expound the full Pakistan demand, which was to be adopted by the Muslim League formally in March 1940. The writer and others present raised all the obvious objections – economic dangers, frontier problems, military and administrative difficulties. Mr. Jinnah brushed them all aside and completely refused to discuss details. This capacity for adhering to a clear-cut idea and ignoring all difficulties of detail and procedure was perhaps Mr. Jinnah's greatest source of strength. From this time onwards, he who had for long been the apostle of the unity of India set his face steadfastly towards partition and would not be deflected either by blandishments or by threats.'

In a general political history of India, the eight years between the outbreak of the Second World War and the transfer of power would require extensive discussion. It would be necessary, in such a work, to explain why Gandhi's instinctive sympathy with Britain's war aims had to yield to the general Congress determination to exploit the war situation and to demand self-government under what they regarded as satisfactory conditions. The failure of the Congress plan, the abstention of Congress from participation in the war effort, and the somewhat ambiguous attitude of the Muslim League,

which gave no official co-operation but nevertheless encouraged individual Muslims to join the armed forces, would
all require consideration. Attention would then have to be
directed to the magnificent contribution made by India to
the war effort in spite of the Congress, and to the share of
soldiers, artisans and industrialists alike in that contribution.
The Cripps Mission of 1942 – which failed chiefly because the
Congress was determined to drive a hard bargain and to surrender nothing to the Muslim League – and the Congress
rebellion later in the same year, would all demand study and
the historian would have to record how the Congress abandoned the theory of non-violence and embarked on a violent
revolution at a time when the war situation in the East was
at its worst. It would be necessary, too, to describe how completely and firmly that rebellion was crushed and how it left
the Congress Party so paralysed and impotent that if Britain
had been anxious to cling to power after the war she could have
done so. None of these matters is strictly relevant to an account
of India today and we can pass them by.

After the war events moved rapidly. The attempts of the
Viceroy to bring the parties together in Simla; the 1946 elections at which Muslims voted so solidly for partition that not a
single Muslim constituency returned a non-partition candidate to the Central Legislature; the Cabinet Mission, which
failed, chiefly because of the constitutional inability of Sir
Stafford Cripps to believe in the reality of what he regarded as
the irrational Muslim demand for Pakistan; and the unhappy
handling by the Viceroy, Lord Wavell, of the arrangements
leading up to an interim Government including the Congress
and the Muslim League – all these happenings were merely
part of the process leading, step by step, to partition and independence and need not be discussed in this book. It need only
be noted that self-government in India dates in effect not from
the final transfer of power on August 15th, 1947, but from the
formation of the Interim Government in 1946. From that time
onwards, the Governor-General was little more than the Chairman of an Indian Cabinet, the members of which were not,
like their predecessors, his personal nominees, but the representatives of the major parties. They were, in fact, the rulers
of the country.

By the end of 1946 India was drifting rapidly to chaos. The real power had passed from British hands; senior officials, anxious about their own future, were conscious that they were caretakers under notice and were disheartened; Ministers, paralysed by the communal situation, seemed unable to come to grips with the problems of administration; and the unparalleled communal riots in Calcutta, together with serious disorders in many parts of India, made it clear that nobody was in effective control. At the Centre, the Interim Government was proving unworkable and, in the spring of 1947, thoughtful men were shocked to see influential members of the Congress Party attempting to sabotage the Budget proposals of Liaquat Ali Khan, Jinnah's second-in-command, while still themselves composing the major wing of the Government in which he was Finance Minister. As a result of a genuine and praiseworthy desire on the part of the British Government to arrive at an agreed settlement of the communal problem and to avoid partition if possible, the transition had been too long drawn out and chaos had resulted.

INDEPENDENT INDIA-
POLITICAL AFFAIRS

Chapter 10

Independence Attained

THE SITUATION IN India at the beginning of 1947 was perhaps without parallel in history, inasmuch as Britain was determined to hand over power, but could find no generally acceptable transferee. Hindus and Muslims agreed that any long continuance of British rule was out of the question, but disagreed about almost everything else. The Congress claim to represent the people of India was indignantly repudiated by the leaders of the Muslim League, who pointed to the solidarity of the ninety million Muslims of India in support of partition. Law and order had broken down in important areas and the present writer recorded about that time that 'life in Calcutta and the other big cities of India today is life on the edge of a volcano which is already giving the premonitory signs of a great eruption'. Effective power had, as we have seen, been transferred to Indian hands when the Interim Government was formed in 1946, but the complete disunity of that Government deprived it of all moral authority and heightened communal tension throughout the country.

The attitude of the major parties was mainly negative. The Congress would not have partition and the Muslim League would not accept a unitary Government. One reason for this negative attitude was the belief held by many Hindus that Britain would never completely part with authority, but would always reserve some measure of control. There was therefore no need for them to find a constructive solution. The resulting stalemate might have continued indefinitely, but for an act of great moral courage on the part of Attlee's Government, which, on February 20th, 1947, declared that India must govern herself by June 1948, whether agreement as to the form of the constitution had been reached or not. The wording of the announcement was significant. It stated that 'His Majesty's

Government will have to consider to whom the power of the Central Government in India should be handed over on the due date, whether as a whole to some form of Central Government for British India, or in some areas to the existing Provincial Government, or in such other way as may seem most reasonable and in the best interests of the Indian people'.

The effect of this statement was electric. Hindus and Muslims alike now realised that the British Government was determined to end its responsibility for India, and for the first time for many years a sense of reality was introduced into Indian politics. The Congress leaders were forced to recognise that partition could no longer be dismissed as fantastic, while the Muslim League could not shirk the uncomfortable thought that power might even be transferred to the existing Interim Government in which they were in a minority. Of necessity, both parties now began to look for a solution to the political problem, and thoughtful men soon began to feel that, in view of the chaotic state into which India was drifting, the transfer of power ought to take place even before the stipulated date.

At this stage, Lord Mountbatten succeeded Lord Wavell as Governor-General and brought to the Indian problem his characteristic fondness for rapid action. This attitude may not always be suitable for the settlement of great political problems, but it happened to be what India needed at that moment. There was a danger that the sense of reality induced by the February announcement might disappear, and a stalemate might recur, with disastrous results.

If the whole issue as to partition had been open at that time, it is doubtful if Mountbatten's forcing tactics would have assisted the deliberations of the leaders. In fact, however, by March 1947 it had become clear, even to the Congress leaders, that partition was completely unavoidable. Ninety million Muslims were determined not to accept a united India, and there was nothing that either the British Government or the Congress could do to resist this determination. The task which faced Mountbatten was, therefore, the limited though difficult and vital one, of securing agreement as to what areas should be included in Pakistan and then ensuring that the Congress did not, at the last minute, shy away from a solution which their heads, but not their hearts, accepted as inevitable. This task he was supremely fitted to carry out, and within three months of taking office he was able to recommend complete self-government, accompanied by the partition of India, with effect from August 15th, 1947.

The statement issued by the British Government on June 3rd, 1947, accepting this recommendation was the fourth great State pronouncement on India in thirty years, the earlier ones being the Montagu-Chelmsford Declaration, the Cripps Memorandum, and, of course, the announcement of February 1947. This succession of documents makes clear the continuity of British policy and the faithfulness of Britain, in spite of many causes of doubt and exasperation, to the ideal of self-government for India.

The Indian Independence Act did three things. It conferred on India full independence; it provided in principle for partition, subject to local ratification; and it ended the relationship between the Crown and the Indian States, leaving the Princes free to decide their own future. The first of these changes has already been discussed at length, and it is only necessary to add that India and Pakistan were to start with Dominion status, but would be fully free thereafter to decide whether they wished to remain within the British Commonwealth or not.

The second and third changes brought about by the Act require some consideration. Although the demand for partition was based on the two-nation theory, the Muslims were not prepared to be satisfied with a true ethnic frontier, but claimed whatever non-Muslim areas might be considered economically or strategically necessary to them. Broadly speaking, this meant that they demanded the inclusion of the whole of Bengal, Assam and the Punjab, besides Sind, the North-west Frontier Province, Baluchistan and the adjacent territories. This claim was clearly untenable. The further claim put forward at one stage by Jinnah for an eight-hundred-mile corridor between East and West Pakistan need, perhaps, not be taken seriously.

Under the Cabinet Mission Plan, a Constituent Assembly was set up towards the end of 1946, and the Provincial delegates were to meet in three groups. One comprised the Punjab, the North-west Frontier Province and Sind; a second was constituted by Assam and Bengal; and a third by the remaining Provinces. The first two groups were Muslim-majority areas, while in the third group the Hindus were in a considerable majority. The Muslim League declined to participate in the Constituent Assembly and when the statement of June 3rd, 1947, came to be implemented, it was therefore necessary to ask the people of certain areas to choose whether they would enter the existing Constituent Assembly and ultimately join the Union of Hindustan, or join a separate Constituent Assembly and thereafter form a separate Union of Pakistan.

It is not necessary to describe the machinery by which this choice was to be registered, though it must be noted that in Bengal, as in the Punjab, the members of the Legislative Assembly were summoned to sit for this purpose in two parts – those representing the Muslim-majority districts in one part and those from non-Muslim districts in another part. It was always clear that the North-west Frontier Province, Baluchistan, Sind, the West Punjab and the Sylhet district of Assam would opt for Pakistan, while it was equally clear that the East Punjab, a predominantly Hindu and Sikh area, would join India. Bengal presented a more difficult problem, and for some weeks before the final partition the issue was in doubt. The population of East and North Bengal were mainly Muslims, while West Bengal, including Calcutta, was predominantly Hindu. During the course of the years, a genuine Bengali nationality had grown up and this, combined with economic considerations, made many educated Bengalis, Hindus and Muslims alike, averse to any idea of a second partition of Bengal. Some leaders of both communities even discussed the possibility that Bengal might remain united, but outside both India and Pakistan. The great mass of Muslims of East Bengal, however, were determined to opt for Pakistan, and Bengali Hindus thus either had to preserve the unity of Bengal at the cost of being included in Pakistan, or to accept what they felt to be the vivisection of their motherland. They chose the latter alternative, and what Curzon had effected for administrative reasons was restored forty years later on political grounds. The partition of Bengal was perhaps the inescapable, logical consequence of the partition of India, but it was felt as a tragedy by many of the most influential and thoughtful Bengalis.

The third change affected by the Indian Independence Act was the release of the Indian Princes from the ties which bound them to the British Crown. The fact that the Princes had stood on their treaty rights and refused to join the Federation contemplated by the 1935 Act presented the British Government in 1947 with a serious problem. The treaties between the Crown and the States had in many cases been declared to be perpetual. They laid on the British Government the obligation of protecting the State territories, while, either by treaty or by the doctrine of paramountcy, the relations of the State with other States and with the world outside were controlled by the Crown. If these relationships were to continue when British India became self-governing, Britain would in fact be committed to maintaining an *imperium in imperio* of the worst possible kind – more than five hundred outposts of Britain scattered throughout territories to which Britain had granted self-government. The independence of what had been British India would, in fact, have been a mockery. There was also a more practical aspect of the matter. The Viceroy was able to protect the Indian States because he had at his command an army and an administration financed by British India. It could not seriously be suggested that Britain herself should finance and provide an army and a Civil Service in the Indian States for the express purpose of allowing those States to remain outside the new self-governing India. The proposition only needs to be stated to be immediately rejected. It was, in fact, clear that, with the transfer of power, the relationship of the Indian States to the Crown must come to an end. This had indeed been stated in the pronouncement of February 20th, 1947, but critics of Britain's policies can justly argue that on all occasions previous to 1947 the British Government had declared its intention of keeping faith with the Princes and that this intention had been reaffirmed even as late as 1942. It is possible to maintain that these assurances should never have been given, but the more practical consideration is that it would have been impossible to implement them without gross injustice to British India. In the view of the present writer, when power was transferred there was no practical or defensible alternative to the annulment of all ties between the Crown and the Indian States – a procedure which left the States, in theory, free to decide their own political future. Many of them in practice found that freedom illusory.

On August 15th, 1947, amidst scenes of great emotion, in which the colourful personality and capacity for friendship of Mountbatten displayed themselves to the full, the vision of the greatest British administrators of India was fulfilled and India became independent. Although the goal had long been clear, none of those concerned could have predicted the path to it. It is, indeed, interesting to notice that, in spite of the practical continuity of British policy in India, on the few occasions when Britain laid down abstract principles they were almost invariably abandoned. The East India Company, for example, began by declaring that its servants must not meddle with the internal affairs of India; a hundred years later the company resolved to limit its territorial possessions to those already acquired; while a little later still the company laid great stresss on the principle of non-interference with Indian customs, however inhuman they might seem to Western eyes. In due course, each of these principles was, in practice if not in theory, completely abandoned. The same process was seen at work in later years, when British statesmen declared that India must learn to govern herself. 'Four conditions were explicitly or implicitly laid down. They were that the new form of government must be based on agreement between Indian parties; that India must remain one and undivided; that minorities must be protected; and that India must remain within the Commonwealth. Not all these conditions were stated initially, and indeed, some of them would have seemed obvious as to require no statement; but all were an integral part of the policy laid down by British statesmen in 1917.'[1] Not one of these conditions has in fact been maintained. The need for agreement was expressly rejected by the announcement of February 1947; India was partitioned; it was recognised that self-government was not compatible with imposed safeguards for minorities; and India was free to leave or remain in the Commonwealth.

This empirical approach to the problems of India was in keeping with the English genius, and although it involved a long period of tutelage, which educated Indians naturally resented, few today would deny that it has been justified by results.

[1] *The Nineteenth Century*, August 1947. Article by P.J.G.

Chapter 11

Early Problems of Independence

THE UNWILLINGNESS of the British Government to admit the necessity of partition until all hope of preserving Indian unity had vanished, had the unfortunate result that no detailed thought was given to the mechanics of division until June 1947, and all preliminary arrangements for the establishment of two independent countries then had to be made in a little over two months. Within this brief interval, three major problems had to be tackled – the settlement of boundaries; the division of the apparatus and personnel of civil government; and the division of military assets and formations. The first of these problems was mechanically the simplest.

The grouping of Muslim and non-Muslim districts in the Punjab and Bengal for the purpose of opting for India or Pakistan was made on a rough-and-ready basis and a much more meticulous examination was required before the final partition of the two Provinces could take place. A Boundary Commission, with Sir Cyril Radcliffe[1] as Chairman, was appointed to make the demarcation, both in the Punjab and in Bengal. The Bengal problem was relatively simple, but the Punjab presented grave difficulties, particularly in connection with the district of Gurdaspur. The Commission had been directed to demarcate the boundaries on the basis of ascertaining the contiguous majority areas of Muslims and non-Muslims, but was also to take other factors into account. These other factors loomed large in the case of Gurdaspur, partly because it would have been unsatisfactory to isolate Amritsar, the great centre of Sikh influence, from India and partly because, as Lord Birdwood puts it, 'it was a case of the needs of an area artificially created by a canal against the sentiments of a majority of the inhabitants'. The matters soon assumed greater importance than

[1] Now Lord Radcliffe.

103

would otherwise have been the case, since the award of most of Gurdaspur to India strengthened India's strategic position against Pakistan in the course of the Kashmir campaign.

It is not necessary to discuss the award in detail. It was deeply and perhaps unfairly resented by the Muslims, and some of the leaders of Pakistan made the unworthy allegation that the settlement had been influenced by Mountbatten in India's favour. The present writer was in Delhi and in contact with all the chief personages concerned at about this time, and he is entirely satisfied that there is no substance in this charge, and that the award was completely unbiased. Its soundness or otherwise will be a matter of controversy amongst historians to the end of time.

In spite of her resentment, Pakistan loyally accepted the award and the boundaries of India and Pakistan were finally settled. Recent boundary incidents on the eastern border are of no importance in themselves, but are merely symptomatic of strained relations between the two countries.

The second problem was the division of the assets and personnel of the civil government. A Partition Council, consisting of two representatives each of India and Pakistan and presided over by the Governor-General, was set up as soon as partition had been accepted in principle. It operated through a Steering Committee, consisting of two officials – H. M. Patel, a senior member of the Indian Civil Service and Mohammad Ali, who later became Prime Minister of Pakistan – whose names deserve to be recorded in view of the signal service they rendered to both countries by reason of their fair-minded approach and their readiness to work together as old colleagues. It is not necessary for us to follow the complicated details of their work and we need only mention two or three of its aspects. Muslim civil servants in India and non-Muslim civil servants in Pakistan were given the option to choose which Dominion they would join. The magnitude of the administrative difficulties which this presented can be realised from the fact that it affected not only a few senior officers, but all grades, and that in the Railway Department alone nearly 160,000 employees asked for transfer from India to Pakistan or from Pakistan to India.

The division of the physical paraphernalia of Government was perhaps less difficult – though Pakistan complained bitterly that she did not get her fair share – but a more complex problem was that of dividing the cash balances, as well as allocating the Public Debt. The attention of politicians was concentrated on the present rather than the future and the allocation of cash balances therefore attracted a good deal of notice. Pakistan claimed a quarter share of the total cash balances of the Government of undivided India, but the Indian representatives maintained that only a small portion of the cash balances represented the real cash needs of the country and that the rest was held as an anti-inflationary measure. Deadlock was reached, but Gandhi's personal intervention led to a settlement which, in spite of protests, was not unsatisfactory to Pakistan. The customs and excise revenue for the year in which partition was effected gave rise to serious disputes, but, on the other hand, a common currency and coinage was maintained until Pakistan set up its own State Bank in 1948.

The division of military personnel and stores, which was the third problem arising out of the mechanics of partition, gave rise to much greater controversy than the arrangements with regard to the civil administration. Feeling between India and Pakistan was bad from the outset, and for a time the possibility of open hostilities – on a wider scale than those in Kashmir – could not be ruled out. Pakistan, as the new creation, felt strongly that it must receive its share of arms and ammunition without delay. A Joint Defence Council, with Auchinleck as its Supreme Commander under Mountbatten, was established and charged with the duty of completing the division of the armed forces and their plant, machinery, equipment and stores. The transfer was to take place in two stages. In the first stage, Muslim-majority units were to be transferred to the Pakistan area and non-Muslim units to India and this was to be done even before the transfer of power. The task in the second stage was 'to comb out the units themselves on the basis of voluntary transfer'. While these processes were taking place, administrative machinery for the armed forces was to be set up in each Dominion and it was expected that all this would be completed by April 1st, 1948, when the functions of the Supreme Commander would be at an end. During his term of office he was to have no operational control and no responsibility for law and order.

The arrangements were well conceived, but the operations of the Joint Defence Council gave rise to much bitterness and on December 1st, 1947, a breakdown was frankly recognised and the post of Supreme Commander was abolished. In the state of feeling which then prevailed between India and Pakistan and between Muslims and non-Muslims, the task of the Supreme Commander had become completely impossible and the termination of the arrangement does not in any way reflect upon Auchinleck.

Pakistan has alleged consistently from 1947 onwards that India refused to send to Pakistan the arms and ammunition which it had been agreed that Pakistan should receive. Without access to confidential documents, it is impossible to pass judgement on this allegation, but it would not be surprising, in view of the tension between India and Pakistan and the dispute over Kashmir, if India did, in fact, keep back arms which she should have sent to Pakistan. The question later became quite academic in view of Pakistan's remarkable success, with American aid, in building up adequate defence services, but it nevertheless rankles in Pakistani minds.

The difficulties arising out of the process of partition paled into insignificance before the appalling problems presented to the Governments of India and Pakistan by the communal massacres in the Punjab shortly after the transfer of power. To understand these developments it is necessary to recall that the Sikhs were, in origin, a puritanical sect which broke away from Hinduism at the beginning of the sixteenth century. Their founder, Guru Nanak, cared little for the things of this world, but the Jats, who were his principal converts, were a hard-headed and practical people who soon aimed at temporal power and determined to build their strength on military discipline, inspired by religious fanaticism. They developed a remarkable cohesion and a highly militant spirit, which soon brought them into conflict with the Muslim rulers of India. The tenth and last Guru, Gobind Singh, was a great organiser who, as the writer has put it elsewhere, 'devoted his whole energies to the organisation of his followers as a great military community whose lives were dedicated to enmity to Islam'. Ranjit Singh consolidated the power of the Sikhs and in the early nineteenth century made them the masters of the Punjab until they were conquered by the British. Even under British rule they never lost their pride in their great past, or ceased to dream that they would reassert themselves if ever British power waned. If the Sikhs had been concentrated in one particular area of the Punjab, the Sikh-Muslim problem could have been solved by the Radcliffe Commission, but unfortunately they were widely scattered throughout the Province. Wherever the partition line might be drawn, nearly two million Sikhs would find themselves under Muslim rule. The apprehension of this possibility caused tension some months before the announcement of June 1947, and fierce communal riots in April were followed by inflammatory speeches by Tara Singh and other Sikh leaders. The Muslim members of the Interim Government strongly pressed Mountbatten, after the June announcement, to arrest the Sikh leaders, and they could justify their demands by the fact that Tara Singh and Gyani Kartar Singh had frankly declared that they would raise the standard of revolt against Muslim rule. Mountbatten apparently took the view that any such action would merely make a grave communal outbreak certain and that the only chance of peace lay in avoiding precipitate action. Responsibility for this decision must have weighed heavily on Mountbatten who had staked his reputation on a peaceful transfer of power and it is impossible to say that at this stage he was wrong. Nevertheless, preparations for an emergency had to be made and it was accordingly arranged that, while the division of the armed forces was taking place, a Boundary Force, consisting of units from both the Indian and the Pakistan armies and operating under British commanders, should be available to aid the civil authorities in keeping the peace.

The situation grew even more explosive a few days before the transfer of power, and critics of Mountbatten maintain that whatever might have been the prudent course of action in June or July, in the first few days of August he should have arrested the Sikh leaders, who were intransigent and inflammatory.

After August 15th, 1947, violence on a scale previously unknown in modern India broke out. It is impossible to pronounce dogmatically as to who began the orgy of murder, but it seems probable that the Sikhs must accept this responsibility. Within a few hours, however, the Muslims retaliated. Before long the cities of the Punjab were in flames, while armed bands of Muslims and Sikhs roamed the country committing unbelievable outrages. District Officers were powerless and the Boundary Force was unable to fulfil its functions, since its members refused to fire on their own co-religionists. The Force was disbanded a little later and few impartial observers will criticise this action.

It is, fortunately, unnecessary for our purpose to dwell on the horror and brutality of the next few weeks, when neither age, nor sex, nor condition offered any protection against murder or mutilation. Before long the common man, unaided and unadvised, realised instinctively that nothing could put an end to these horrors except the physical separation of the Sikhs and the Muslims. Towards the end of August 1947 there began one of the greatest and most tragic mass-migrations of history. Innumerable multitudes, from towns and villages alike, left their homes and all their wordly possessions, except perhaps what they could carry with them, and trekked wearily to the hoped-for safety of the west if they were Muslims, or the east if they were Sikhs or Hindus. They had no plans, no idea of how they would live and in most cases no known destination. The imagination is numbed in the attempt to conceive the suffering and the sense of helplessness of these wretched cavalcades. Nor did flight necessarily bring safety. Many groups of refugees were attacked on the road and put to death, while refugee trains were derailed and their passengers murdered.

When the first news of what was happening reached Delhi and Lahore, both Governments not unnaturally believed that it was still possible to restore confidence and discouraged great movements of population. Within a few days, however, they realised that this was now out of the question and they applied themselves with great vigour to the task of somehow feeding and protecting the terror-stricken refugees. That task might well have broken a long-established Government and it is to the eternal credit of India and Pakistan that their newly formed Governments succeeded, little by little, in bringing order out of chaos.

A Joint Military Evacuation Organisation was set up at Lahore. Every possible form of transport, including the air services, was laid under requisition to facilitate movement;

composite Muslim-Sikh escorts were provided for convoys of refugees; and, where possible, evacuees were gathered together in temporary camps until they could be sent on to safety. The greatest of all these temporary camps was in Delhi, where it is said that one hundred thousand Muslims took shelter in the Purana Qila. The story of these operations is graphically told in a publication of the Government of India, and a short extract from it will give some idea of what was involved. 'Fleeing from towns and villages close to the Indo-Pakistan border, non-Muslims began to enter India in large numbers in small disorganised parties towards the end of August and the early part of September 1947. Later, when the Indian army began to help them, huge foot convoys, each 30,000 to 40,000 strong, started upon a 150-mile march from the fertile colonies of Lyallpur and Montgomery districts. Thus in forty-two days (September 18th to October 29th), twenty-four non-Muslim foot columns, 849,000 strong, with hundreds of bullock-carts and head of cattle, had crossed the border into India.

'The movement of these columns raised problems of baffling complexity. When the supply of food failed, the Government of India had to drop cooked food as well as food grains and sugar by R.I.A.F. planes which flew from Amritsar and Delhi to Jaranwala, Lyallpur, Churkhana, Dhabhansinghwala, Balloki head-works and Bhai Pheru. Drugs, vaccines and doctors were rushed by air and motor transport. A field ambulance unit was sent to Raiwind to inoculate refugees before they crossed the border. On the way the columns were often attacked and sometimes suffered heavy casualties. Women and children were abducted, and unauthorised search deprived them of the few valuables they carried. The columns suffered at the hands of not only man but also nature. Exposure and devastating floods thinned their ranks. Nevertheless, the determined caravan moved on.'

The railways, in spite of the disorganisation resulting from the distribution of personnel between India and Pakistan, and the even greater difficulties caused by floods of unusual severity, also played a great part in the movement and, according to the publication just quoted, between August 27th and November 6th, 1947, they carried 2,300,000 refugees inward or outward across the Indian frontier.

The failure of the Boundary Force to fulfil its proper function has already been mentioned, and from August 31st each
Government took over separate responsibility for the maintenance of law and order in its own territories and used its
own army for that purpose, as well as for the assistance of
evacuees. This proved a more satisfactory arrangement,
and the magnificent part played by the armies from this stage
onwards did much to atone for the break-down of discipline in
certain units of the Boundary Force.

By November the main movement was at an end and it was
estimated that eight million refugees had crossed the frontier.
During the three months since partition, human nature in the
Punjab and other affected areas had sunk to the lowest depths
and risen to the greatest heights of which it is capable. There
are nauseating but well-documented stories of troops and police
of both communities who fired on the very convoys they were
engaged in protecting. On the other hand, there were Sikhs
who died defending Muslims and Muslims who gave their
lives for Sikhs and Hindus – and there were British officers
and women who cared only to protect the Indians or Pakistanis in their employ.

There can be little doubt that the instinct of the common
man was right, and that only the tragic process of segregation
of Muslims and Sikhs could lead again to peace and security.
Nevertheless, it provided the Governments of both countries
with the appalling problems of housing, feeding, clothing and
providing medical attention and sanitation for the vast numbers
of refugees, who realised their helplessness more than ever
now that the physical danger was over. When these more
immediate problems had been solved by means of the construction of vast temporary camps, the Government of India had to
take up the harder task of rehabilitation – or, to put it in more
concrete form, of finding permanent occupation for the great
army of now landless peasants or urban workers. Agricultural
lands left vacant by Muslims were allotted to the cultivating
classes amongst the refugees, but loans also had to be given on a
considerable scale for the purchase of implements and seeds,
as well as for maintenance until harvest time. The urban classes
were more difficult to settle, particularly as the occupational
structure of the non-Muslim refugees was unlike that of the

Muslim refugees who had migrated to Pakistan. Industrial training classes were instituted; the All India Spinners Association organised cotton-spinning centres to provide work for 100,000 spinners; and public works were undertaken to furnish employment. None of these schemes was of much help to a man who had spent his life in an office, or to the small trader, and though the Government gave loans and grants to assist refugees of these classes to set up in business, many remained for long without any real occupation. They swelled the unhappy ranks of the unemployed and increased the magnitude of a problem which finds a prominent place in the national plan.

Every thoughtful Englishman must ask himself from time to time if this great tragedy, humiliating and painful to Britain as to India, could have been avoided, and three suggestions have been made in various quarters as to how the Punjab massacres could have been prevented. The first is that the Governor-General should have arrested Tara Singh and his colleagues when they began to inflame the minds of the Sikhs in the middle of 1947. Although it is reasonable to contend that they should have been arrested, to believe that action against a few individuals would have arrested the flood of communal passion in the Punjab at the time is gravely to underestimate its depth and intensity. The second suggestion, that a peaceful transfer of population should have been arranged before partition was effected, ignores the traditional attachment of the Punjab peasant to his land. It is extremely improbable that any degree of persuasion or, indeed, anything short of the communal massacres which actually occurred, would have induced either the Sikhs or the Muslims to migrate, and there is also the possibility that propaganda directed to this end might have precipitated the very tragedy it would have been intended to prevent.

Thirdly, it is said that the British army should have been left with responsibility for law and order in the Punjab for a limited period after the transfer of power. This is an over-simplification of the problem. Under whose orders would the army have acted? Clearly, it could not have been under the control of two mutually hostile Governments and the only possible arrangement would have been one in which law and order had not been completely transferred by the British

Government. Neither India nor Pakistan would have accepted such an encroachment on their newly-gained sovereignty. The time had at length come when India and Pakistan had to govern themselves and no form of continued surveillance was compatible with that decision. Britain had discharged her responsibility by establishing in undivided India a reliable and well-trained administration, and it was because that administration was strong enough to stand the strain imposed on it by the events in the Punjab that order was at length brought out of chaos.

Chapter 12

The Federation of India

WE HAVE ALREADY SEEN that, when the transfer of power took place, the treaties between the States and the Crown were annulled. At the same time paramountcy came to an end, for, in spite of pressure from Indian politicians, the British Government rightly took the view that 'it could not and will not in any circumstances transfer paramountcy to an Indian Government'. All political relationships with either British India or the Crown thus terminated in 1947 and a void remained. The 562 States were left in isolation from the new Union of India, and in theory, could have remained 562 separate kingdoms. If they had formed a solid geographical block, a third dominion existing side by side with India and Pakistan might have been a possibility, but, in fact, the Indian States, occupying forty-five per cent of the area of undivided India and containing a population of ninety-three million people, were scattered all over the map. A few of them could perhaps have made out a case for remaining independent, but it was unthinkable that the States as a whole should stand aloof from the Uhion of India. As Coupland has put it, 'An India deprived of the States would have lost all coherence. For they form a great cruciform barrier separating all four quarters of the country. If no more than the Central Indian States and Hyderabad and Mysore were excluded from the Union, the United Provinces would be almost completely cut off from Bombay, and Bombay completely from Sind. The strategic and economic implications were obvious enough. The practicability of Pakistan must be admitted, but the more the separation of the States from British India is considered, the more impracticable it seems: India would live if its Muslim links in the north-west and north-east were amputated, but could it live without its heart?'

One of the first tasks of the Union Government was thus to find 'a common centre for the whole country, including the Indian States, able to function effectively in the Provinces and States alike in matters requiring all-India action'.

This task was taken in hand before the transfer of power and on July 15th, 1947, Sardar Vallabhai Patel, the member of the Interim Government in charge of the States Department, invited the States to accede to the Indian Union in respect of defence, foreign affairs and communications, while preserving their sovereignty in all other matters. There was at that time a great deal of loose talk of a possible federation, outside the Union of India, of the great southern States of Travancore, Mysore and Hyderabad. If this talk ever had any foundation at all, the Nizam of Hyderabad held the key to the situation, but fortunately for the Union of India, his vacillation, together with the relentless pressure exercised by Patel, destroyed any illusions that might have been entertained by the Government of Travancore, or its forceful Dewan Sir C. P. Ramaswami Aiyar as to the possibility of holding aloof. By the date of the transfer of power, all the States within the geographical limits of India, except Hyderabad, Kashmir and Junagadh, had acceded to the Indian Union. Critics of India have declared that many of the States were dragooned into accession by that great administrator Vallabhai Patel, but the alternative would have been chaos and disintegration, and credit must go to the Sardar for having preserved the unity of India.

Hyderabad presented a difficult problem. It was a province of the Mughal Empire until, early in the eighteenth century, the Viceroy Asaf Jah succeeded in making himself independent of Delhi, though he never formally renounced allegiance. Later in the century, after a defeat by the Marathas, the Nizam put himself under British protection and the treaty then made placed the external relations of Hyderabad under the control of the Crown. In the nineteenth century the doctrine of paramountcy still further strengthened the authority of the Crown and attempts made by the Nizam from time to time to assert that his position was different from those of other Indian princes vis-à-vis Britain were unsuccessful. The supremacy of the paramount power was decisively affirmed by Lord Reading in a famous letter in 1926.

The old system of personal rule had continued in Hyderabad without much radical change from Mughal times and all important posts were held by relatives and friends of the ruling family who were, of course, all Muslims. In many ways the State was well run and progressive, though not democratic, but the Hindus, who formed eighty-five per cent of the population, were an insignificant minority in superior Government service.

When the transfer of power took place, the Nizam was in an indecisive frame of mind, but his real desire seemed to be to remain independent of the Indian Union. He had every legal right to do this and was urged to such a course by many of those closest to him. The arguments used in favour of it were threefold. First, with a population of seventeen million, a revenue of Rs. 26 crores and a highly organised administration, Hyderabad was fully capable of existing as a separate State and her special traditions demanded that she should do so. Secondly, it was likely that India would become a republic and the Nizam was not prepared, after an association of one hundred years, to dissociate himself from the Crown. Thirdly, accession to either Union would almost certainly provoke the communal strife from which Hyderabad had hitherto been free. A little later, a fourth argument was added to the effect that, with its mixed population, Hyderabad could not contemplate taking sides with either Union in the struggle for Kashmir.

The Government of India refused to recognise Hyderabad's claim and urged that India was an economic and political entity, that the Union Government was the natural successor to the Crown in respect of relations with the States and quoted Sir Reginald Coupland's dictum that 'an India deprived of the States would have lost all coherence'. Neither side seemed inclined to give in, but in November 1947 a stand-still agreement for one year was made to cover the period until the question of accession should be decided one way or another. Relations between the Nizam and the Government of India rapidly worsened and disorder, for which both sides were to blame, grew rapidly in Hyderabad. The State Congress Party, organised largely from Madras, advocated the overthrow of the Hyderabad Government and launched a mass civil disobedience movement which soon led to widespread violence. Meanwhile, the Muslims in the State had been equally ready to resort to the use of force. The Ittehad-ul-Muslimeen'[1] with its semi-military organisation known as the Razakars, took a bitterly communal line. Each Razakar vowed to 'fight to the last to maintain the supremacy of the Muslim power in the Deccan'. Individuals who sought union with India were terrorised and arms and ammunition were smuggled into Hyderabad on a considerable scale ready for the impending struggle.

The Communists naturally made the most of this opportunity. They established themselves firmly in the two districts of Nalgonda and Warrangal and were, in the initial stages at any rate, welcomed by the State Congress Party. According to the official Hyderabad report, 'Communists and Congress flags were hoisted together; violence, arson and murder increased; grain was looted or destroyed; attempts were made to prevent the collection of taxes by force and by promises that, with the advent of the Congress and the Communists to power, taxation would cease and land be handed over to the peasants; those who refused to join were threatened with death'. In fact, there was little to choose between Hindus and Muslims in the practice of violence and there was no chance that it would be brought to an end until the question of accession was settled.

In the meantime great pressure was brought to bear on the Nizam by Sardar Vallabhai Patel. More than once negotiations seemed to be on the point of success and on at least one occasion there was some ground for thinking that the Nizam was about to agree to the Indian demands, but he was deterred at the very last minute by the threats of the Razakars. At another stage there was talk of the substitution for accession of an agreement giving India control of defence, foreign affairs and communications, but here, again, at the last moment the Nizam raised fresh stipulations and the discussions were infructuous.

While these discussions were going on, the Government of India steadily increased its pressure. An economic blockade was imposed and according to the special correspondent of the *Daily Telegraph*, the Reserve Bank of India 'closed down on Hyderabad's requirements of Indian currency'. At length the

[1] Muslim Association.

negotiations finally broke down and in September 1948 India settled the question once for all by sending troops into Hyderabad to take possession. Their action in Hyderabad was ruthless and effective, though the complete restoration of order proved a long and difficult task.

It is difficult to feel that this long-drawn-out dispute reflected credit on any of those concerned. Razakars, Congressmen and Communists showed an equal readiness to resort to violence; the Government of India exerted a degree of pressure which is difficult to justify in view of the undoubted right of the Nizam to remain independent if he so chose; while the Nizam, by reason of his vacillation and his inability or unwillingness to consider the long-term interests of his people, cut indeed a sorry figure. Whether India was justified or not in the action she finally took is a matter about which historians may well argue for generations to come, but the practical man is bound to consider that the inclusion of Hyderabad in India was the only satisfactory conclusion possible.

The accession of the States meant only that they had handed over to the Union responsibility for defence, foreign affairs and communications, while in all other respects they were autonomous – free even from the limitations which paramountcy had imposed on them before the transfer of power. The existence of these strongholds of autocracy presented a challenge to the new Congress Government of India. There were, it is true, some States in which Legislative Assemblies and Councils had been established, but in most cases these bodies were only advisory. According to the White Paper on the States issued by the Indian Government, 'These institutions served to create an illusion of democracy while retaining the autocratic set-up with the help of large blocks of members nominated by the Executive. . . . The position on the eve of the transfer of power in India was that in most cases autocracy continued unmasked and in a few States it was covered by a thin veneer of democratic façade.'

The disparities between the different States in size, resources and stage of development were great. There were States like Travancore, which compared favourably with most parts of British India in education and other aspects of progress; while at the other end of the scale were small States which have been described as little more than the demesne lands of their rulers, where elementary forms of feudalism provided the only pretence at administration. There were sixteen States each of which had a population of over one million and at the other extreme there were in Saurashtra 222 States having a total population of three and a half million people. Again, there were nineteen States each of which had had a revenue of more than one crore of rupees[1] a year, while there were, according to the White Paper, petty principalities which 'showed a revenue approximating to an average artisan's wage'. It was clear that it would be difficult, if not impossible, to modernise some of these small States and to introduce democratic forms into them, and yet the official view was that 'with the advent of independence the popular urge in the States for attaining the same measure of freedom that was enjoyed by the people of the Provinces, gained momentum and unleashed strong movements for the transfer of power from the rulers to the people'. The present writer believes that this account of the popular movements in the States was exaggerated and that the urge for change operated in Delhi rather than amongst the peoples of the States. However this may be, the Government of India was determined to introduce popular government throughout India and for this purpose decided to merge the States, where necessary, into sizeable units.

Three different processes were involved, of which the simplest was the merger of 216 States into the neighbouring Provinces. This treatment was mainly applied to small units such as the seventeen Deccan States with an average population of a hundred thousand, or the Orissa States with an average area of fifteen hundred square miles and an average population of less than two hundred thousand. There were also a few larger units, such as Baroda and Kolhapur, which for geographical and administrative reasons, were included in the Bombay Province.

The second process was that by which sixty-one States were consolidated into seven centrally administered areas. These States were in the main small, though some larger States were included in this category for strategic or administrative reasons, or because there was no Province to which they could con-

[1] One Crore = 10,000,000.

veniently be attached. The important State of Bhopal was taken under central administration at the express wish of the Nawab. The rulers of the merged and centrally administered States signed agreements providing for the cession by them to the Dominion Government of full and exclusive authority, jurisdiction and powers. They ceased altogether to be concerned in the government of their States and became pensioners who, on the whole, were well treated by the Government of India.

Thirdly, there were five groups of States which 'with due regard to geographical, linguistic, social and cultural affinity of the people could be consolidated into sizeable and viable units existing entirely of States'. The numerous petty States of Kathiawar and the Rajputana States obviously lent themselves to this treatment and, in all, 275 States, containing a population of nearly thirty-five millions, were included in six groups— namely, Saurashtra, Rajasthan, Madhya Bharat, Patiala and East Punjab, Travancore-Cochin and Vindhya Pradesh.[1] Each group was to have at its head a *Rajpramukh*, who was to be elected by The Council of Rulers from amongst the former rulers of the States in the group.

It would be idle to pretend that in all cases the surrender of power was purely voluntary. A great deal of pressure was exercised on some States by the Government of India, and the freedom that Britain bequeathed to the States to decide on their own relationships with India was illusory. The justification for the pressure was the plain fact that in many of the smaller States the rulers rendered no service to their people. They had become an anachronism and it was desirable that an independent India should sweep them away. It is, indeed, reasonable to maintain that the British Government should have abolished them before the transfer of power.

These mergers and consolidations were all completed before the end of 1949 and the only princes then exercising authority were the *Rajpramukhs* and the rulers of Mysore, Jammu-Kashmir and Hyderabad, which had not been affected by the integration. The *Rajpramukhs* executed covenants transferring to the Union Government jurisdiction over all federal

[1] The Union State of Vindhya Pradesh became a centrally administered area before the Constitution came into force in 1950.

matters (except taxation, which was dealt with later), and
their own position was at the same time assimilated to that of
Constitutional Governors of Provinces. In June 1949, Mysore,
which had hitherto only acceded to the Union for the purposes of defence, foreign affairs and communications, accepted the authority of the Centre in all Federal subjects,
except taxation. Somewhat similar arrangements were made
with Hyderabad.

It only remained to bring about the financial integration of
the Indian States with the rest of India. This was done by a
process too complicated to be described here, but of which the
essential elements were the abolition of internal customs
duties, the increase of income tax to the same level as in British
India and financial adjustments between the Centre and the
States by way of transitional payments to make up for loss of
revenue.

After the enactment of the constitution in 1949, the five
Rajpramukhs, and the rulers of Mysore, Hyderabad and Jam-
mu-Kashmir, executed instruments accepting it. The process
of integration was thus complete and India consisted of twenty-
seven States, namely nine Part A States[1] corresponding to former
Governors' Provinces, nine Part B States, comprising the six
Union States together with Hyderabad, Mysore and Jammu-
Kashmir, and nine Part C States or centrally administered areas.
There was also a fourth class of State described as Class D,
consisting of the Andaman and Nicobar Islands.

However tidy the situation may have appeared on paper, in
many parts of the new Union there was virtually no administration at all. The British Government had carried the policy
of non-interference with the Indian States so far as not even
to insist on the establishment of regular judicial machinery
and in some of the smaller States only the crudest forms of
feudal organisation existed. The personnel necessary for a
modern administrative system were not available, and in some
States the people may even have been worse off as a result of the
destruction of the old feudal forms, which could not yet be
replaced by anything better. Steps were taken to fill the void,
but the process is by no means complete yet.

The danger that the unwillingness of some of the Princes to

[1] The old term "province" was dropped in the new Constitution.

join the Union would lead to the disintegration of India had been avoided, but it was thought by some observers that a similar danger would arise from the demand for the formation of what were described as linguistic provinces. Until 1919 the Government of India was a unitary and undemocratic government and the division of British India into Provinces was mainly a matter of administrative convenience. It was of little consequence whether or not the Provincial boundaries corresponded with ethnic or linguistic or even geographical frontiers. As political consciousness grew, the question became of greater importance, and both the Montagu-Chelmsford Report and the Simon Commission suggested that some redistribution of the Provinces on linguistic and ethnic lines might receive consideration. In its own organisation, the Indian National Congress made tentative advances in this direction in 1908, but it was not till 1920 that it accepted the linguistic redistribution of official Provinces as a definite objective. The Nehru Committee in 1928 declared emphatically that it was most desirable for Provinces to be regrouped on a linguistic basis. Thenceforth this policy was uniformly followed by the Congress until independence and new responsibilities compelled a more practical approach. In 1948 a committee known as the J.V.P. Committee, consisting of Nehru, Patel, and Pattabhai Sitaramayya, said frankly that 'when the Congress had given the seal of its aproval to the general principle of linguistic Provinces, it was not faced with the practical application of the principle and hence it had not considered all the implications and consequences that arose from this practical application'. Nehru now set his face steadily against linguistic Provinces, on the grounds that if the units of the Federation corresponded too closely with ethnic and linguistic divisions, fissiparous tendencies might develop and indeed the Provinces might loom larger than India in the eyes of their inhabitants. This was indeed the crux of the matter. If Indian nationality was a reality, it was difficult to understand why people attached so much importance to provincial boundaries. If it was not yet an unqualified reality, linguistic Provinces might be dangerous. This was an over-simplification of the issue, however, for there were many Indians who were gradually becoming conscious of their Indian nationality, but who were more immediately aware that they were Bengalis, or Biharis, or Telugus.

Nehru might have been able to postpone this problem indefinitely if the Communists had not skilfully exploited the Telegu demand for an Andhra State[1] in the elections of 1952. The Communists adopted 'Andhra for the Telugus' as their slogan in that area and romped home in the Telugu-speaking part of Madras. It was probably this fact, rather than the fast unto death of Shri Potti Sriramulu in support of the Telugu demand, that led Nehru to surrender and to agree, in 1953, to the formation of an Andhra State. This led inevitably to the opening of the larger question of State boundaries and to the appointment of the States Reorganisation Commission.

One of the most complicated of the problems with which the Commission was faced was that of the great Marathi-speaking people lying athwart India from Bombay to Madhya Pradesh and Hyderabad. The people of the eight Marathi-speaking districts of Madhya Pradesh,[2] known collectively as Vidarbha, had long claimed separation from the rest of that Province, and the Hindi-speaking inhabitants had more or less become reconciled to the idea of the bisection of the Province. It was urged by important sections of the Maharashtrians[3] that Vidarbha should be consolidated with Maratha areas in Bombay and Hyderabad to form a Samjukta[4] Maratha State. Opinion, however, was divided about this in Madhya Pradesh, particularly in view of the fact that Vidarbha had a financial surplus which its inhabitants did not wish to see spent elsewhere. The States Reorganisation Commission was opposed to the splitting up of the Bombay State and accordingly abandoned the idea of a united Maharashtra, but recommended the formation of a separate Marathi-speaking State of Vidarbha. The Maharashtrians would thus be almost entirely included in Vidarbha and Bombay. This proposal was overtaken by events in Bombay which will be described below.

[1] Andhra – i.e., the north-east portion of the Madras Presidency inhabited principally by Telegus.

[2] Formerly known as the Central Provinces.

[3] The Marathi-speaking people are now often called Maharashtrians instead of Marathas.

[4] Samjukta = united.

There remained the problem of how to deal with the Hindi-speaking districts of Madhya Pradesh. It was ultimately decided to consolidate them with Bhopal, most of Madhya Bharat (old Central India) and the rather unsatisfactory Centrally administered area of Vindhya Pradesh. The new State, known as Madhya Pradesh, is a prosperous and compact unit and has Bhopal as its capital.

The Bombay State was in many ways the most advanced in India. Its literacy rate was high, the State was well administered and progressive, and civic-consciousness was perhaps more developed than in any other part of India. On general grounds, the case for leaving it unchanged was strong. Unfortunately, there was in Bombay a serious communal problem which led both the main elements in the population to clamour for partition. The Maharashtrians, who formed forty-four per cent of the population in the Bombay State and about the same proportion in the City of Bombay, are an energetic martial people who had for long urged the formation of a united Maharashtra comprising the Marathi-speaking areas of the State of Bombay, Madhya Pradesh and Hyderabad, with Bombay as its capital. The other main element in the population of Bombay State consisted of the Gujeratis, who, for historical reasons, have long had great influence in the councils of the Congress Party. They had at times demanded a consolidated Gujerat State, including the States of Saurashtra and Kutch in the north, together with the Gujerati-speaking areas of Bombay.

When this matter was examined by the J.V.P. Committee, it was recognised that the cosmopolitan character of Bombay City, and its position as 'the hub of Indian financial and industrial activity', made it unthinkable that it should become the capital of a purely Maharashtrian State. 'It should continue,' reported the Committee, 'the meeting place of all communities, their source of pride and affection, and a convenient centre for their joint labour and enterprise. It will be incongruous to make this multilingual, cosmopolitan city the capital of a unilingual Province.' This sentiment was echoed by every impartial observer and there was therefore general approval outside Bombay for the recommendation of the States Reorganisation Commission that Bombay City and State should be left more or less *in statu quo*. The writer was in

India when this recommendation was made and it seemed probable to him that, in spite of Maharashtrian agitation, the people of Bombay as a whole would accept it. Unfortunately, the Congress Working Committee took a hand and decided to make Bombay City into a separate State and to break up the rest of Bombay State into Gujerati and Maharashtrian areas. Violence and disaster broke out at once, on such a scale that Delhi felt bound to intervene. The Government of India then made the astonishing decision that the City of Bombay should be administered from Delhi, while the residual Gujerati and Marathi areas should be formed into separate States. The greatest and most progressive city of India was thus to be treated in the same way as the backward tract of Manipur. It can only be assumed that this was a tactical move on Nehru's part, designed to bring the contestants to a sense of reality. After some months' unrest, the Government of India ultimately decided to create a new State consisting of the whole of the old Bombay State – including alike Bombay City and the Maratha and Gujerati areas of the State – together with the Maratha areas of Madhya Pradesh and Hyderabad, and certain Gujerati areas to the north. In other words, the united State which the Maharashtrians had so long demanded was established, but it had included in it the commercially important Gujerati areas of the old Bombay Province, as well as Saurashtra and Kutch to the north. It had a populaton of over fifty million people and an area of more than one hundred and eighty thousand square miles and it might well be regarded as too large for an administrative unit. The settlement naturally satisfied the Marathas, except for certain extremists, but profoundly disturbed the Gujeratis, who feared that their interests would be subordinated to those of the Marathas. Severe rioting broke out in Ahmedabad and elsewhere when the decision of the Government of India was announced, and after two years of intense Gujerati agitation, the new State of Bombay was partitioned. From May 1960 a separate State of Gujerati came into existence, with its capital at Ahmedabad. Bombay City remained the capital of Maharashtra.

Hyderabad also presented special difficulties, since it consisted of the three areas of Telangana, Karnataka and Marathwada, the populations of which differed from one another in race, language and character. Advocates of the dismemberment of Hyderabad maintained that it had remained an artificial unit, that 'the progress of the people who have remained backward cannot be accelerated unless its three component regions are attached to more advanced units', and that this step was necessary for the liquidation of the undemocratic position of the State. As against this, it was urged that the area had been integrated for more than six hundred years from the time of the Bahmani kings, and that a real cultural synthesis had taken place. It is not easy to weigh these conflicting arguments, but it is probable that Hyderabad's resistance to the pressure on it to join the Indian Union in 1947 had somewhat prejudiced its case. The Reorganisation Commission came to the conclusion that all organised parties in the State desired its disintegration. It accordingly recommended that the Telangana area should be reconstituted as a new State to be called Hyderabad, and that the Maratha areas should be merged in Bombay, while the districts of Raichur and Gulbarga should be included in the proposed Karnataka State[1] – which was to consist of the former State of Mysore and the Kannada-speaking districts surrounding it. Ultimately, the Government decided to merge Telangana into the Andhra State, and Hyderabad as a State ceased to exist. The decision may possibly have been right, but it is impossible for an Englishman not to regret the disappearance of what was once the faithful ally of the British Crown – a State which, though considered backward by those who equate progress with democracy, was of great cultural and historical interest.

In dealing with the problem of the Punjab and the Patiala and East Punjab States Union (which formed an *enclave* within the East Punjab), the Commission was confronted with what appeared to be a linguistic claim, but was in reality a demand for a separate Sikh-majority State. The Sikh organisation known as the Shriromani Akali Dal declared, in effect, that the Punjab really consisted of two distinct areas, in one of which Punjabi was the principal language while Hindi was mainly used in the other area, and they demanded the formation of a separate Punjabi-speaking State. The Commission was not impressed with his demand. It pointed out that there were

[1] Eventually named Mysore.

many Hindus in the so-called Punjabi-speaking area who attached nearly as much importance to Hindi as to Punjabi and that in any case the distinction between Punjabi and Hindi was far from clear cut. Punjabi was regarded by the best authorities as a dialect of western Hindi and, according to the Commission, 'the line of demarcation between the Punjabi and Hindi spoken in the State has become more theoretical than real'. It went on to say that the problem of language in the Punjab was primarily a battle of scripts and sentiments and it seemed to it that, however the State might be divided, Hindi and Punjab would have to exist side by side.

Closely linked with the demand for a Punjabi-speaking State was the claim that the artificial unit known as PEPSU should, in view of the fact that 49 per cent of its population were Sikhs, be maintained as a separate State and not merged with the Punjab. The Commission did not consider that PEPSU could be regarded as administratively or economically viable and it recommended its merger. Similar treatment was proposed for the Himachal Pradesh and the Commission wrote enthusiastically in support of its proposal for these two mergers. 'The whole of the Punjab from the Sutlej to the Indus was obviously intended by nature to be a single natural area. Even after the division of the State, the areas within the Union of India commanded by the Ravi, Beas and Sutlej constitute a compact unit fertilised by a single river system. The central part of this unit consists of an area on both sides of the rivers Beas and Sutlej. This central part, however, has vital economic links with the hill districts of Himachal, where the catchment areas of this river system are located; and the portion which is to the south also has important economic links with this central part, because the most important irrigation work which has been undertaken since partition is intended to serve this southern portion, either directly by means of new irrigation canals, or indirectly by means of augmenting the available supply in the old canals. . . . Apart from the fact that the irrigation system of the whole of the Indian Punjab is thus one and indivisible, the power potential of this region, which is also dependent on this system, is also immense; and the Uhl and Bhakra-Nangal electrical power grids together are intended to command the entire area of united Punjab. . . . In our opinion, the formation of a united Punjab will facilitate planning of the kind which seems to be so obviously indicated.'

There can be little doubt that this reasoning was sound. The Commission's proposals regarding the merger of PEPSU and West Punjab were accepted and in due course became law, but after much discussion it was decided to leave the relatively backward Himachal Pradesh under Central administration. The Government of India's rejection of the Sikh claim for a separate Punjab-speaking State was a great disappointment to the Sikhs, and before long they made it clear that they were not prepared to accept defeat. When Nehru declared that a Punjabi Suba was unthinkable, the Sikhs remembered that Andhra had once been unthinkable, and they embarked on a prolonged and bitter agitation. In August 1961 Master Tara Singh began a 'fast unto death', but he abandoned it on the 1st October and was then compelled by the highest Sikh religious authority to undergo humiliating penances for breaking his vow. The Government of India then appointed a Commission to enquire into the grievances of the Sikhs, but the main Sikh organisation – the Akali Dal – refused to co-operate with the Commission. Tara Singh's loss of prestige did not lead to any abatement of the Sikh demand, but after the Chinese attack on India in 1962, the problem was put aside for a time. It must not be assumed that it has been settled – India cannot afford to have a disaffected State on the borders of Pakistan.

In eastern India the reorganisation of the States presented no problems comparable with those of Central or Western India, but at one time relations between West Bengal and Bihar seemed likely to give rise to trouble. The real issue was as to the transfer of certain border areas from one of those States to the other, but Dr. B. C. Roy, the Chief Minister of West Bengal, threw a bombshell into the arena by announcing that he and the Chief Minister of Bihar had agreed to a complete merger of their States. For those who knew either State, it was difficult to take this proposal seriously. There is little love lost between the Bihari and the Bengali, and while the Bihari was naturally jealous of the superior wealth and education of the Bengali, the Bengali on his part resented the prospect of being swamped by the numerical strength of Bihar. The proposal was greatly disliked in both States and has been quietly dropped. It is not easy to understand why it was made, since Dr. B. C. Roy was perhaps the most astute and experienced Chief Minister in India, and was not likely to have made this proposal without good reason. The Congress High Command presumably backed it out of anxiety to reverse the process of disintegration which they feared might set in as a result of the formation of linguistic States, but it is unlikely that the Government of India expected the merger to go through.

Apart from these territorial questions, the Commission found itself bound to deal with two matters of policy. In the first place it recommended the abolition of all the different classes of State and the organisation of the entire Union, apart from the Andamans and the Nicobars and the Laccadive group of islands on the basis of fourteen[1] States and the four centrally administered territories of Delhi, Manipur, Tripura and Himachal Pradesh. Secondly, it abolished the posts of *Rajpramukhs*, apparently on the grounds that they would maintain undesirable loyalties to the past, and would ill-accord 'with the essentially democratic framework of the country'. In other words, all units of the Federation were to be assimilated to the uniform democratic pattern of the old Provinces.

The ultimate result of all these protracted and complicated discussions has been a substantial reduction of the number of units in the Federation. India now consists of sixteen States, nine Union Territories and the North East Frontier Tract, which includes some of the Hill people of Assam. The units are listed in an appendix.

Many Indians regard Nehru's handling of the Bombay situation – as indeed of the whole problem of the States reroganisation – as his greatest failure. To the outsider it seems difficult to acquit the Government of India of the charges of vacillation and of failure to appreciate the strength of the emotions associated with the various communal and linguistic demands. Nehru himself is completely indifferent to local as distinct from India patriotism, and has regarded the question of States reorganisation as a matter mainly of administrative detail. His view is logical, but is not accepted by large sections of the Indian public.

[1] Subsequently increased to sixteen by the creation of the States of Gujarat and Nagaland.

The desire of the Government of India to put in reverse the centrifugal forces which seemed to be operating, led it to establish five zonal councils, each comprising Ministers and other representatives from the various geographically contiguous States and one Union Minister, who presides. The Councils have no powers and are purely advisory and it is not easy to see that they can have many important functions. They are designed to encourage co-operation among the States in major development projects and also to deal with such matters as State border disputes, the position of linguistic minorities, and inter-State transport. Their real value is psychological and, if Nehru's hopes are realised, they may in due course lead the people of India to recognise that State boundaries are purely matters of administrative convenience and that the only patriotism required or justified is of an all-India character. There are no signs of any such development at the moment.

The growth of provincialism in recent years is indeed most disturbing. In 1960 it led in Assam to widespread anti-Bengali riots, the underlying cause of which was the bitter rivalry between Assamese and Bengalis for employment. A little later the introduction of Assamese as the official language of the State gave rise to serious troubles in Cachar, many of the inhabitants of which have a dialect of Bengali as their mother tongue. The Assam Government have been censured in some quarters on the ground that they made no real effort to control the Assamese rioters, but took swift action against the Bengali trouble makers in Cachar. Nehru has also been widely criticised for his inability to deal with a State Government generally regarded as extremely parochial in its outlook.

Even with the integration of the States, the unification of India still remained incomplete, in view of the existence of the French and Portuguese *enclaves*. After some hesitation, the French took a realistic view and their territories, of which Pondicherry and Chandernagore were the most important, were formally ceded to the Indian Union. The Portuguese proved more intractable and declared that, since Goa was part of the metropolitan territories of Portugal, it could in no way be affected by the withdrawal of the British and French from India. The Government of India on the other hand asserted that by all ethnic and cultural tests the people of Goa were

I

Indians and they were determined to sweep away what they regarded as the one remaining outpost of colonialism. Indian feeling on this subject was very strong and in 1955 large numbers of Indian volunteers assembled along the boundaries of Goa with the intention of invading that territory. At this time Nehru still considered that questions of this kind must be settled peacefully and he insisted that the volunteers should abandon their project.

Towards the end of 1961, however, speeches made in the course of the campaigns for the forthcoming all-India elections again whipped up public feeling. Krishna Menon, the Defence Minister, took a leading part in demanding that this matter should be settled once for all, by force if necessary. Allegations were then made that Indians in Goa were suffering serious oppression and much was made of the fact that a Portuguese frigate had fired on an Indian vessel. A considerable Indian military force was disposed along the frontier of Goa. Nehru declared that his patience was exhausted and at midnight of 17/18th December the Indian army invaded Goa. In spite of much brave talk, the Portuguese put up very little resistance and in a few days the operation was concluded and Goa was incorporated into the Union of India. When Goa, Daman and Diu were declared to be Union Territories in December 1961, they were at first placed under a Military Administration, but on 6th June 1962 a Civil Administration as a Union Territory, with T. Sivasankar as Governor, was established in accordance with the Twelfth Amendment to the Constitution. Elections were held in December 1963 and a popular Ministry was sworn in during that month.

Generally speaking, western peoples have disapproved of India's action and regard it as a breach of the spirit if not the letter of the United Nations Charter. Most Asian and African peoples on the other hand have applauded what was considered to be a blow against colonialism. In India itself there is no doubt that the overwhelming majority of the people were behind Nehru and Krishna Menon in this operation.

Quite apart from those of the Hill people of Assam who were included in the North East Frontier Tract, the Nagas presented a difficult problem on the periphery of the State. They were a proud and independent people who did not regard themselves as Indians, and a considerable proportion of them quite un-realistically demanded complete independence. For some years Nehru was equally unrealistic in not recognising the genuine-ness of Naga feeling and in ascribing the trouble entirely to Christian missionary interference.

The Naga movement soon assumed the character of a rebellion and it was not until 1957 that a group of Naga repre-sentatives demanded the establishment of a single Naga ad-ministrative unit under the direct aegis of the Government of India. This raised difficult problems of jurisdiction. The somewhat parochial Assam Government saw no reason why the Govern-ment of India should come into the picture. During the long drawn out tripartite discussions between India, Assam and the Nagas, those Nagas who opposed inclusion in India – described officially as 'Naga hostiles' and led by A. Z. Phizo – continued their rebellious activities. In 1960 Phizo visited England and put the case for his people. For some years the preparation of plans for a Naga State went on with the collaboration of a majority Naga Group, while simultaneously armed 'rebel' Nagas continued to struggle for independence.

By December 1963 sufficient progress had been made for Nagaland to be incorporated into the Indian Union as the sixteenth State, with Shilo Ao as Chief Minister. Elections were then held and of the forty-six seats in the Assembly, eleven were won by the Democratic Party, which is believed to be associated with the underground movement against inclu-sion in India.

A number of 'hostiles', however, still remained in armed rebellion. A Peace Mission led by the Chief Minister of Assam and including the Reverend Michael Scott, undertook negoti-ations with the rebels and a somewhat vague agreement to cease military activities appears to have been reached. This led to exploratory peace talks between the Governor of Naga-land and the hostile Nagas, but so far there has been no concrete result.

If it can be assumed that the Naga troubles have been settled, the only serious outstanding demand for alteration in the political map of India is that of the Sikhs which, as we have seen, has been put into cold storage. The separatist claims made by the Dravida Munnetra Kazagham before the

Chinese attack perhaps need not be taken seriously, provided the Hindi fanatics make no attempt to force their language on the South.

Subject to those two qualifications, it would seem that the internal political reorganisation of India has now been completed.

Chapter 13

The Constitution of India

THE CIRCUMSTANCES of constitution-making in India were different from those in which the other great federations of the world have been fashioned and a brief reference to the differences may be profitable. When the U.S.A. came into existence, a number of independent States, previously unconnected with one another except through their common subordination to the British Crown and subsequent rebellion against it, accepted the necessity of federation somewhat grudgingly to meet particular dangers and difficulties. They were therefore determined to limit the authority of the Federal Centre and insisted on retaining for themselves all powers not specifically transferred to the Union. In Canada, on the other hand, a federation was adopted for generally accepted reasons of convenience, after a somewhat unsatisfactory period of unitary government and since the Canadian Federation, according to Berriedale Keith, 'grew up under the shadow of the great conflict between North and South in America' the makers of the constitution were determined not to repeat the American error of leaving the powers of the States undefined. They decided in favour of a strong Central Government with which the residuary powers should rest. In the case of Australia, the Colonies had been autonomous, the Federation was a convenience rather than a necessity and the Federal Government was only given those powers deliberately surrendered by the States.

None of these three patterns obtained in India in 1947. From August 15th the Constituent Assembly was a fully sovereign body, competent to frame either a unitary or a federal constitution without consultation with any outside authority. There were, of course, provincial rivalries and loyalties, but in the first flush of newly gained freedom they

133

counted for little against the universal pride of independence. The leaders of the Congress Party were the unquestioned repositories of authority and the nation was prepared to accept their guidance. This had not been so when the Constituent Assembly was first summoned in December 1946. At that stage the necessity for partition had not been accepted and regard had to be paid to the strong Muslim demand for a strict limitation of the powers of the Central Government. The historic Objectives Resolution, moved by Nehru, had therefore declared that the territories comprising British India and the acceding States 'shall possess and retain the status of autonomous units, together with residuary powers, and exercise all powers and functions of Government . . . except such powers as are vested . . . in the Union'.

When the Constituent Assembly reassembled after the transfer of power, this reason for limiting the power of the Centre no longer existed and it was at once agreed that, except as regards the Indian States, residuary powers should vest in the Union. During one hundred and fifty years, Britain had succeeded in building up for the first time in history a measure of unity. How could self-governing India destroy it?

Indian politicians had for long studied the constitutions of the world and the Constituent Assembly drew on many sources. The Government of India Act, 1935, acknowledged as a masterpiece of draftsmanship, provided the framework; the constitution of Eire suggested the enunciation of directive principles; the idea of fundamental rights was inspired by the constitution of the U.S.A.; while the influence of the Canadian pattern is apparent in the sections of the constitution dealing with Federation. Above all, in spite of the necessary differences between a federal and a unitary system of Government, the constitution drew heavily upon English principles and concepts.

Perhaps the most important characteristic of the Indian constitution is that the balance of power necessary in any federation is tilted in favour of the Federal Centre against the constituent States. This is apparent in three ways. In the first place, though the respective legislative powers are enumerated in the Federal, Concurrent and States Lists, residuary powers are specifically declared to reside in the Union. Secondly, in cases of emergency, arising either from threat of external aggression or internal disturbance, or in a situation where the President considers that the government of a State cannot be carried on in accordance with the provisions of the constitution, the Federal Government has wide powers of intervening in State matters and in some circumstances of assuming the entire functions of any or all of the State Governments. A more limited power of financial intervention is given to the Centre in circumstances where the President is satisfied that the financial stability or credit of the country, or part thereof is, threatened. Action under any of these provisions has to be approved by Parliament within a limited time.

Thirdly, the predominance of the Federation is assured by the fact that defence, international relations, ports, railways and currency are the prerogative of the Centre alone, and in the case of ports and aerodromes the Central Government can modify or supersede legislation, whether enacted by the Centre or the States.

There can be no doubt that the framers of the constitution have succeeded in creating the strong Centre which was always the aim of the Indian National Congress. The States, nevertheless, cling jealously to the considerable powers they possess and are not unduly influenced by the advice of the Federal Government. In 1954, for example, they steadily resisted the attempts of the Central Finance Minister to bring about some uniformity in the administration of State sales taxes, while some of them have initiated a policy of prohibition, against the consistent advice of the Central Government. On the other hand, some States have had to be more pliable than they would wish, in view of their need of grants from the Centre for development and other purposes. In this matter they are to some extent protected by the fact that, though the most important sources of revenue are federal, the States have a specific constitutional right to receipts from certain heads of federal revenue and to a share of the proceeds of income tax. In reality, the relations between the States and the Centre depend more on politics and personalities than on legal definition, and some observers doubt whether the ascendency of the Centre will be maintained now that Nehru is no longer alive.

As must be the case in a written, federal constitution,

Parliament is not supreme in the sense that applies in the United Kingdom. It is itself bound by the Constitution, the supremacy of which is safeguarded by the authority of the Judiciary to pronounce invalid any Act of Parliament that offends against the Constitution. Thus Parliament is debarred from enacting legislation to compel a person to give evidence against himself; or to allow a child of under fourteen to work in a factory or mine; or to appropriate revenues to the propagation of any particular religion. In the United Kingdom, Parliament could, if it chose, do all these things and since the Indian concept of Parliamentary Government is modelled on that of Britain, Indian politicians have not in their hearts accepted this right of the Judiciary to over-rule Parliamentary authority. They have therefore shown themselves very ready to amend the Constitution whenever the decisions of the Courts have seemed to limit the freedom of Parliament or even of the Government.

Although Parliament is thus not supreme, it approaches nearer to that position than its counterpart in the U.S.A., since Parliament itself, acting under a special procedure, is the authority for changing the Constitution. Any such amendment must be passed by a majority of the total membership of each House and by a majority of not less than two-thirds of members present, while in the case of certain changes affecting the Judiciary, the distribution of powers between the Centre and the Provinces, or the representation of the States in Parliament, any amendment must also be ratified by not less than half of the State Legislatures.

It will be seen that amendment of the Constitution is easier in India than in most federal countries. The Constitution is in that sense flexible and there is indeed a risk that amendment will be so easy as to prevent the Constitution from acting as a safeguard in the way originally intended. In the U.S.A., where the Constitution is much more rigid than that of India, there have only been twelve amendments in the last century and a half, and twice during that interval periods of over forty years have passed without any amendment of the Constitution. The Indian Constitution has already been amended seventeen times.

Another important characteristic of the Constitution is the

incorporation in it of certain fundamental rights. During the framing of the Constitution, some of the Government's advisers urged strongly that abstract principles should be avoided and that the Constitution should be kept simple and practical. Probably Indian leaders today, with a vastly greater experience than in 1947, would agree as to the soundness of this advice, but at the time of the transfer of power the current of political opinion was strongly in favour of treating the Constitution as the bulwark of the liberties of the people. Political thought had been greatly influenced in this matter by the American pattern, while some of the earlier Congress leaders had been led in the same direction by their studies of the constitution-making experiments of revolutionary France. It may seem strange that the exponents of a newly gained democratic system should so distrust democracy itself as to demand constitutional safeguards – but this is not without historical precedent.

At an early stage, the Government of India discovered how completely it had fettered itself by these declarations of fundamental rights and it was not long before steps were taken to amend the Constitution. The first and fourth amendments are of particular interest.

In June 1951 the first amendment of the Constitution was passed to relieve the Government from three major difficulties. The first of these arose from an attempt of the Madras Government to improve the position of the backward classes by reserving seats for them in certain educational institutions. The Supreme Court held that this amounted to discrimination and was therefore unconstitutional. The Government of India rightly felt that action to uplift the backward sections of the community could not be against the spirit of the Constitution, and it therefore secured an addition to Article 15, specifically permitting the State to make special provision for the advancement of the backward classes. The other two important changes effected by the first amendment to the Constitution were more open to question and that relating to the freedom of the Press aroused bitter controversy. Article 19 (1) of the Constitution laid down that all citizens should have the right to freedom of expression. This had been interpreted by the Courts with so much liberality that a newspaper could, with impunity, inflame feeling against a foreign power, and indeed this had been done freely in regard to Pakistan in 1950, when the tension between that country and India was at its height. In a speech in which he seemed to be ill at ease and struggling between his new responsibilities and his former belief in unlimited freedom, Nehru urged that Parliament must have power to legislate 'when something written or said continuously may endanger the peace of the world or our country'. This view was accepted and the relevant amendment removed the bar to the imposition of reasonable restraint on freedom of expression, in the interests of the security of the State, of friendly relations with foreign States and of certain other matters.

The other main provision of the first amendment started a process which was carried further in the fourth amendment four years later. One of the most important safeguards in the Constitution was embodied in Article 31, which laid down that a law providing for the compulsory acquisition of property must fix the amount of compensation, or specify the principles on which the compensation would be calculated. The abolition of the landlords had long been a main plank in the Congress platform and in the early years after the transfer of power several States passed legislation with this object in view. Some of the relevant acts were challenged on the grounds that they infringed the right to hold property or otherwise curtailed the fundamental rights provided in the Constitution. In Bihar, the Patna High Court held the Act concerned to be unconstitutional inasmuch as it involved discrimination between one class and another. It thus appeared that the States might be unable to implement their policy of agrarian reform.

An article was therefore included in the first amendment to the Constitution which excluded laws for the acquisition of estates from the limitations imposed by the articles of the Constitution dealing with fundamental rights. It was, however, still possible to maintain that an acquisition law could be challenged in the Courts on the ground that the compensation provided by it was derisory and that the very word "compensation" implied something commensurate with the value of what was acquired. Against this view it was argued that the absence of any qualifying adjective such as "reasonable" made it clear that the adequacy of the compensation was not justiciable. The matter soon took on a wider aspect when other forms of property besides estates began to be concerned. Further doubt was cast on the whole position by the interference of the High Court of Bombay with the action of the Government of that State in taking over the Sholapur Mills under the Sholapur Spinning and Weaving Ordinance afterwards replaced by an Act.

At this time 'planning' had led the Government to the exercise of increasing control over economic affairs and Nehru was not prepared to allow the achievement of what he regarded as social justice to be delayed by judicial interpretations of the Constitution. He accordingly introduced the fourth amendment to the Constitution. The resulting changes in Article 31, together with the addition of Article 31A, had a twofold effect. First, they barred the Courts from examining the adequacy of the compensation specified in any law for the acquisition of property, and secondly in certain important cases they relieved the State of the constitutional obligation to pay compensation for the acquisition of rights or property.

It appears probable that the authors of the Constitution did not intend these matters to be justiciable and that, at any rate in its first aspect, the amendment merely reaffirmed the original purpose of the Constitutent Assembly. Nevertheless, it came as a great shock to business men, whether British or Indian, particularly as it was followed a little later by the declaration of the Congress Party that the Socialist State was one of its aims. Nehru's assurances that Government did not in fact in general intend to acquire property without payment of adequate compensation, did little to allay the resulting uneasiness. Perhaps the real cause of anxiety sprang not so much from the amendment itself, as from the obvious determination of the Government not to let constitutional safeguards interfere with the execution of its policy and from the speech of the Prime Minister in support of the amendment. It is difficult to exaggerate the extent to which this amendment shook confidence both inside India and in the world at large.

It is in fact clear that the initial concept of fundamental rights, which was an important characteristic of the Constitution, has been weakened considerably. At the same time, the importance of the Directive Principles in the constitution has grown. These may be regarded as amplifications of the aspirations expressed in the preamble to the Constitution and attributed to the people of India. They are not enforceable by any Court, but it is declared to be the duty of the State to apply these principles in making laws. They are, indeed, a kind of blueprint, within the general design of which Central and State Governments are expected to work. In his speech on the first amendment to the constitution Nehru treated the Directive Principles as the dynamic part of the constitution which must grow at the expense of the fundamental rights or static part. His words on this occasion are worth quotation. 'The real difficulty which has come up before us is this. The Constitution lays down certain Directive Principles of State policy and after long discussion we agreed to them and they point out the way we have got to travel. The Constitution also lays down certain fundamental rights. Both are important. The Directive Principles of State policy represent a dynamic move towards a certain objective. The fundamental rights represent something static, to preserve certain rights which exist. Both again are right. But somehow and sometime it might so happen that that dynamic movement and that static standstill do not quite fit into each other.

'A dynamic movement towards a certain objective necessarily means certain changes taking place; that is the essence of movement. Now it may be that, in the process of dynamic movement, certain existing relationships are altered, varied or affected. In fact, they are meant to affect those settled relationships and yet if you come back to the fundamental rights they are meant to preserve, not indirectly, certain settled relationships. There is a certain conflict in the two approaches, not inherently because that was not meant, I am quite sure. But there is that slight difficulty and, naturally, when the Courts of the land have to consider these matters they have to lay stress more on the fundamental rights than on the Directive Principles of State policy. The result is that the whole purpose behind the Constitution, which was meant to be a dynamic constitution leading to a certain goal step by step, is somewhat hampered and hindered by the static element being emphasised a little more than the dynamic element and we have to find out some way of solving it.'

Some of the Directive Principles may be taken for granted as forming the background of policy of any modern, civilised Government – for example, that the State must endeavour within ten years to provide free compulsory education; that satisfactory conditions must be secured for employees; and that children and young people must be protected against exploitation.

The second group of Directive Principles, however, may be regarded as introducing the concept of the welfare state. Article 41, for example, clearly foreshadows public assistance in cases of unemployment, old age and sickness, and the main criticism of it springs from a doubt as to whether the Indian economy is yet ripe for elaborate provisions of this kind. The socialist pattern of society towards which India is now tending is also foreshadowed in Article 39, which lays down *inter alia* that 'the operation of the economic system must not result in the concentration of wealth'. It was no doubt this principle which, some years later, led the Taxation Enquiry Commission to suggest the imposition of a ceiling on personal incomes. The Planning Commission endorsed this idea and suggested that personal incomes in the higher ranges should, after tax, not exceed thirty times the prevailing average family income. Nehru rejected this idea as impracticable, but it is likely to be a recurring *motif* in Indian political thought.

It is interesting to note that, at the time of the drafting of the Constitution, the Congress leaders, like British Socialists at an earlier date, seemed to be concerned solely with the distribution of wealth and not with its production. It is thus only in the sphere of agriculture and cottage industries that the State is directed to take active steps for development and there is no reference at all to the desirability of industrial expansion or the participation of the State in industrial activity. In fact, this part of the constitution bears the stamp of the Gandhian economic thought which the Congress party of late has largely discarded. A further carry-over from pre-independence thought is the directive to the State to separate the executive from the judiciary – a principle the wisdom of which may well be doubted by those with practical experience of Indian administration.

One other Directive Principle of some interest lays down that the State shall endeavour to bring about prohibition of the consumption of alcohol. This principle has not only been impugned as infringing the personal liberties safeguarded by other articles of the Constitution, but has led from time to time to considerable disagreement between the Centre and some of the States. Prohibition is almost an article of faith with Morarji Desai and some of his contemporaries, but many of the younger generation take a different view and there are now signs of some relaxation of prohibition in those areas where it has been introduced.

The wisdom of inserting in a constitution statements of social and economic policy may well be questioned, but it was in keeping with the exalted and idealistic mood which possessed the educated people of India just after the transfer of power – a mood perhaps best illustrated by the preamble to the constitution:

WE, THE PEOPLE OF INDIA, having solemnly resolved to constitute India into a SOVEREIGN DEMO-CRATIC REPUBLIC and to secure to all its citizens:

JUSTICE, social, economic and political;

LIBERTY of thought, expression, belief, faith and worship:

EQUALITY of status and of opportunity; and to promote among them all

FRATERNITY assuring the dignity of the individual and the unity of the Nation;

IN OUR CONSTITUENT ASSEMBLY this twenty-sixth day of November, 1949, do HEREBY ADOPT, ENACT AND GIVE TO OURSELVES THIS CONSTITUTION.

To English readers, inherently suspicious of abstract statements of doctrine, this preamble may sound a little unreal, but it represented the sincere aspirations of those who framed it.

It is not necessary for our purpose to describe the mechanism of the Constitution in detail. It is perhaps enough to state that the legislatures in the Centre and in the larger States are bicameral; that members are elected on the basis of adult suffrage – though for a period of ten years seats were reserved for the scheduled castes[1]; that the President of the Union is elected by an electoral college consisting of the elected members of

[1] Formerly known as the untouchables.

Parliament and the State Legislatures; and that the Governors of States are appointed by the President. As in the British Constitution, it is nowhere laid down that either the President or the Governors must act on the advice of their Ministers and, since all executive authority is vested in the President, he could, without offending the letter of the law, govern despotically. In practice, the convention that the President acts on the advice of his Ministers has been followed and it has until recently been taken for granted that the President is a strictly constitutional head of the State and not, as in the U.S.A., its chief executive. At a meeting of the Indian Law Institute in November 1960, however, the President, Dr. Rajendra Prasad, cast doubt on this assumption and suggested that a study should be made of the President's powers. The reasons which led Dr. Rajendra Prasad to raise this issue are not clear, but it has not so far become of any practical importance. The Central Ministers are collectively responsible to the House of the People and, as they are appointed by the President and hold office during his pleasure, it can be presumed that the usual English convention regarding the results of a defeat in Parliament would apply, though the matter has not yet been put to the test.

It only remains to add that the independence of the Judiciary is assured by provisions parallel to those which operate in the United Kingdom and that this independence has been honourably and courageously maintained by the Judges of the Supreme and High Courts.

The only other clause of the constitution requiring mention here is that relating to the use of English as the official language. Important elements in the Congress Party had for long felt the conduct of official business in a foreign language to be derogatory to the dignity of India, and when India attained independence they pressed strongly for the replacement of English by Hindi in all Government proceedings and correspondence. Before the transfer of power the problem was complicated by the existence in Upper India of two languages – Urdu and Hindi – each of which claimed to be the most suitable Indian *lingua franca*. Basically, Urdu was merely a form of Hindi into which a large Persian element had been introduced after the Muslim invasions of India, while in the course of centuries literary Hindi had undergone a high degree of Sankskritisation. The division between the speakers of Urdu and those of Hindi did not by any means coincide with the division between Muslims and Hindus, but politicians had nevertheless come to identify the two languages with the respective communal cultures. When partition took place, the claim of Urdu to be the *lingua franca* thus disappeared and the demand that Hindi should be the official language of India was greatly strengthened.

There was, however, the practical difficulty that the majority of the people of India did not know Hindi and that English was the only medium in which Indians from the north, the south, the east and the west could communicate with one another. Moreover, considerable opposition to the substitution of Hindi for English sprang from three sources. In the first place the people of South India, who speak languages having no etymological affinity with Hindi, were bitterly opposed to the use of Hindi and regarded the proposal as an attempt by the politicians of North India to dominate the South. Secondly, there were objections from the Bengalis, who were justly proud of their own language, which they regarded as superior to Hindi as a literary vehicle. Thirdly, many thoughtful men felt that a sound knowledge of English would be even more important in the future than in the past if India were to take her rightful place in the modern world. In diplomacy, international trade, science and technology a thorough knowledge of English would be essential – and yet doubt might well be felt as to the wisdom of burdening students with the task of learning Hindi and English, as well as their own regional language.

On the other hand, it could well be argued that, without a national language, India would never attain real unity and in the early years of independence this argument outweighed all other considerations in the minds of many Indian politicians. The Constituent Assembly made a sensible compromise between the two views, and under Article 343 of the constitution it laid down that though the official language of the Union would be Hindi, for a period of fifteen years the English language would continue to be used for all official purposes as previously. The President was empowered, during that period, to authorise the use of Hindi in addition to English for any official purpose. At the end of fifteen years Parliament was to consider the whole matter again.

In the following year the States were directed to introduce the compulsory study of Hindi in secondary schools and, in view of the importance of stenography in Government service, classes in Hindi shorthand and typewriting were started in Delhi. Unfortunately, the South Indians concerned were bitterly opposed to the innovation and, as most of the best stenographers in the Government of India come from Madras, the scheme fell rather flat. In 1952, South Indian Members of Parliament showed their attitude by walking out when the Railway Minister spoke in Hindi.

The movement for the increased use of Hindi nevertheless continued to gather strength and in June 1955 an Official Language Commission was appointed to make recommendations for the progressive use of Hindi for official purposes. Its report was not published until 1957, but in the meantime the President had issued an order authorising the use of Hindi in addition to English for all purposes. The Commission's report was brilliantly non-committal. It approved of the ultimate replacement of English by Hindi, but expressed no view as to when this should be effected. At its annual session in January 1958, the Congress Party was equally non-committal and the Parliamentary Commission which examined the report of the Official Language Commission made the masterly suggestion that though the change over to Hindi should take place in 1965, English might thereafter be used as the official language for any purpose and period laid down by Parliament. In August 1959, Nehru made the statesmanlike pronouncement that English would continue as 'an associate additional language' as long as people required it and that there would be no imposition of Hindi on non-Hindi speaking people. This assurance was implemented in the President's order on May 1960. In 1963 the Official Languages Act laid down that English would continue to be used as an official language. It has not fully allayed suspicion in the South, but it seems fairly clear that as far as the Central Government is concerned, no change is likely in the foreseeable future. It is interesting to

K

note that English is still the medium of instruction in the Defence services.

Nine States have passed official language orders, but it appears that letters from the Secretariats are still written in English.

Chapter 14

Politics and Parties

I T IS PERHAPS not fanciful to trace in modern Indian political thought three main elements, which have come down from particular historical phases. First, there is the readiness to accept control and regulation as part of the normal pattern of life, which may reasonably be connected with the traditional authoritarianism of the Hindu and Muslim periods; secondly, there is an impatience to advance at an impracticable *tempo*, which springs naturally from the sense of time lost under alien rule; while, thirdly, the almost superstitious regard for Parliamentary forms and for the rule of law is clearly the result of the injection of British ideas of freedom and democracy into the Indian system.

Historical causes have in fact generated certain motive forces which, in varying degrees, operate in all the political parties of India today. The most important of these forces is a passionate devotion to new-found independence. Englishmen of the old school revisiting India after some years are apt to be misled by the nostalgic remarks of old friends and colleagues – and still more by their contacts with old servants – into believing that large sections of the Indian public 'wish the British could come back'. Nothing could be further from the truth. Pride in Indian independence is universal and the determination to maintain it against all encroachments, real or imaginary, is common to all parties and all classes.

The second motive force in Indian politics is the belief in neutralism or as it is now called non-alignment. This belief, as we shall see later, has been considerably modified by China's recent aggression, but it has by no means been abandoned. India still suspects all treaties and alliances and looks with particular disfavour on those pacts which seem to bring the struggle between the West and the Communist countries nearer to South Asia.

Thirdly, there is the belief of the great majority of educated Indians in democratic forms of Government. Their interpretation of those forms may differ greatly from that of Western people, but they regard freedom and parliamentary government as synonymous terms. Nehru perhaps exercised greater authority than any contemporary statesman in the West, but he did it in and through the legislature and it would be a reasonable guess that if dictatorship lay ahead in India, the way to it would lie through Parliament.

A fourth and more sinister influence in Indian politics is suspicion of Pakistan. In the Hindu Mahasabha, or militant wing of Hinduism, that suspicion seems to degenerate into hatred, but in a lesser degree it is prevalent in all Indian parties and helps to mould policy in all its branches – defence, finance and economic affairs.

Finally, a powerful factor in Indian politics is boundless belief in the future. In spite of the fears and doubts engendered by the mid-term appraisal of the Third Plan it is regarded as almost self-evident that a period of great prosperity lies ahead and that this can be achieved without the evils that attended on industrial development in Europe, provided the economy is properly controlled. Planning is in the air and all parties believe in it.

The most important problems that have confronted Indian politicians since the transfer of power – the framing of the constitution, the demand for linguistic States, relations with Pakistan, and economic planning – are treated in separate chapters, but we must now consider the main political parties and their approach to these problems. Small splinter groups may be ignored and we shall consider only the Indian National Congress, the Socialists, the Hindu Mahasabha, the Communists and the Swatantra Party and we shall begin with the Indian National Congress as the oldest and the greatest of them.

Before the transfer of power, the Congress Party was a curious agglomeration of individuals of every conceivable shade of political and economic thought, united only by their common longing for independence and their devotion to their great leader, Mohandas Karamchand Gandhi. The achievement of independence left them without any common body of thought and aspiration, and the murder of the Mahatma seemed to create a blank which nothing could fill. Fortunately, there was at hand one who in due time would fill the gap left by Gandhi's assassination. Few men could be outwardly more dissimilar than Gandhi and Jawaharlal Nehru – the ascetic, semi-mystic man of the people and the secular-minded, polished, Harrovian aristocrat – and yet they have both in their day been the idols of the masses, the inspiration of all India. Like Gandhi, Nehru had a certain enigmatic quality, defying analysis. He was a man of moods, impulses and contradictions; at one moment clear cut and dogmatic; at another groping for the truth; one day volatile and talkative, the next taciturn and inscrutable; by temperament, at once a democrat and a dictator. He lacked the subtlety and worldly wisdom of Gandhi, and his impatience over detail and intolerance of criticism were a sore trial to his colleagues and advisers, but it was impossible to be with him without realising his greatness and his single-ness of purpose. He might be right or wrong over Kashmir or socialism; he might, without knowing it, be a pacifist or an imperialist; but the one unchanging element in his complex character was a passionate desire for the welfare of the masses. To most men, such a desire is an intermittent and somewhat abstract feeling; to Nehru it was the mainspring of life. It mattered to him far more than political forms or theories, and a very acute observer in Delhi once suggested to the writer that, if Jawaharlal ever found that he could not raise the stand-ard of the people by democratic methods, it would not be long before he jettisoned democracy. Nevertheless, he was a true democrat in the sense that he enjoyed the presence of ordinary folk. However tired he might be at the beginning of a tour, he drew spiritual refreshment from contact with crowds, and came back with renewed energy and hope.

Nehru, however, was neither a good administrator nor a prac-tical party chief, and, in the early years after the transfer of power, India was above all in need of sound administration. Fortunately, Sardar Vallabhai Patel, a veteran of the Congress with a high reputation as a 'party boss', possessed qualities complementary to those of Nehru. A man of few words and theories, decisive by nature and training, he gave India the stability and direction which at that time Nehru could not have supplied, and under the guidance of these two men the new Government coped successfully with the problems of the rehabilitation of refugees, the restoration of order and the integration of the States.

By the end of 1948 the Congress had thus begun to find its new leadership. It still had to discover some new guiding principle to replace the old struggle for independence, and it was not easy to see how such a principle could emerge in so heterogeneous a party. Clearly, one of India's most immediate problems was that of achieving balanced economic development and it was perhaps unlikely that the industrialists and well-to-do men who then formed the economic right wing of the Party would ever see eye to eye in this matter with Professor Ranga and other apostles of socialism. The two wings were, indeed, as far apart as the Socialist and Conservative parties in England. An uneasy compromise lasted for the first four or five years, but in 1952 the first general elections under the new constitution changed the situation in an unexpected manner. The Congress Party secured 367 out of the 497 seats in the Lower House, but its composition had undergone a radical change. The eminent doctors and lawyers, the large landholders and the successful business men, who had formed the most important section of the Congress Party before and just after independence, now largely disappeared. A competent observer noted, at that time, that the middle classes as a whole had given little support to Congress during the election and that the Congress victory was due almost entirely to the loyalty of humble folk. The typical new Member of the Congress Parliamentary Party was, in fact, the 'small man' and it was only necessary to stand outside Parliament, when the members emerged at the end of the day, to realise the difference in social status and wealth between the average new Congress member and his pre-election predecessor.

Many of the new members were men whose experience had been confined to the affairs of their own districts. Their horizon was limited and such economic ideas as they possessed were coloured with Gandhian thought and with the suspicion that their leaders had not fulfilled the promise of a new heaven and a new earth for a self-governing India. Could it be that Nehru, whom they knew not to be greatly interested in economic affairs, had been led away from the straight path of socialism by Ministers who had fallen under the spell of the capitalists? Big business had been a bulwark of the Congress Party of old. Was it counting for too much now? These thoughts simmered in the minds of the new Members for a year or so, while they familiarised themselves with Parliamentary procedure and began to feel at home in the House and the Lobbies alike. From about the end of 1953 it seemed to the outside observer that the back benchers of the Congress Party, who had previously been generally content to do what they were told, were now beginning to assert themselves – not so much in Parliament as in party meetings – and more than once Ministers had to give in to them. It was noted, too, that where economic affairs were concerned, the influence of 'the Party' was always exerted in a leftward direction. This pressure soon began to influence Government policy and legislation, and frank expositions of the socialist aims of the party were given at the Avadi and Amritsar Congress Sessions in 1955 and 1956 respectively. These developments will be discussed in a later chapter and we need only note here that although it was an open secret that the Cabinet was divided into a left and a right wing, the latter had practically no support inside the Parliamentary Congress Party, Those few Congressmen who were inclined to take a non-socialist view moved into the new Swatantra Party. Even today big business counts for little either in the Congress Party or in Parliament and there is the unfortunate result that, when important commercial and industrial matters are discussed, there are few members present with any practical knowledge of what is involved.

This did not mean, however, that Government had everything its own way. After the 1952 elections question time in the Lok Sabha became more lively and the slightest suspicion of any irregularity or any attempt to hide a mistake, led to a merciless barrage of questions. India appeared to have discovered a way in which, in spite of what was virtually a one party system, public opinion could make itself felt. This fact was well illustrated in 1958 when in spite of Nehru's affection for him, the Finance Minister T. T. Krishnamachari was forced to resign on account of certain investments made by the public sector Life Insurance Corporation in companies in which a

Marwari business man, Hari Das Mundhra, was interested. The investments could well have been defended on their merits, but the Lok Sabha felt that it had not been told the whole story and like the English House of Commons, it will not tolerate evasion.

In the following few years, two developments occurred. In the first place the Congress Party lost much of its old discipline and cohesion and corruption began to become serious. This deterioration was to some extent reflected in the results of the 1962 election, when although it still retained a huge majority, the Congress Party lost seats to both right and left wing parties. In the Uttar Pradesh a shameless personal struggle for power – in which the Chief Minister and the President of the State Congress Party were the chief contestants – split the Party so badly that many Congressmen voted for the Socialist, Dr. Rammanohar Lohia rather than for the veteran Congress candidate Dr. Keshkar. The electoral contrast between N. Dandekar of the Swatantra Party and R. R. Gupta of the Congress Party well illustrates the sorry state of affairs in that State. Two thousand ballot papers were declared invalid, and when a recount was ordered they simply disappeared. In the Punjab, the Congress Chief Minister, P. S. Kairon, broke the power of the main Sikh party and ruled the State with a rod of iron, but allegations that he was using power for his own personal ends were openly made and in spite of Nehru's defence of Kairon, led to several hundred resignations from the Party. Ultimately the Chief Justice was asked to investigate the allegations and he found Kairon guilty of abusing his position for the benefit of himself and his family. The Punjab Home Minister was also censured in the report. Similar conditions prevailed in some other States and only in Maharashtra, West Bengal and Madras did the Congress remain unaffected by the general deterioration.

Not even the Chinese attack availed to pull the party together and in August 1963 an emergency meeting of the All India Congress Committee was called in response to a request of eighty of its members, to investigate the reasons for the numerous defeats of the party in by-elections.

To some extent this deterioration was the natural result of a long period of virtually unchallenged power, but a contributory factor was the decline in the personal prestige of Nehru amongst sections of the educated public. The first outward sign of the change was seen in 1956 when Nehru's initial failure to condemn Russia's behaviour in Hungary exposed him to such severe criticism that he was compelled to modify his attitude to Russia in the Lok Sabha. Two years later his unwillingness to condemn Chinese aggression created a storm in the Lok Sabha, and influential Congressmen, anxious to defend him, began to put the blame on the Defence Minister, Krishna Menon, whose Chinese sympathies were well known and who was frankly described in some quarters as Nehru's evil genius. Matters were made worse when in the 1962 elections Nehru declared that he would resign if Krishna Menon were defeated in a Bombay constituency by Acharya Kripalani and the hostility towards Krishna Menon which grew as the Chinese threat came nearer seriously affected Nehru's own position. When the Chinese advanced into the Brahmaputra valley in October 1962, Nehru was forced to eject Krishna Menon from his Cabinet. The shock given to the obviously ageing Nehru by the collapse of his foreign policy was profound and he never really recovered from it either physically or mentally.

None of these vicissitudes affected his relations with the masses. The criticisms of his policy were only from the intelligentsia and the common people continued to pay him an almost idolatrous devotion. At his death, even his critics felt a deep sense of loss and recognised that his true greatness had consisted in his holding India together in the early years of independence.

While Nehru's influence in some quarters was declining, a star of altogether different quality was rising in the South. Kamaraj Nader, the non-Brahmin, non-English-speaking Chief Minister of Madras since April 1954 was little known outside his own State until recently, but sprang rapidly to prominence in 1962. At the emergency meeting of the All India Congress Committee in August 1963, Kamaraj propounded the theory that the Congress had lost touch with the masses and needed to be vitalised. He therefore proposed that Ministers at the Centre and in the States should abandon office to devote themselves to Party work. In Madras he no doubt had in mind the need

to combat the Dravida Munnetra Kazagham which was skilfully exploiting the general alarm in Madras at the attempts of
politicians in the North to foist Hindi upon them, and he set
the example by resigning his office. It was generally believed
that Nehru had for some time been anxious to free himself from
right wing elements in the Cabinet and the Kamaraj Plan gave
him the opportunity of doing so. All the Central Ministers
agreed to hand in their resignations and those of six of them
were accepted. Prominent amongst those who went out were
Morarji Desai, S. K. Patil and Lal Bahadur Shastri, the Finance,
Food and Home Ministers respectively. It was an open secret
that Desai and Patil were strongly opposed to the Prime
Minister's economic ideas and it was no doubt for this reason
that they were compelled to go. The resignations of Krishna
Menon and Malaviya earlier in the year had reduced the left
wing element in the Cabinet and these new changes may be
thought to have redressed the balance. The case of Lal Bahadur
Shastri was quite different. He was not a good administrator
but was deeply respected in the Party and had for long been
the accepted arbiter in Congress disputes. He was indeed the
one man who might be able to help in pulling the Party together
and his departure from the Cabinet was not in any sense
regarded as a step down.

T. T. Krishnamachari, who had been brought back into the
Cabinet in 1962 now became Finance Minister – a fact which
filled Morarji Desai's cup of bitterness to the full, since there
is no love lost between the two men – while G. L. Nanda, a
labour leader of long standing, was moved from the Labour to
the Home Ministry.

A few months later, Nehru suffered a mild stroke and Lal
Bahadur Shastri was brought back into the Cabinet as Minister
without portfolio, to relieve the Prime Minister of some of his
duties.

As Nehru's health continued to give cause for anxiety, an
intriguing situation developed. In Nehru's absence Nanda
presided over Cabinet meetings, but Shastri represented the
Prime Minister in the Lok Sabha. No Deputy Prime Minister
was appointed and Nehru steadily refused to give any indication of his desires as to the succession.

When Nehru died, on 27th May 1964, as the senior-most

Cabinet Minister Nanda was sworn in as Prime Minister, but this was only a caretaking appointment and a great struggle for office went on behind the scenes. Shastri, Morarji Desai and Nanda were regarded as the possibles, though some observers would have added Indira Gandhi, Nehru's daughter, to the list. Kamaraj's remarkable power now came into play. He insisted that after all the argument was over there must be a unanimous choice and in a few days he secured the election of Shastri, with the support of all the Congress Provinces. In Shastri's new Cabinet, T. T. Krishnamachari remained as Finance Minister and a very bitter Morarji Desai was excluded. That redoubtable fighter, S. K. Patil, who had been dropped from the Cabinet with the Kamaraj Plan, was brought back – and it is significant that in slang parlance he is said to have been 'de-Kamarajed'.

Shastri's illness almost immediately after he became Prime Minister created considerable anxiety as to the stability of the new Government, but he recovered rapidly and is now firmly in the saddle and except perhaps for Morarji Desai, there does not appear to be any serious opposition to him inside the Party.

It appears that Shastri and Kamaraj are determined to restore the health of the Party and it is perhaps for this reason that in September 1964 Biren Mitra, the Chief Minister of Orissa, resigned in the face of a demand for an enquiry and that the Chief Minister of Madhya Pradesh invited an enquiry into the charges against him.

The importance of the conflicts inside the Congress Party which we have described must not be exaggerated. They do not vitiate the fundamental fact of Indian nationalism, but they do illustrate the way in which the Congress Party has lost some of its old power to weld together the separate elements in the country. It is not yet possible to tell whether that party will ultimately survive the old guard who led it before the Transfer of Power, or whether it will break up either on a geographical, linguistic or doctrinal basis.

The Party is, by reason of its origin, amorphous and in spite of its general bias to the left, different sections of it interpret its socialist aims very differently. Those aims will be discussed in a later chapter, but the divergences came to light very clearly in the meeting of the All India Congress Committee at Bhubaneswar in January 1964. High sounding resolutions marked 'a transition from the socialistic pattern of society to democratic socialism as the Congress ideal', but only a well-trained metaphysician could explain the different meanings attached to this phrase by different sections of the Party. From the practical point of view it is to be noted that the High Command refused to countenance resolutions demanding nationalisation of banks, and that the attempts of Krishna Menon and Malaviya to sponsor full-blooded socialist resolutions failed ignominiously – partly because President Kamaraj would not allow them to shirk the issue by postponing a vote on their proposals.

The Congress Government today faithfully reflects these differences. The Prime Minister is generally described as somewhat right of centre; S. K. Patil is a staunch right winger; Nanda is a doctrinaire socialist – and the brilliant T. T. Krishnamachari – T. T. K. to his many friends including the writer – believes in capitalism provided it is firmly under his control. The mixture may be illogical, but in the context of India's needs, it makes a good deal of sense. Above all Kamaraj backs Shastri and dislikes Krishna Menon, Malaviya, and the other left wingers.

The ramifications of the various Socialist Parties since the transfer of power are of too little permanent significance to justify description here. The main Socialist Party, of which Jai Prakash Narain was the moving spirit, came into existence at a time when right wing influence in the Congress Party was strong. The Socialists advocated the abolition of *zemindaris* without compensation, attacked the Government for favouring the capitalist system and demanded a minimum wage of Rs.100 per month as well as a 'ceiling' of Rs.1,000 per month on personal income. From the outset the party was badly organised and in 1948 it took a bad beating in the District Board elections in its main stronghold, the United Provinces. It had discredited itself with thinking people by its lack of any positive, constructive policy. A little later it attempted to remedy this defect by a general demand for nationalisation of British interests, banks and insurance companies and key industries; and at the same time it ventured into the labour field. The textile mills strike which it organised in Bombay was a

failure and it therefore turned its attention to the Kisans[1] only
to find itself forestalled by Professor Ranga and Prakasam, who
left the Congress Party some months before the 1952 Parliamentary elections and formed the Praja Party. In spite of the
accession to the Socialist Party of Acharya Kripalani, for many
years one of the most respected figures in the Congress, the
Socialists did badly in the 1952 elections and secured only
twelve seats, another ten going to the Praja Party in a new
guise. The simple fact was that the various socialist groups did
not differ sufficiently from one another or from the rank and
file of the Congress Party to justify their existence. The right
wing of the Congress Party was almost eliminated in the
elections and thenceforth personalities rather than principles
were the real grounds of separation between it and the Socialists.

In 1954 the Praja Socialists, though only securing nineteen
out of the 117 seats in the State Assembly of Travancore-
Cochin, were able to form a government there by sufferance of
the Congress and Communist members, but they had little
influence elsewhere and the defection of some of their leading
personalities in September 1954 still further weakened them.
In Andhra, where they had built high hopes, they secured only
thirteen seats out of 196 in the 1955 elections to the Provincial
Legislature, as against 146 seats won by the United Congress
Front. In 1964 further fissures occurred amongst the Socialists.
The practical minded Asoka Mehta left them to become Deputy
Chairman of the Planning Commission, and when the national
executive of the Praja Socialist Party decided to expel him, a
considerable number of the [Praja Socialists followed Asoka
Mehta into the Congress fold. The residue merged with Dr.
Rammanohar Lohia's Socialist Party to form the Samyukta
Socialist Party but quarrels have already broken out in the
new group and Dr. Lohia himself has not yet joined it. The
socialist party leaders have been strong individualists, not likely
to be happy in any party or to give it cohesiveness, and at no
time has it appeared likely that any of the socialist groups would
count for much. Today, when the Congress itself has become a
frankly socialist party, it is difficult to see how these splinter
groups can survive.

Just as the Socialist Party must be thought of as a somewhat

[1] Peasants.

ineffective left-wing offshoot from the Congress, the Hindu Mahasabha must be regarded as a more significant deviation to the right. Although it did not come into existence until 1928, the Mahasabha may properly be described as the spiritual successor of Lokamanya Tilak, the arch-priest of militant Hinduism at the end of the nineteenth and beginning of the twentieth century. It was intended to be a cultural organisation for the revivification of Hinduism, but the communal tension of that time, together with the fiery and aggressive character of its leaders, V. D. Savarkar and Dr. Moonjee, soon turned it into a truculent, political party. It embarked on a movement to reconvert those Muslims who had previously been Hindus and at the same time it organised the semi-military training of Hindu youths. The training was generally understood as being intended to fit them equally for service against the British or the Muslims, and the activities of the Hindu Mahasabha at this time were an important cause of the communal riots in many parts of the country. The Mahasabha had two aspects. On its political side it joined hands with the Congress in demanding independence, but was far more communal in its attitude and fought strenuously against separate electorates or any other political concession to the Muslims. On its religious side it stood for the most orthodox forms of Hinduism and was bitterly opposed to any social reform which appeared to be contrary to the teaching of the Hindu scriptures, or even to Hindu tradition. Unlike the Congress, it was prepared on certain conditions to co-operate with Britain in the Second World War – chiefly for the purpose of securing military training for the Hindus, who would thus be strengthened against the Muslims.

It goes without saying that such a body fought hard against partition and, even after August 1947, showed no signs of willingness to accept a *fait accompli*. Its openly professed aim was to undo partition by hook or by crook, and either persuade or force Pakistan to rejoin India. Its more extreme members were bitterly critical of Gandhi, who accepted the fact of partition and strove to damp down antagonism between India and Pakistan, as well as between Hindus and Muslims in each country. Although the murder of Gandhi can in no sense be laid at the door of the leaders of the Hindu Mahasabha, it was generally felt that their teachings had created the atmosphere which made the assassination possible, and for some time thereafter they had to withdraw from politics.

A little before this time, the leadership of the Hindu Mahasabha had passed to Dr. Shyama Prasad Mookerjee, and in August 1948 he announced the intention of the party to re-enter politics. His party had suffered a measure of persecution after the assassination of Gandhi, but this perhaps strengthened its position in the country and the Mahasabha and other connected bodies were able to take a frankly communal and militant line which caused Nehru much anxiety. At the General Session of the Mahasabha in December 1949, resolutions repudiating partition and calling for the restoration of undivided India were passed, and Dr. Khare spoke openly of the inevitability of a fight with Pakistan. Dr. S. P. Mookerjee was described in 1952 as the best parliamentarian in either House and, even though the better mind of India was turned against a militant attitude towards Pakistan, he was able to keep up a pressure in the House of the People quite disproportionate to the small number of seats won by the Hindu Mahasabha and connected parties in the General Election. The party throve on bitterness between India and Pakistan and made the Kashmir situation worse by supporting the *Praja Parishad* agitation in Jammu for immediate full acccession to India, with the abandonment of any idea of a plebiscite at any time. Riots broke out in Delhi and Dr. Mookerjee was arrested. On his release he again entered Kashmir and was arrested, but shortly afterwards, in June 1953, he died.

Dr. Mookerjee's death was a great loss to the Hindu Mahasabha and to his own particular branch of it, known as the Jan Sangh. More important, however, was the fact that feeling towards Pakistan was at this time becoming less bitter. India now took her possession of most of Kashmir for granted and the resulting loss of interest in this subject weakened the principal motive force of the Mahasabha on its political side. Nehru's secularism seemed for the time to have triumphed over the militant communalism of the Hindu Mahasabha, and friends of India rejoiced at the discomfiture of what was, from the outset, a reactionary body. Recently, however, the Mahasabha has shown signs of staging a comeback and in the

1962 elections to the Lok Sabha, the Jan Sangh secured fourteen seats. Its most important figure today is the remarkable
Hindu orator Vajpaye and it has enrolled a considerable
number of voluntary workers in the Uttar Pradesh and Delhi.
It is believed to be financed by a wealthy industrialist, but its
economic policy has not yet crystallised and it must be regarded
mainly as a body dedicated to the maintenance of the Hindu
way of life.

The Communists, who provide the only effective opposition
in Parliament today, are likely to be of much greater importance in years to come than either the Socialists or the Hindu
Mahasabha. In the early 'twenties, Russian leaders frankly
declared their intention of attacking Britain in India and set
themselves to organise and finance a Communist Party of India.
Money was poured into the country freely. Workers' and
peasants' bodies were formed in certain areas and every kind
of subversive activity was encouraged by Communist agents.
In 1924, the trial of four Indian Communists for sedition
brought to light a good deal of information about the methods
employed by the organisers, and still greater knowledge of
these matters was obtained in the course of the trial of the
Meerut conspiracy case in 1929. The Government of India
was able to curtail the receipt of financial assistance from
abroad and to take effective measures against the Communist
Party. It is doubtful, however, if any of these measures would
have produced much result if the initial approach of the Communists had been on right lines. As it happens, they presented
the Indian peasant with those anti-God and anti-private
property aspects of Communism which were least likely to
appeal to him and, on the whole, their rural activities between
the two wars were not very successful. In the urban areas their
task was easier, but even there they were not able to create as
much trouble as they had hoped. Shortly before the Second
World War, however, they seemed to develop a new technique
and to present a Communism shorn of those features which
had made it unattractive to the Indian masses. In 1937 and
1938 they fomented numerous strikes in Calcutta, Bombay and
elsewhere, some of which led to violence.

In the early years of the war, resolute action was taken against
subversive movements and the activities of the Communists

were severely circumscribed. In 1941, when Russia came into the war, the Communist Party came right out in support of the allied war effort. A number of Communists who had been under detention were released, and in 1942 the Communist Party of India was removed from the list of unlawful associations. Certain sections of the Party did active propaganda to keep labour steadily at work in munitions factories and mills, and when the Congress launched its ill-fated 'Quit India' movement, P. C. Joshi, the General Secretary of the Indian Communist Party, declared that 'we Indian Communists are trying to convince our fellow patriots that the course of action suggested by Congress leadership does not lead to freedom, but cuts the nation away from freedom's battle and divides progressive forces in Britain and India'.

This helpful attitude naturally stood the Communists in good stead with the authorities and at the time of the transfer of power they found themselves in a much stronger position than before the war. Communist influence was in fact greater than the numerical strength of the Party might have suggested. In the third decade of the century many Indian students and intellectuals had made the same mistake as the British Socialists and hailed the Russian Revolution as the triumph of liberty. Their own struggle for independence naturally led them to sympathise with such a movement and though at the time of the Second World War the Western world had shed any illusions it once possessed about Russian Communism, in India the glow of admiration still lingered. It would probably be true to say that from the 'thirties onwards a large proportion of Indian university students were attracted by Communist ideas.

Nevertheless there were serious elements of weakness in the Party. Its teachings ran counter to the main current of middle-class thought, and it had incurred the hostility of the Congress by its collaboration with and its receipt of funds from Government in the War effort.

The operations of the Communists in India between the transfer of power and the Chinese attack on India fall into three distinct phases. For the first three years or so they pursued openly subversive activity and made it their business to stir up violence wherever possible. In this phase they bothered little

L

about ideologies, but seized on concrete grievances and in-flamed the minds of the sufferers to the point where violent outbreaks were inevitable. It goes without saying that the volatile city of Calcutta was the scene of much violent Communist activity. Under the guidance of that great anti-Communist, Sardar Vallabhai Patel, Dr. B. C. Roy, the Chief Minister of West Bengal, outlawed the Communist Party of India and took drastic action against those connected with it. Communist violence in Calcutta nevertheless continued during most of 1948 and 1949. Crude bombs were frequently used, serious jail riots occurred, four Europeans were brutally murdered and for some months no manager, European or Indian, went to his factory in the morning without a haunting fear that he would be the victim of violence before the end of the day. The position was not made easier by the decision of the High Court that the action of the West Bengal Government, in outlawing the Communist Party, was unconstitutional. Vallabhai Patel and B. C. Roy were tenacious of their purpose and gradually the situation was brought under control. Nobody who knows Calcutta would ever risk predicting long-continued peace, but it could safely be said that the fears, so widespread in 1948 and 1949, that the forces of disorder would gain the upper hand in that city, no longer prevailed.

The situation in South India and particularly in Hyderabad after the transfer of power lent itself naturally to subversive activity. The Communists in Andhra entered into alliance with various subversive groups, and in the middle of 1948 two districts of Hyderabad were practically controlled by Communists with headquarters at Bezwada. A parallel Government was set up which distributed all land to the cultivators, cancelled all debts, fixed agricultural wages, and controlled the rates of interest which might be charged by moneylenders. A reign of terror was established under which the most ruthless action was taken against those who dared to oppose the will of the Communists.

Great Communist activity was reported in all the eastern parts of the Madras Presidency and in Orissa, and there were also strong Communist groups in Assam and Malabar. At one time the danger that a Communist belt would be established right along the coast from Madras to Calcutta was not remote.

Subversive activities in this area were thus catalogued by an official spokesman: 'Open defiance of authority; frequent skirmishes with the forces of law and order; espionage and pilfering of military secrets; murder and dacoity; parallel governments and "courts" (which sentenced Congressmen to death); obstruction of official food procurement; incitement not to pay taxes and to seize land; fomenting of strikes in which they win either way – if the strike succeeds they gain prestige; if it fails, discontent gains them more adherents.'

The 'police action' against Hyderabad in 1948 enabled the Central Government and the Army to take effective measures against the Communists and to restore the writ of Government in the Warrangal and Nalgonda districts of Hyderabad. At the same time, the Madras Government followed the example of West Bengal and dealt severely with all persons concerned with subversive activity. Satisfactory steps were also taken to build up an intelligence service adequate to cope with these new difficulties. In all these measures against terrorism, the directing brain and will was that of Vallabhai Patel and it is satisfactory to record that before his death, at the end of 1950, the situation had been brought fully under control and the danger of a Communist insurrection, which at one time had been real, had passed away.

Nevertheless, the Government was prepared to run no risks and, in February 1951, the Preventive Detention Bill, arming Government with necessary powers to deal with unlawful activities, was introduced. The Bill was criticised bitterly by the representatives of those at whom it was directed, but the unshakable determination of Government to put an end to the menace of violent Communism was matched by a marked swing of public opinion against the movement in the areas principally concerned – a swing which led villagers in West Bengal to deliver up Communist agents to the authorities.

The Communist Party now embarked on its second post-independence phase in which it abandoned violence and sabotage as its normal methods and took to constitutional agitation. It began to preach that the Government of India were merely the camp followers of the Anglo-American imperialists and to urge the formation of a working-class front to resist capitalist and governmental exploitation. The new policy of non-violence led to the release of many Communists who had been arrested and the accession of field strength thus obtained was directed to the task of taking up local grievances of all kinds. In spite of this new approach, in the 1952 elections the Communists secured only twenty-seven out of the 497 seats in Parliament. The Party nevertheless had some striking local successes, particularly in Andhra, where it made the Telugu demand for a separate Province the main plank in its election platform. These tactics were highly successful and the number of seats secured by the Communists in the Andhra elections to the Madras Legislative Assembly would, but for Rajagopalachari's superb party management, have made it difficult for the Congress to form a Government there. In Travancore-Cochin, too, the Communists did fairly well in the 1952 elections. The Communist Party in that State set up 'Peoples' Courts' and urged the public to boycott the official Courts. The demand gained strength from the fact that the Peoples' Courts dealt with cases very expeditiously, but the Travancore Government soon arrested the members of the Courts and suppressed these illegal bodies.

In the next year or so Communist influence in India steadily declined and even in Andhra, at the elections held in 1955 after the demand for a separate Andhra State had been conceded, the Party did badly. This decline, together with the new international Communist policy, led the Party once again to change its tactics and to enter on a third phase in which it supported Nehru's foreign policy, attempted to form a popular front of left wing parties and at the same time aimed at infiltration into the Congress Party.

This new policy made it possible for the Communist Party to play an open part in the All-India 1957 elections. It appears that the Party decided to concentrate its resources on two or three areas, of which Kerala – a newly-formed State consisting of nearly all of Travancore-Cochin together with the district of Malabar – was for several reasons the most hopeful. A progressive education policy, followed for a long period in the State of Travancore, had produced a large educated middle class for whom no suitable employment was available. Sir C. P. Ramaswami Aiyar, the well-known Dewan of Travancore, used to boast that in his State even the bus drivers were graduates. Unfortunately, this also meant that graduates had to be bus drivers and discontent was the inevitable result. Moreover, the last Congress Government of Travancore-Cochin had been notoriously inefficient, inattentive to its duty, and hopelessly divided into communal factions. It completely lost the respect of the public, so much so that in 1956 it had to be superseded by the Government of India, a period of President's rule being imposed. In the 1957 elections, many non-Communists voted for the Communists simply because, above all, they did not want to see the former Congress Ministers in power again. The Communists secured sixty out of 127 seats in the State Legislative Assembly. Five Independents aligned themselves with the Communists who were then able to form the first Communist Government in the Commonwealth.

The first impact of Communism on Kerala was profoundly disturbing. The Police became rapidly demoralised and the Chief Minister issued a statement which, whatever his intentions may have been, appeared to mean that employers were not to be protected against violence at the hands of labour. Law and order broke down over widespread areas, and planters, whether Indian or British, lived for a time in a state of insecurity. The Government of India kept a watchful eye on the proceedings, and it soon became known that certain important members of the Central Cabinet favoured immediate intervention. The Communists, with their usual flexibility, rapidly adjusted themselves to this threat. Fresh instructions were issued to the Police, law and order were rapidly restored and for a time the Government of Kerala behaved with such propriety that there was no excuse for Central intervention. During this period considerable freedom of speech was allowed, the Press enjoyed a licence to abuse Government which would probably not have been tolerated in a Congress State and Communist Ministers seemed anxious to delude the outside world into believing that they were not really Communists but merely advanced Socialists.

The Communists used this interlude to carry on mass indoctrination on orthodox Party lines. The apparatus of the Polit Bureau was introduced and put under the control of a Minister; village committees of the Party were set up to supervise the work of officials; and several thousand 'village welfare workers' were recruited from amongst Party members and were expected to spread the Communist doctrine. At the same time steps were taken to bring the schools – many of which were staffed and financed by Christian missionaries – under State control. It would be difficult to criticise this change in principle, but the assumption of close supervision of education by a Party which despised religion was bitterly resented by many Hindus and Muslims, as well as by the Christians. The opposition to this move grew even stronger when it became clear that deliberately 'doctored' textbooks were being forced on the schools by the Communist Government.

The phase of apparent Communist moderation was soon at an end. The State Police were again expected to play a pro-Communist role; Government sought to break non-Communist labour unions and when this led to violence, gave them no protection against their Communist rivals; and all sections of society were made to feel that only the Communists had any rights or could look for help from Government. Anger and resentment mounted and the determination of the non-Communists to get rid of the Communist Government at all costs soon resulted in such widespread disorder that in July 1959 the Central Government suspended the State Constitution and took Kerala for the time being under President's rule. This action was warmly approved throughout India and indeed Nehru had been under considerable pressure to intervene at an earlier stage.

President's rule in Kerala lasted until fresh elections were held in February 1960. Although the number of votes then cast for the Communists was larger than in 1957, they lost thirty-six of their seats and a non-Communist Government was formed with a Praja Socialist as Chief Minister and a Congressman as Finance Minister. The new Government enjoyed the somewhat unhappy support of the Moslem League, but the coalition was an uneasy one and the position was further weakened when the Praja Socialist Chief Minister, Pattom Thanu Pillai, left Kerala to assume the governorship of the Punjab. Since then the Kerala Congress Party itself has been badly split over the choice of a State Congress President and other matters. In September 1964 the Congress Party government was defeated in a non-confidence motion in which fifteen

Congress members joined hands with Socialists, Communists and members of the Moslem League. The Government resigned and as the Opposition were unable to form a government, the President assumed the administration which he placed in the hands of the Governor, Giri.

During the past two years the Communists throughout India have suffered a serious setback as a result of Chinese aggression. The Party itself has been divided between those who take a nationalist line and those who seek excuses for defending China. More important still, the thinking public has become aware of the dangers which might arise from an Indian Party owing allegiance to a foreign organisation. There are, it is true, areas such as West Bengal and the East Punjab where volatile elements can be stirred up or factions exploited. In such areas the Communists had some local successes in the 1962 elections, but in India as a whole they have taken a severe knock.

The situation is so confusing that any clear cut analysis would be misleading, but it is approximately true to say that the pro-Russia anti-China Rightist Group is led by S. A. Dange; that the pro-China Leftist section has A. K. Gopalan as its moving spirit; and that E. M. S. Namboodiripad and Bhupesh Gupta are the most important Centrists of the Party.

At a meeting of the National Communist Party in April 1964, Dange was taken to task over letters alleged to have been written by him to the British Government twenty years previously and when he refused to leave the chair while the matter was discussed, thirty Party members walked out. They were suspended, and since they included such important Party members as Gopalan and Namboodiripad confusion was made worse confounded. There are now two parallel organisations each claiming to be the Communist Party of India. Dange's party calls for a national democratic front of all progressive elements in all parties and supports Government's attitude to international affairs. Gopalan's party on the other hand, condemns Government's party policy, seeks to form a workers-peasants party and even regards Public Sector industry as an 'instrument of building capitalism'.

In September 1964 the Communists tried to rehabilitate themselves by exaggerating the seriousness of the food situation and condemning Government roundly for its failure to cope with this problem. They soon overstepped the mark and a considerable number of them were arrested on the ground that they were stirring up violence.

We have used the word Communism for want of a better term, but it is an unsatisfactory name by which to designate the beliefs of the amorphous collection of individuals and groups in India who call themselves Communists. True Communists in India are not numerous and the great majority of Party members are almost completely ignorant of the works of Marx and Engels. The few genuine apostles of Communism, however, are very intelligent and until recently have worked with greater devotion and singleness of purpose than the members of any other party. They have, moreover, been supported by powerful propaganda agencies from abroad. Although it is no longer as easy as it once was in India to buy well printed and handsomely bound Communist works at a nominal price, it is still true that the main stock in trade of many hole-in-the-wall bookshops consists of pornography and Communism. Before the Chinese attack the Communists therefore exercised an influence out of all proportion to their numbers. They exploit skilfully the sense of frustration which is so widespread amongst the middle classes of India today, and in the field of industry they pose as the stout defenders of the rights of labour. Their labour unions are as a rule better organised and disciplined than unions affiliated to the Congress Party, and employers often find it easier to make a firm settlement with them than with their Congress rivals. The Party appeals simultaneously to the idealism of some and the cupidity of others and it is important not to underestimate the influence of this double appeal. In a country where illiteracy is still the rule, where people are now awakening to a new sense of their rights, and where emotions are more easily aroused than in Britain, intelligently organised Communism must always be a danger and though it can safely be asserted that there is no likelihood of a successful Communist insurrection in the near future, it is clear that there will be a protracted struggle between the Congress and the Communists.

In the middle of 1959 a new political group, known as the Swatantra – or Independent – Party was formed under the sponsorship of that veteran statesman Rajagopalachari. Its main theses are that the Congress Government of India is excessively control-minded; and that the present trend of Congress policy will lead naturally to the suppression of liberty. The aim of the movement is the liberation of the individual from the clutches of the State.

Opinions differ widely as to the long term prospects of the new Party. Its founders maintain that many present supporters of the Congress are perturbed at the increasingly socialist trend of thought in that Party and will welcome the opportunity of voting for a non-Communist Party which believes in private enterprise. They point to the large crowds which gather to hear Rajaji on his tours of North India and claim this as a sign that the Party fulfils a real need. Opponents of the Party on the other hand assert that its leadership is a hotch-potch of politicians with nothing in common except their dislike of Congress; that in underdeveloped countries where National Planning is inevitable, it is meaningless to cry for freedom from economic controls, and that while the Party may appeal to a few wealthy business men, it has nothing to attract the common man. They add that Rajaji's personal popularity is so great that any tour of his would attract popular enthusiasm, and that when he ceases to be active the Party will have no focal point.

In the 1962 elections they secured twenty-two seats and so became the third largest party in the Lok Sabha. The Party leaders have cleverly exploited factions inside the Congress Party and have gained strength from alliances with other anti-Congress groups. In Rajasthan the Party has been supported by the Maharaja and its right wing character secures for it support from the traditionalist and anti-modernist feelings which are still strong in that State. The Swatantra Party may well secure a considerable number of seats as a result of these factors, but it is doubtful whether there is any considerable long-term future for a really right wing party in India. The current of thought is so strongly to the left, that even the Congress right wing would elsewhere be regarded as mildly leftist. In the meantime, however, the Party leaders can fairly claim that their outspoken criticism of the Congress Government and of the socialist philosophy of the Congress Party, has not been without its effect on Government thought and policy.

In Parliament we have the curious situation that the only effective opposition is that of a party whose secret aim is to destroy the parliamentary system. That system is indeed developing on lines somewhat different from those to which we are accustomed in Britain. The overwhelming majority of the Congress is perhaps not just the temporary and accidental result of the last elections, but may well be part of the long-term pattern of Indian politics. Members of that Party may criticise the proposals of their own Government, but they will walk obediently into the correct division lobby. There is thus no possibility that Government might sustain a defeat on an important matter. Parliament is indeed becoming not a place where policies are settled and Governments born or overthrown, but the forum in which a virtually irremovable executive expounds its ideas and policies. This does not mean that the Indian Cabinet is in the position of a dictator. It often has to fight hard in defence of its policies, but the struggle takes place in Party meetings rather than in Parliament. Some observers suggest that India is in fact, without conscious design, evolving a new form of Parliamentary Government – a form in which, instead of the periodical interchange of Government and Opposition which characterises the British system, there may be one party permanently entrenched in power, representing the great majority of the nation and sensitive through its party organisation to public opinion. As long as that sensitivity remains, the system may perhaps be well suited to Indian conditions, but in any one-party system there must always be an inherent danger of its ultimately approximating to the Fascist type. That danger has been avoided so far, but it is a little disturbing that so few Indian politicians seem to realise the implication of an invulnerable Congress Party, or to realise how easily a parliamentary government, left too long without an effective opposition, could cease to be democratic.

Chapter 15

India and Pakistan

A YEAR OR SO BEFORE the transfer of power, C. R. Raja-gopalachari, the wisest of the Congress leaders, in-curred unpopularity with his party by suggesting that, if the Muslims really wanted Pakistan, the Hindus would be wise to accept their demand. If this advice had been taken at that time, partition might have resulted in the creation of two friendly States, anxious to co-operate and ready to enter into agreements covering matters of common interest over a wide field. The worst evils of the division of India would thus have been avoided. Unfortunately, this did not happen and in 1947 most Congressmen accepted partition with unconsenting minds, in the absence of any practicable alternative. The Hindus as a whole bitterly resented partition and, in spite of Gandhi's wise advice, the more militant sections amongst them openly declared that, before long, an India free from British control would reunite the two parts of the sub-continent. Pakistan was very conscious of this feeling and regarded her powerful neighbour from the outset with fear and suspicion, which were strengthened by the belief that she had been unjustly treated by India in the division of the assets and par-ticularly the military stores of undivided India.

Any chance that this suspicion and bitterness might grad-ually fade away was destroyed by the Punjab massacres in 1947, which we have already described. Every refugee fed the fire of hatred with his own tale of horror and brutality, and since India and Pakistan were now in the main the lands of the Hindus and Muslims respectively, the mounting com-munal antagonism naturally exacerbated the bad feeling between the two countries. They were thus in no mood for a calm approach to the three dangerously controversial issues of Kashmir, evacuee property and economic relationships, with

171

which they were almost immediately confronted. We must now deal in some detail with these matters.

When the rulers of the 562 Indian States had to choose whether they would join India or Pakistan, or remain aloof from both countries, the guiding considerations were geography, religion and their own wishes. In most cases all these factors pointed to the same answer, but in Kashmir, for historical reasons, this was not so. During the eighteenth century, Kashmir proper, with its almost entirely Muslim population, was under the cruel rule of the Afghans, but in 1819 the powerful Sikh ruler, Ranjit Singh, conquered the country, to the great relief of its inhabitants. At about the same time he installed as ruler of the State of Jammu, which is immediately to the south of Kashmir, a Dogra Rajput chief, Gulab Singh. In the course of the next two decades, Gulab Singh, who, though often un-scrupulous and cruel, was a man of considerable ability and efficiency, conquered the neighbouring States of Ladakh and Baltistan. In 1846, at the conclusion of the First Sikh War, Kashmir was ceded by way of indemnity to the British, who installed Gulab Singh as its ruler. His domains thus included most of the modern State of Jammu and Kashmir, with the exception of Gilgit and some petty territories.

At the time of the transfer of power, the population of Kashmir and Jammu was about four million, of whom over three million were Muslims. Nearly all the 800,000 Hindus were in the State of Jammu. The ruler of this mainly Muslim population at this time was Sir Hari Singh, grandnephew of Gulab Singh. It was alleged that, as a high-caste Hindu, he made no pretence of treating his Muslim subjects fairly, or of taking any interest in the welfare of his people. Taxation was extortionate, cow-slaughter was a capital offence, Muslims were not allowed gun licences and nearly all important posts in the State were held by Kashmiri Brahmans, known as Pandits. All outside observers condemned the cynical indifference of the Maharajah and his entourage to the well-being of their people, and the fact that the British Government had been content to maintain a régime of this character in existence is a just ground of criticism of British rule.

Muslim antipathy to the régime led, in 1931, to serious disorder and then to the foundation of the Kashmir Muslim

Conference which captured most of the elected seats in the new Legislature. In 1938 a minority of Muslims broke away from the Muslim Conference to form the National Conference under the leadership of Sheikh Abdullah, who soon became a close friend of Nehru, himself a Kashmiri Brahman. This new body, which included Hindus as well as Muslims, worked in conjunction with the Indian National Congress and the prolonged struggle between the Congress and the Muslim League in India was reflected in the bad feeling between the Kashmir Muslim Conference and the Kashmir National Conference. Nevertheless, the two bodies were at one in their desire to be rid of the Maharajah and all connected with him.

The position of the Maharajah in 1947 was thus delicate in the extreme. Geographical considerations and the wishes of the majority of the population might perhaps have led him to join Pakistan, but in this case it was certain that he would be ejected by the Government of that country. If, on the other hand, he acceded to India, it was highly improbable that support would be forthcoming for a corrupt, unprogressive and autocratic régime. Inside the State itself, nobody, except a handful of highly privileged Hindus, was in the least anxious for him to remain as Maharajah.

Hari Singh was not the man for decisive action in such circumstances and he decided to play for time. On August 12th, 1947, he declared his intention of making a stand-still agreement with both India and Pakistan, which would preserve existing postal and economic relationships until Kashmir decided her future. That experienced observer, Lord Birdwood, considers that in view of the strong Kashmiri-Muslim feeling against India, an imaginative approach by Jinnah to Hari Singh in the early days after partition might well have led the Maharajah to accede to Pakistan. That approach was not made and within a few weeks events had moved out of the control of the Maharajah. Jinnah's stern aloofness was thus partly responsible for the later complications.

At that time the Kashmir Government was having considerable trouble with the Muslim inhabitants of the subordinate State of Pooch, who strongly favoured accession to Pakistan. Their position was greatly strengthened when, towards the end of October 1947, Muslim tribesmen from the north-west, animated partly by their traditional love of raiding and partly by anger at the innumerable stories of atrocities told by Muslim refugees from the East Punjab, bore down into Kashmir and allied themselves with their co-religionists against the Maharajah and the Hindu ruling classes. The cry of 'Islam in danger' engendered fanaticism and hatred, and as they moved on towards Srinagar the tribesmen struck terror into the hearts of the local Hindu inhabitants.

It is almost universally believed in India that the Pakistan Government had deliberately incited the tribesmen to invade Kashmir and, not unnaturally, that belief still further embittered Indian feeling. It is impossible to be dogmatic on this matter, but the judgment of the present writer is that the Pakistan Government at the highest level had no previous knowledge of the movement at all, though the Chief Minister of the North-west Frontier Province may have facilitated it and a number of highly placed Pakistani officials certainly connived at it.

The tribesmen advanced rapidly and something like panic seized the Maharajah and his court. They appealed to India for help and were told that, unless Kashmir acceded to India, no aid could properly be given. On October 26th, 1947, the Maharajah accordingly acceded to India and the accession was accepted. It was reported by the Indian representative in Kashmir that 'the troops left in Srinagar had no prospect whatever of holding the invaders, for they consisted merely of one squadron of cavalry'. Indian troops were therefore flown into Kashmir the day after the accession.

Opinions will continue to differ as to the wisdom and propriety of India's action. Her supporters argue, first, that the Maharajah was perfectly entitled to accede without consulting his people, and that neither in Kashmir nor in any other State was it India's business to interfere in the domestic question as to how the decision to accede had been reached; secondly, that Vallabhai Patel had told Kashmir frankly that if she chose to accede to Pakistan, India would not resent her action; and, thirdly, that had there been any further delay in sending in troops, the situation would have been irretrievable and large numbers of Europeans and Hindus would have been massacred.

Critics of India maintain that her acceptance of accession against the probable wishes of the population at that time was inconsistent with her general professions, as well as with her attitude over Hyderabad and that her proper course would have been to send troops in for the sole purpose of driving back the tribesmen and to invite Pakistan to join her in this venture. They allege that the opportunity of securing the accession of Kashmir was too tempting to be missed by the Government of India, and that Mountbatten, who was biased against Jinnah, succumbed to the sophistries of Delhi.

Mountbatten's own attitude is thus summarised by his biographer:

'He said that while urging the Maharajah to make up his mind about accession before the transfer of power, he had all along, from his visit in June onwards, exerted his whole influence to prevent him from acceding to one Dominion or the other without first taking steps to ascertain the will of his people by referendum, plebiscite, election, or even, if these methods were impracticable, by representative public meetings. When during the past forty-eight hours it became clear that the Government (i.e., of India) were determined, against the military advice both of their own Chiefs of Staff and of himself, to send in troops in response to a request from Kashmir for aid, he returned to the charge about accession.'

It is not necessary for our purpose to follow in detail the course of the strange war which now ensued. We need merely note that the tribesmen were rapidly driven back to the west, where they joined forces with the Azad Kashmir Army, consisting of Muslim members of the Kashmir State Forces who had deserted some months before the transfer of power and who sought to establish an independent Kashmir Government. The Indian Army succeeded in driving the opposing forces back to the Kotli-Poonch-Uri line, but the absence of good roads from India and the long line of communications prevented any further advance. At a somewhat indeterminate date early in 1948, the official Pakistan Army entered Kashmir and took part in the campaign.

At this stage, neither country wanted to promote a general Indo-Pakistan war and both countries were thus hampered in these movements of troops by their desire to respect each other's territory outside Kashmir. It is for this reason that Radcliffe's award of Gurdaspur to India has been so bitterly attacked in Pakistan. Without Gurdaspur, India could not have used the Pathankot railhead on which her force at Jammu was based. A condition of stalemate was rapidly reached, which continued until a cease-fire was arranged on January 1st, 1949. From 1948 onwards India has, in fact, occupied all Kashmir east of the Kotli-Poonch-Uri line, while Azad Kashmir, west of that line, has formed part of Pakistan. The history of the controversy over Kashmir since that time is dreary indeed and the charges and counter-charges between India and Pakistan – many of which can be fully sustained – are too unedifying to justify detailed study here. In theory, both India and Pakistan agreed at the outset that the future of Kashmir must be determined by a plebiscite, but attempts to implement this principle always broke down because of disagreement as to who was to control the country while the plebiscite was taking place. The line taken in Delhi for some years was that Kashmir is legally part of India and India must retain responsibility for its Government unless and until the people decide otherwise. India also urged the danger of leaving Kashmir a vacuum into which either Pakistan or some other hostile power could easily enter. Pakistan, on the other hand, has consistently argued, in the light of all modern experience elsewhere, that a plebiscite held while the local officials and the army were servants of the Government of India would be a farce.

The Kashmir issue was referred to the United Nations by India at a time when the military situation was difficult for her and that body has made numerous efforts to solve it, including the appointment of one Commission, two arbitrators and a Plebiscite Administrator who has never been allowed to function.

On an impartial study of the records, one is bound to conclude that Pakistan has been more ready than India to accept outside arbitration, or to abide by plebiscite conditions which she does not like. In India there was never any enthusiasm for a plebiscite – which, at any rate in the early days, would probably have gone against India – and she was not therefore prepared to run risks, or to accept a position which she regarded as unsound, merely in order to enable a plebiscite to be held.

In 1951 a further obstacle to a plebiscite was created when India agreed to the election of a Constituent Assembly in Kashmir – though Nehru asserted that it would not stand in the way of any implementation of a decision of the Security Council. In the following year, Sheikh Abdullah, the Chief Minister of Kashmir, showed signs of desiring for Kashmir a greater independence of Delhi than the other States of India enjoyed. A decision to elect the Head of the State and to adopt a separate Kashmir flag were significant pointers in this direction. Agreement was reached with Delhi on these particular matters, but a year later Sheikh Abdullah was arrested and replaced by Bakshi Ghulam Mohammad, whose leanings towards India were not doubted. The *Hindustan Times*, the leading Delhi newspaper, at this time made an interesting comment which illustrates India's lack of enthusiasm for a plebiscite – 'The situation today is that the people of Kashmir have no yardstick other than their religion to determine their affiliation – no plebiscite in India's view can be fair and impartial if it is influenced by an appeal to religion.'

In 1954 Bakshi Ghulam Mohammad felt sufficiently well established to declare that 'the question of our accession to India is no longer an outstanding problem for the people of Kashmir. It is part of India and will remain so'.

This was undoubtedly the view of the man in the street of India. If he came from the south or the east he was not much interested in the Kashmir problem, but in any case he regarded possession as ten-tenths of the law and did not believe that there was any problem to be solved.

In 1956 Nehru openly lent his support to this view when he stated, with almost brutal frankness, that the idea of a plebiscite was now out of date and suggested a partition on the basis of existing possession. Pakistan angrily rejected this proposal. The enactment of a Constitution for Kashmir as part of the Indian Union was greatly resented in Pakistan, where it was regarded as an act in defiance of earlier United Nations resolutions demanding a plebiscite for Kashmir. The Constitution of

M

Kashmir came into force on January 26th, 1957, and shortly before that date Pakistan raised the matter in the United Nations. Her spokesman proposed the withdrawal of all Indian and Pakistani troops from Kashmir, the stationing of United Nations troops in that country as a preliminary to a plebiscite and the postponement of the operation of the new Constitution.

There was a good deal of sympathy in the United Nations with Pakistan's demands, and a 'holding resolution' sponsored by Australia, Colombia, Cuba, the United Kingdom and the U.S.A. was passed on January 24th by ten votes to nil, with Russia abstaining. Reaction in India was rapid and adverse, and the Press was quick to make it clear that foreign troops would not be tolerated in Indian Kashmir, while it was alleged by some Indian leaders that the resolution was the result of a desire in certain Western countries to put Nehru in difficulties. Nehru declined to postpone the inauguration of the Kashmir Constitution and contended that any such action would be meaningless, as Kashmir had been legally part of India since her accession in 1947. In the middle of February 1957, Australia, Cuba, the United Kingdom and the U.S.A. sponsored a new resolution in the Security Council to the effect that the Council's current President should proceed to India and Pakistan to discuss conditions of progress towards the settlement of the Kashmir problem, 'bearing in mind the proposal for the use of a temporary United Nations force'. The resolution was accepted by Pakistan, but India strongly opposed it and Russia exercised the veto. A new resolution was then put forward by the U.S.A., the United Kingdom and Australia, directing the President of the Council to visit India and Pakistan and report. This resolution was carried.

By this time anger in India was widespread and intense. For the first time since the transfer of power, Nehru spoke harshly and unfairly of Britain. His words must perhaps be discounted to some extent, since they were uttered in the middle of a general election campaign and it is probable that when the electoral excitement was over he regretted having accused Britain of 'trying to weaken India internally by the same tactics the British practised in the days before independence'. It was nevertheless clear that India had no intention of compromising on this issue and the United Nations made no serious attempt to follow up its resolutions.

Fortunately the other main dispute – that relating to the waters of the Indus and its tributaries – has proved less intractable than the problem of Kashmir.

Although the Kashmir dispute is primarily a matter of strategical considerations, coloured also by emotion and prestige, it has also an economic aspect arising from its connection with the irrigation system of West Pakistan. Undivided Punjab is an area of scanty rainfall, over two-thirds of which falls in a normal year between June and September, and cultivation is therefore very largely dependent on irrigation. It is watered by the Indus and her five tributaries and the six rivers are conveniently divided into two systems – the western rivers, namely, the Indus, Jhelum and Chenab, and the eastern rivers, namely, the Ravi, Beas and Sutlej. Some idea of the magnitude of these rivers can be gained from the fact that the Indus carries roughly as much water as the Nile, while the Jhelum and the Chenab each carry about a third of that volume. The eastern rivers are on a smaller scale and their combined flow is about one-fourth of that of the western system. The Indus rises in Tibet and passes through Kashmir into Pakistan; the Jhelum has its source in Kashmir and flows thence into Pakistan; while the Chenab rises in India and flows through Kashmir into Pakistan. Of the eastern rivers, the Ravi rises in India and flows into Pakistan; the Beas lies wholly within India; and the Sutlej rises in Tibet and flows through India into Pakistan.

The great irrigation works constructed in the basin of the Indus and its tributaries during the British period were not spread evenly throughout the Punjab, and it so happened that partition, effected on a communal basis, resulted in the inclusion in Pakistan of twenty-one million acres of the irrigated area of the Punjab, as against five million acres which fell in India. Pakistan nevertheless felt herself to be in a weak position, inasmuch as she depended wholly on rivers the upper reaches of which lay in Indian territory or in Kashmir. This involved a treble risk. Her supply of water might be deliberately diverted at a time of strained relations; or, in the absence of a fair-sharing agreement, she might fare badly in a year of drought; or even if relations between the two countries were good, India's own need to increase her irrigation facilities might leave Pakistan short of water, since the total available supply of the system is inadequate for desirable developments in the West and East Punjab. It may seem strange that rivers, the joint flow of which is more than twice that of the Nile, should not be sufficient for the needs of the surrounding country, but the difficulty arises from the uneven distribution of the flow throughout the different seasons of the year. In the Indus, for example, the volume of water carried in the six months of the summer is over seven times that carried in that of the rest of the year, and the figures for the other rivers are somewhat similar. Much of the summer flow is wasted, and it is reckoned that half of the annual volume of water in the system flows unused into the Arabian Sea. In the absence of adequate storage arrangements the water available, in the dry season, is barely sufficient in a normal year, and any diminution of the flow to Pakistan might well be disastrous to her.

There is, moreover, a second respect in which Pakistan felt herself vulnerable. Water for irrigation is led from the rivers by canals which in many cases take off from dams or head-works. Some of the Pakistan canals have their head-works in Indian territory and one of them flows for many miles through India before reaching Pakistan. It would be simple to cut or divert these canals if India so wished.

Soon after partition, India and Pakistan entered into a stand-still agreement, the effect of which was that the same proportion of the water of the rivers concerned would be allowed to flow downstream into Pakistan, as before partition. That agreement lapsed on March 31st, 1948, and on the following day India discontinued the supply of water to the Central Bari Doab and the Dipalpur Canals in Pakistan. The result in loss of crops and distress in Pakistan was considerable. Pakistan alleges that supplies in the rivers were also cut off, but India denies this and the charge has never been substantiated.

A month later an agreement was reached under which India reopened the canals, subject to the levy of *seigniorage* charges for water and the adjustment of the capital cost of certain head-works and carrier canals. Before long, serious misunderstandings arose over this new agreement. India claimed that it was meant to be a temporary arrangement to give Pakistan time to tap new sources and, since Pakistan had made no such effort by September 1948, India threatened to discontinue supplies to the two canals. Nehru intervened and the threat was withdrawn, but India distinctly laid down that it was her intention to diminish supplies gradually, giving Pakistan time to have recourse to new sources of supply. Any further negotiations, she stated, would be on this basis. Pakistan, which had made certain difficulties over payment of *seigniorage*, demanded a reference to the International Court of Justice. While that proposal was being discussed, in September 1951, the World Bank offered its good offices to work out a settlement.

Matters dragged on uneasily, but without any particular flare up, until the winter of 1952–3, when a serious drought all over the Indus Basin left an absolute shortage of water for irrigation. Both countries suffered from this shortage, but Pakistan alleged that India took more than its stipulated share of water for the head-works on the eastern rivers, and that this action, together with India's withdrawals above the head-works for new canals, left Pakistan seriously short of water. There were also reports that the Government of India proposed to abandon the Ferozepore head-work, on which important cotton and wheat growing areas in the West Punjab depended and that new Indian irrigation works contemplated on the Sutlej would still further reduce supplies.

There is no evidence to suggest that India was behaving unfairly and there is no doubt that the danger to Pakistan at this time was exaggerated. For the West Punjab cultivator, however, irrigation is a matter of life and death and the suggestion, however unjustified, that India was deliberately keeping Pakistan short, raised tempers to fever-pitch. David Lilienthal, of the Tennessee Valley Authority, happened to be present at a place in Pakistan where, for some perfectly good reason, the supply of water was temporarily reduced and his description of the local excitement will illustrate the way in which water disputes can lead to bloodshed. 'I saw the source of water supply for Lahore and the surrounding farming country near the border when (probably for some operating reason) India had cut down the flow; every passer-by could

see how low the canal's waters had fallen. An hour later I talked
to Pakistanis so furious and worried they were ready to fight
with their bare hands. Later in the day the waters were up
again.' It is not therefore surprising that, in 1953, the canal
water dispute loomed as large as Kashmir in the minds of many
Pakistanis.

Fortunately, the following monsoon was good. The danger
to Pakistan's food supply receded, tempers became calmer,
and the World Bank Working Party was able to proceed
quietly with its investigations. The plans put up by India and
Pakistan to that body were wholly irreconcilable. Pakistan
claimed that existing uses of water must be continued from
existing sources, whereas India claimed that, though existing
uses must be continued, they need not necessarily be from the
old sources. The water in the eastern rivers, India contended,
could in due course be released for use in India and replaced as
far as Pakistan is concerned by water from the western rivers.
India's view was much the more rational of the two. The
Working Party then put forward its own proposals, which
involved rejection of the Pakistan claim with regard to the
existing sources. They envisaged the exclusive use of the
western rivers by Pakistan (except in Kashmir) and of the
eastern rivers by India, after a transition period during which
India would construct the link canals needed to replace supplies
from India. Under this plan the cost of the new work required
would be shared between the two countries. Sir William Iliff,
who represented the World Bank in these discussions, displayed
almost superhuman patience over a long period and it is largely
due to him that a settlement on the principles proposed by the
World Bank was reached in 1960. The construction of the link
canals and other necessary works in 1960 was estimated to cost
about Rs.500 crores or £375 million, but it is now clear that
the actual cost will be nearly double that sum. A large part of
this expenditure will be financed by loans from the World
Bank, the United Kingdom, the U.S.A. and other friendly
countries. It is reckoned that it will take from ten to thirteen
years to complete the engineering works concerned.

Unfortunately, the struggle for Kashmir and the canal
waters dispute were not the only issues between India and Pakistan in the early years of independence. The disposal of the

property of the millions of people who had abandoned their homes would have been a difficult problem even if the two countries had been in a co-operative mood. Since they were not, it was insoluble, and to this day the great majority of the refugees have been unable either to sell or to receive compensation for their immovable property and have almost ceased to hope for it. Some idea of the magnitude of the problem can be gained from the fact that, according to the Pakistan census of 1951, seven and a quarter million Muslims had migrated to Pakistan from India since 1947, while C. N. Vakil tells us that up to about the same period over six and a half million non-Muslims had left Pakistan to settle in India. Further migration has taken place since then and indeed it is a continuous process.

The migrations fall into three phases. Before the partition of India, serious disorders in several parts of the country had resulted in the departure of half a million non-Muslims from what was to be Pakistan, and of a relatively small number of Muslims from India. The Punjab massacres of 1947 then produced a displacement of population on a much larger scale and, by March 1948, the number of Hindus and Muslims who had left West Pakistan for India, or the East Punjab for Pakistan, was well over twelve million. The third phase began in 1948 and went on until 1952, during which period it is estimated that nearly four million Hindus left East Pakistan and nearly one million Muslims left Calcutta or other parts of West Bengal for East Pakistan. The total displacement of population up to that time must have been in the neighbourhood of seventeen million, or one-third of the population of Great Britain.

The numbers of Muslim and Hindu refugees give no idea of the relative losses of the two communities. Many of the Hindu refugees from Pakistan were large landed proprietors or industrialists. According to C. N. Vakil, 'Lahore Hindus and Sikhs accounted for five crores of rupees out of six crores of rupees total investment in Lahore factories, and owned 167 out of 215 indigenous factories in that city.' The Muslim refugees were in the main small cultivators or traders. Reliable figures do not exist, but in 1949 it was estimated in India that property left behind by Hindus or Sikhs in Pakistan amounted to Rs.1,400 crores against perhaps Rs.200 crores worth left in India by Muslims. However inaccurate these figures may be, there is no doubt as to the existence of a great disparity. The result was that in the words of a very competent observer in the middle of 1949, 'If Kashmir is written on the hearts of every Pakistani, it is evacuee property which is more apt to make the gorge of Indians rise.' It would be unfair to say that Pakistan is not prepared to settle this problem while India holds Kashmir, but it is certainly the case that Pakistan has no sense of urgency about evacuee property and cannot understand why India spends on it time which could, according to Pakistan, be more profitably devoted to a solution of the Kashmir problem.

When the first great mass movement took place in 1947, both Governments were inclined to regard it as the temporary result of panic and to assume that their main problem would be repatriation. By September, however, it had been realised that this assumption was wrong and that the overwhelming majority of those who had fled would never return. The immediate task was the reception of the new-comers, which we have described in an earlier chapter, but this was necessarily linked up with the disposal of refugee property. From the point of view of Government, abandoned lands would be needed for the new-comers, while the refugees themselves were desperately anxious to sell their old property. The practical difficulties of sale by a Pakistani in India, or by an Indian in Pakistan, at this time of chaos and hatred, were in most cases insuperable. Governments clearly had to take a hand. The Governments of India and Pakistan agreed on a common policy, appointed custodians of evacuee property, and undertook to give full facilities for sale. The Government of West Punjab, however, took a much tougher line and in December practically made it impossible for a refugee to India to sell his property. Endless conferences were held, but little practical result ensued and the countries grew farther apart. India took the practical view that the problem could only be solved on a Government to Government basis, each Government taking over, on proper valuation, the abandoned property and making payment through the Government of the other country. Pakistan, however, realised that under any such arrangement she would have to pay a considerable balancing charge to India and this she was not prepared to do. It is not necessary to follow the history of the many discussions in detail, but there can be little doubt that the main cause of failure to arrive at any arrangement was lack of determination on the part of the Government of Pakistan to reach a settlement. The results of the failure have been disastrous for many hundreds of thousands of people, and today, if one meets a well-to-do Hindu who formerly lived in Pakistan, he is almost sure to say that he has lost the whole of his property. It is not surprising, therefore, that this evacuee problem has greatly embittered relations between the two countries.

Apart from these three specific disputes, feelings in the early years after partition were exacerbated by what can only be described as a trade war between the two countries. The partition of India was based on political rather than economic considerations, and resulted in the creation of a Pakistan which might be regarded as the perfect example of a colonial economy, whereas the new India had a better balance between agriculture and industry. Thus all the jute mills of the subcontinent were located in India, while in 1947–8 Pakistan produced 78 per cent of the total yield of raw jute in both countries. Similarly in the case of cotton, Pakistan produced 40 per cent of the total output of raw cotton in undivided India, but contained less than 5 per cent of the cotton mills. It would have been well for both countries if an arrangement could have been made, at least for the first year or so, under which Pakistan would have continued to supply and India to manufacture jute and cotton on the basis of a sharing of the export duties and the foreign exchange earnings. It is generally understood that a proposal to this effect was made to India by Pakistan shortly after partition. Unfortunately, the Punjab massacres and the Kashmir dispute had made the atmosphere wholly unpropitious for any such arrangement. India's attitude was soon made clear, when the Joint Expert Committee had to apportion the revenue collected on account of the jute duty in the year of partition. India insisted on the retention by each Dominion of the revenue collected at its own ports – a principle which would have given Pakistan only about 25 per cent of the jute duty, though 78 per cent of the raw jute came from her territories.

It was in fact clear that the economic relations between India and Pakistan were to be based on conflict rather than co-operation and from this stage Pakistan determined to set up her own jute mills and deprive Calcutta of raw jute. India, for her part, planned a considerable increase of jute cultivation. At the same time, Pakistan imposed a customs duty on raw jute crossing the land frontier between East and West Bengal. The Government of Sind next took a hand and placed drastic restrictions on the removal of commodities by Hindu emigrants to India from the Province, to which India replied by threatening to withhold the cash balances due to Pakistan under the financial agreement which had just been made. Every action an the part of one of the Dominions seemed only to provoke retaliation by the other.

A few months later, wiser counsels began to prevail and in June 1948 two important agreements were signed. The Payments Agreement provided *inter alia* that there would be no exchange control between the two countries, while the Trade Agreement envisaged the supply of cotton and other commodities by Pakistan in exchange for jute goods and cotton goods, coal, iron and steel and other essentials. Perhaps because the agreement was too general in its nature and did not fix prices, each party complained of the failure of the other to carry it out, and the levels of trade contemplated were not reached. Pakistan, in particular, alleged that the high proportion of her output committed to India resulted in the exercise of unfair pressure on Pakistan exporters, and when the agreement was renewed in June 1949 the stipulated qualities were reduced.

In September 1949, when Britain and India devalued their currencies, Pakistan decided to maintain the value of her rupee and the resulting outburst of indignation in India made all economic agreements between the two countries meaningless. What should have been regarded as a cold, unemotional act of financial wisdom, or unwisdom, was treated as a deadly blow to Indian prestige. Pakistan was exultant and the common man in both countries entered with deep emotion into a controversy of which he can have understood nothing. One of the most intelligent Hindus in Delhi said to the writer at this time, 'I would rather see both countries ruined than agree that the Pakistan rupee should be worth one iota more than the Indian rupee.' Apart from this hysterical approach, there was the hard fact that Pakistan jute and cotton would now cost India 40 per cent more than before in terms of Indian currency. The Government of India, therefore, refused to recognise the Pakistan rupee at its old value, or indeed at any value at all. For many months, India cherished the hope that the International Monetary Fund would bring pressure on Pakistan to devalue, but in the meantime no monetary transactions between the two countries were possible on an official basis. Trade was at a complete standstill, except in so far as it could be financed by black-market operations and the operators were quick to recognise that, on the land frontier of East and West Bengal, the Pakistan rupee was worth about thirteen Indian annas in spite of Pakistan's non-devaluation. The ban on remittances bore harshly on Hindus in East Pakistan, though Pakistanis working in Calcutta gained considerably from the unfavourable black-market rate for Pakistan rupees.

The conflict was particularly bitter in the jute world. Pakistan, without any justification, refused to allow the export to India of jute fully paid for before devaluation. India countered by an attempt to discontinue buying jute for some months and indeed some sections of the Indian jute industry went so far as to try to persuade American buyers to hold off the market altogether. In December, India retaliated for the detention of jute already bought by stopping supplies of coal to Pakistan. The jute was subsequently released; but delay on the part of India in resuming coal supplies caused further deterioration in relations. On January 20th, 1950, through booking of goods by rail and river between Assam and Calcutta, via East Pakistan, was discontinued and not reopened for some weeks.

By April 1950 it was recognised in Delhi as well as in Karachi that neither country could long stand the loss resulting from the deadlock, and a new interim agreement, providing for the sale of jute by Pakistan, and of steel, jute manufactures and other commodities by India, at prices expressed in Indian rupees, was negotiated. Cotton from Pakistan and coal from India were not included in the agreement.

This was followed in February 1951 by a trade agreement which recognised the *par* value of the Pakistan rupee and, although Indian feeling was still sore on this subject, the devaluation war was at an end. Many other trade matters still remained unsettled, but during the next three years there were innumerable conferences to discuss them and a number of useful agreements were negotiated. Much progress in this respect was made in 1953. In that year, imports of coal from India and jute from Pakistan were substantially raised; the harassments and complications in connection with passports between India and Pakistan were lessened; and it was agreed to aim at widening the scope and expanding the volume of trade between the two countries. In July 1955 Pakistan devalued her rupee to the Indian level and this further eased the strain. The improvement has continued and today it may be said that trade relations are as good as is possible between two countries which are politically hostile – though both countries have reorientated themselves economically and the volume of trade between them has therefore declined considerably since 1948.

Of the four factors which have embittered feelings between India and Pakistan since 1947, three have thus lost much of their importance. The Kashmir problem, however, is as intractable as ever. The assumption of power in Pakistan by Field-Marshal Ayub created nervousness in India, where it was quite wrongly thought that a soldier would necessarily be bellicose. Nevertheless in 1959 and 1960 the quarrel seemed to have been put into cold storage. India took her possession for granted and Pakistan for a time saw no hope of any effective action.

Early in 1961 Pakistan drew closer to China and agreed to demarcate the boundary of Pakistan-occupied Kashmir with China. This assumption of the permanence of the Pakistan occupation of Azad Kashmir angered Nehru, who declared, somewhat unreasonably, that he was not prepared to discuss Kashmir while part of that country was occupied by Pakistan. This new mood unfortunately coincided with anti-Hindu demonstrations in Pakistan and communal clashes in Jubbelpore. Ever since the transfer of power there has, indeed, been a vicious circle in this field. When the tension between India and Pakistan over Kashmir is heightened there are communal clashes in both countries – and when communal friction becomes serious the Kashmir issue assumes greater prominence.

In 1962 Pakistan again pressed the Security Council of the United Nations to consider the Kashmir dispute, but that request was soon overtaken by events. The Chinese invasion of India affected the matter in two ways. In the first place Pakistan politicians gloated over India's difficulties and saw in them an opportunity of bullying India into surrender over Kashmir. The inevitable result was the heightening of antagonism between the two countries. Secondly, the attempts of Duncan Sandys, the British Secretary for Commonwealth Relations, to find a solution of the Kashmir problem irritated India beyond measure and the series of discussions between India and Pakistan, which involved six high level meetings spread over five months in 1963, simply exacerbated the prevailing bad feelings, and did nothing towards producing a solution. Discussion in the United Nations merely added fuel to the fire and the announcement by Bakshi Ghulam Mohammad that direct election to the Indian Parliament would take place as soon as the Chinese emergency was over simply inflamed feeling in Pakistan. At the same time, important sections of the Indian public genuinely believed that before long Pakistan would take advantage of India's difficulties to launch an invasion.

At the end of 1963, when relations between the two countries were as bad as they have ever been, the hair of the Prophet was stolen from the Hazratbal shrine near Srinagar in Kashmir. It was, of course, assumed in Pakistan, without any evidence, that this was a Hindu outrage and the resulting anger led to serious anti-Hindu riots in Khulna in East Pakistan. Unfortunately, these troubles coincided with strong action by the Government of Assam against illegal immigration into that State by Moslems from East Pakistan. This immigration was not a new phenomenon. Mymensingh cultivators, far superior in skill and diligence to the peasants of Assam, have for some decades been infiltrating into Assam, but the problem now took on a communal aspect and the preventive action taken by the Government of Assam worsened relations between India and Pakistan. The anger resulting from all these occurrences – and particularly from the suspicions engendered by the theft of the hair of the Prophet – led to serious communal disturbances both in India and Pakistan. The anti-Hindu riots in East Pakistan produced their counterpart in Calcutta. The stream of Hindu refugees from East Pakistan further inflamed Indian feelings and outbreaks of communal violence occurred in Assam, Bihar and Madhya Pradesh. The Government of India took strong action to suppress these disturbances, but it was clear to all observers that relations between India and Pakistan and between Hindus and Moslems in both countries had reached a low level.

Personal friends of Nehru report that he was now profoundly depressed over these developments and felt that in the short time remaining to him, he must somehow settle the dispute with Pakistan. Sheikh Abdullah, the Lion of Kashmir, was released from his long detention and was used as an intermediary between India and Pakistan. Nothing whatsoever is known as to what was in Nehru's mind. Abdullah stood firmly for the right of Kashmir to determine its own future. Whether or not he meant by that that Kashmir would become independent alike of India and Pakistan is anybody's guess and there is certainly no evidence that, in spite of Nehru's desire for peace with Pakistan, he was at all inclined to surrender India's claim to unqualified sovereignty in Kashmir. Even if such a thought had been in Nehru's mind, it is doubtful if he could have persuaded the Indian public to accept it. The writer does not believe either that a settlement of the quarrel was in sight at that time or that it is to be expected in the near future. A general desire for a settlement is no substitute for a readiness to compromise – and of any such readiness there are no signs in India today.

The existence of this weak spot so near where it used to be said that 'three empires meet' is, indeed, important and suggests two general reflections, the first of which is as to the inability of the United Nations to settle a straightforward international quarrel, or even to pronounce an opinion regarding it. Shortly before his assassination, Liaquat Ali Khan, the Prime Minister of Pakistan – not a man given to impassioned outbursts – said to the writer: 'Why on earth cannot either the United Nations or the Commonwealth tell us if we are wrong. We could understand that, but we do not understand how India and Pakistan can both be so right that you have to be smooth with both of us.' He went on, 'Your United Nations is rather like a policeman who, when a burglary has taken place, makes no attempt to pin down any particular party as the culprit, but calls a conference to decide how much of the swag the householder must surrender.' There is much force in this criticism, and unless the United Nations can develop the moral fibre required to give judgment in matters of this kind, it is unlikely that they will ever have the authority to prevent war.

The second and general reflection, also arising from a discussion with Liaquat Ali Khan, is concerned with the structure of the British Commonwealth. Was the Commonwealth wise to disclaim any responsibility for helping to settle a family quarrel in the initial stages? The objections to, and the dangers of, Commonwealth intervention are obvious and, amongst its older members, perhaps over-ride all other considerations, but if the new members find themselves referred summarily to an outside body for the settlement of family disputes, they may begin to attach more importance to that body than to the family. These reflections, however, are now academic and there appears to be not the slightest chance that any outside agency could usefully intervene.

As a result of the varying phases in the disputes described in this chapter, feeling between India and Pakistan has naturally fluctuated from time to time. The 'near-war' state in 1947 was succeeded by the partial economic *rapprochement* of 1948, and the further *detente* resulting from the Kashmir 'cease-fire' agreement in January 1949. The hopes raised by that agreement were nevertheless soon disappointed and, thanks to a combination of political and economic factors, low level was reached in the winter of 1949–50, when important sections of the Press in both countries frankly demanded war. At that time the writer, who was then on tour in India and Pakistan, saw Nehru rise to his full stature and by sheer personal ascendancy, both in the Cabinet and in Calcutta – where 'make war on Pakistan' was scribbled on every electric standard or poster site – drive his people back to sanity. Liaquat Ali Khan performed a similar though less dramatic service for Pakistan. Since then there have been innumerable ups and downs, but not until 1963 were relations quite as bad as they had been in 1950. It is too early yet to see signs of improvement and it is not to be expected that relations between the two countries should in the foreseeable future become good. It will be enough if they remain tolerable.

Chapter 16

India and the World

A T THE TIME OF the transfer of power, most of the members of the Indian Cabinet were almost wholly without experience in the conduct of foreign affairs. In the Provinces they had become familiar with the handling of public finance, the maintenance of law and order and the organisation of the nation-building departments, but they had neither participated in, nor co-operated with, the Central Government, which alone was concerned with external relations. The Indian delegates to the Peace Conference and other important international bodies, and the High Commissioners who represented India in several capitals, were necessarily chosen from outside the ranks of the Indian National Congress, and the members of that party had thus no opportunity of familiarising themselves with the mechanism of diplomacy. Most of them, indeed, had concentrated their attention so exclusively on the struggle for power that they were but faintly interested in world problems, except where, as in the case of South Africa, those problems had a direct bearing on Indian interests.

The outstanding exception to this general rule was Jawaharlal Nehru, who had pondered long and deeply on international affairs and who came to be regarded by the Party as the expert to whom such matters could safely be left. For most Indian politicians of that time the stock in trade of thought on world problems was fondness for China, respect for Russia, deep-seated suspicion of the old 'colonial powers' and disillusionment over America.

In 1947 and 1948, partly because of this lack of interest and partly on account of preoccupation with grave domestic troubles, the Government of India was manifestly uncertain of itself in the international sphere and not at all anxious to tie itself too definitely to any line of policy. Nehru himself had occasion to rebuke some of his followers for talking as though India at that stage could really count in world affairs. The anxiety of the Government of India was, indeed, not so much to influence the world, as to make sure of maintaining India's new-found freedom.

A year or so after the transfer of power, India had to make up her mind with regard to one important aspect of her external relations. She had to decide for or against continued membership of the British Commonwealth. In the bitter days of the struggle for power, Congress leaders had committed themselves deeply to a complete severance of the Common-wealth tie and had indeed assumed that Dominion status was an inferior and incomplete kind of freedom. Experience had shown this assumption to be wrong, and throughout 1948 enlightened Indian opinion began to veer towards some form of association with the Commonwealth. At the end of the Dominion Premiers' Conference in October 1948, Nehru stated that: 'We may not agree about everything, but it is surprising what a large measure of unanimity there was, not only in the objectives to be aimed at, but also in the methods to be pursued. . . . This meeting has shown me that there is great scope for the Commonwealth.' In December 1948, at the Jaipur Session of the Indian National Congress, Nehru declared that membership of the Commonwealth had involved not the least interference with her foreign policy, and he plainly advocated remaining in the Commonwealth. The advantages of the connection were indeed obvious and there must have been present in many Indian minds the thought that India's position vis-à-vis Pakistan would be greatly weakened if India left the Commonwealth and Pakistan remained in it. Nevertheless, the old revolutionary sentiment died hard, and when Nehru finally decided in favour of keep-ing the Commonwealth connection, he found himself faced with strong though uninformed opposition. At this stage the Commonwealth countries displayed an imaginative flexibility of a kind rare in political history. A formula was found which enabled India to become a republic while remaining in the Commonwealth through the common headship of the King. The ultimate effect of this development on the structure of the

N

Commonwealth as a whole cannot yet be foreseen, but from the point of view of Indo-British relations the result was most satisfactory, and the acceptance of the formula by the Constituent Assembly was a remarkable personal triumph for the Indian Prime Minister.

In September 1949 India again had occasion to review her relationship with Britain – this time in an economic context. For years before the transfer of power, Indian politicians and economists had condemned the link between the rupee and sterling as unnatural and harmful to Indian interests and the freeing of the rupee had been one of their foremost aims. It came, therefore, as a surprise to the world when in 1949, within a few hours of the devaluation of the pound by Sir Stafford Cripps, the Indian Cabinet decided on a corresponding devaluation, on the ground that the close connection of the economies of Britain and India made it essential that they should keep in step. Thus, on the two important issues of Commonwealth membership and the relation between the rupee and sterling, Indian statesmen were able to conquer the understandable prejudices of the old unhappy days and to recognise the community of interest of Britain and India.

India was now beginning to find her feet in the international world and a new note of confidence crept into Nehru's speeches on foreign affairs. The part played by India in bringing about a *détente* in the Far East at the time of the Korean War strengthened this confidence, and Nehru began to give more emphatic utterance to that policy of neutralism which America found so hard to stomach and by which most British people were somewhat puzzled.

Although neutralism has been greatly modified in the last year or so by anxiety with regard to China, it has by no means been abandoned and it is important to understand the factors which contributed to it. In the first place, India saw the world divided into two opposing groups of powers and she believed that all historical precedent pointed to the inevitability of war unless some third party could bridge the gulf between them. It seemed to Nehru that India was cast in this role and many of his countrymen regarded India as particularly well fitted for that part by reason of her close ties with the democracies. India, they then felt, was the natural interpreter of the West to China and perhaps to Russia.

Secondly, they were at this time suspicious of the U.S.A. and wrongly believed that she was as likely as Russia to start a war – a belief that sprang partly from unfamiliarity with American politics, and from the resulting tendency to read into the wild speeches of Dulles and certain other American politicians more than they really meant.

The third element in neutralism was the Gandhian doctrine of non-violence, supported in the minds of many Indians by a completely unhistorical view of ancient India as a land of peace. The facts do not support this view and it is one of the ironies of Indian history that even the doctrine of *Ahimsa*, or non-violence, was first formulated in the course of a philoso-phical discussion which justified the prosecution of a war of conquest. Nevertheless, many middle-class Indians do believe that India's neutralism is an historical continuation of her traditional attitude, and they do not see any inconsistency be-tween that attitude and India's invasion of Goa.

There was also the belief, now considerably shaken by the recent evidence of Chinese imperialism, that India can, by re-maining neutral, avoid the devastation of the next world war. A prominent Indian business man stated this view quite frankly to the writer some years ago. 'We have been lucky enough to escape the ravages of two wars,' he said, 'and if we play our cards properly we can escape the next one too.' However unreal this belief in the possibility of neutrality may seem to us in the West, its existence has to be accepted as a fact.

Finally, there were a few far-sighted men who felt that India must play for time, and build up her strength under the shelter of neutrality, until she could cope with external threats.

It is impossible to guess in what proportion these different elements were combined in Indian thought after Independence. It is, however, quite clear that neutralism was not just a creation of Nehru himself, but was the dominant mood of India in the first decade or so of independence. This mood was difficult for the West to understand, but it may nevertheless be that the existence of one great country which, though neutral, cherished the same political and humanitarian ideals as Britain was not without value in the stage of world affairs then existing.

Nearly all writers on India in recent years have commented on the complete transformation of Indian feeling towards Britain since the transfer of power and the warmth of the relations now existing between the two peoples. It is impossible for an Englishman to visit India today without feeling this warmth wherever he goes, but the importance to both countries of maintaining this friendship makes it desirable to remember that there have been several occasions when serious differences of opinion on important matters might have impaired those relations. The first such occasion was at the time of the action taken by the Government of India to compel Hyderabad to join the Indian Union. The present writer regards that action as justified by expediency, but it came as a great shock to a large section of the British public, who already had a slightly guilty feeling about the abrogation of Britain's treaties with the princes. Frank comment in the British Press caused great anger in India, but, fortunately, it was soon recognised in Delhi that at least part of the trouble arose from the ineptitude of the handling of the British Press by the Indian High Commission at that time. Simultaneously, it began to be realised in London that India had no real alternative to the action taken.

A second difficulty was the failure of the Indian leaders, in the early years of independence, to understand the British neutrality over the Kashmir issue and the consequent growth of a belief that Britain was biased in favour of Pakistan. Even today when the present writer visits India he is apt to be told that Britain is pro-Pakistan. His consolation is that in Karachi he frequently has to defend Britain against the charge of being pro-India.

In 1956 events in Egypt gave rise to a more serious disagreement between Britain and India. The merits or demerits of the British action are not relevant to the purpose of this book, and we are only concerned with the fact that the overwhelming majority of educated Indians – politicians, officials and members of the public alike – were genuinely shocked by it. Typical of the general feeling was the comment of one influential Indian: 'We thought you were leading us out of the jungle – now you have taken us back into it.' Some British writers have argued that this attitude is inconsistent with India's use of force in

Hyderabad and Kashmir, but it is perhaps more profitable to reflect that those in India who were most deeply upset by the Anglo-French intervention were not Britain's traditional critics, but her closest friends. It is important, therefore, to understand the reasons for their attitude. Two main factors seem to have been at work. In the first place there was the feeling of Afro-Asian solidarity symbolised by the Bandoeng Conference, which will always lead to resentment at any attack on Asian or African countries by a European power, however great the provocation or justification may be.

Secondly, there was the fact that Indians had not outgrown their unconscious fear that colonialism might somehow or other be revived. To British people the fear seems unreal, but it existed – and perhaps still exists.

These reasons may not appear convincing to those Englishmen who believe that the Anglo-French action was wise and justifiable, but they should at least help to an understanding of the Indian attitude. Fortunately the basic good feeling between Britain and India is strong and the estrangement did not last long. Relations once more became close and cordial and were well symbolised by the tumultuous welcome given to Her Majesty the Queen when she visited India in 1961. Nothing could better illustrate the breadth and flexibility of the Commonwealth than Her Majesty's presence on January 26th, 1961, side by side with the President of India at the Republic Day celebrations.

Since then there have been several misunderstandings, the first of which related to British policy in the Congo and to the quite unjustified but widespread Indian belief that in some vague way Britain was supporting colonialism there. The next occasion of strain arose from anxiety as to the possible effect on the Indian economy of Britain's proposed entry into the Common Market. Reflection subsequently showed that fears on that score had been greatly exaggerated, but before a more sober appraisement had been generally made, the introduction of the Bill to regulate immigration into the United Kingdom administered a second shock. It is not relevant to our purpose to discuss the merits of that Bill, but there can be little doubt that the British Government's handling of these matters was inept and left well-disposed Indians with a feeling that Britain was turning away from the Commonwealth to Europe. Fortunately the Commonwealth Immigrants Act has worked smoothly and has perhaps ceased to be a cause of irritation.

A little later the Goa episode provided an additional complication. Her Majesty's Government sought to dissuade India from invading Goa and expressed disapproval after the invasion had taken place. In so doing they correctly represented the feeling of the people of Britain, but Nehru was unable to understand why his action should have been criticised and the British attitude was strongly and perhaps unreasonably resented in India.

These, however, were minor incidents compared with the upsurge of gratitude when, towards the end of 1962, Britain and the U.S.A. rushed to assist in the defence of India against Chinese aggression. Unfortunately that feeling was to some extent dissipated by the attempts of Duncan Sandys, the British Commonwealth Secretary, to effect a settlement of the Kashmir dispute and so bring India and Pakistan closer together for purposes of defence. In 1964 a speech by Sir Patrick Dean in the Security Council of the United Nations urging agreement between India and Pakistan regarding Kashmir also aroused anger in India. Important sections of the Indian public were so convinced that their position over Kashmir was wholly correct that any attempts to secure a compromise seemed to them to be an indication of bias in favour of Pakistan. On the other hand, in May 1964 the imaginative action of the British Prime Minister in rushing to the funeral of Nehru touched Indian hearts and perhaps cancelled the effect of the irritation over Kashmir – though anger was again caused by the reference to Kashmir in the communique issued at the end of the Commonwealth Conference in July 1964.

It is too early to judge what effect these events will have on relations between Britain and India, but they nevertheless serve as a warning. Indians are undoubtedly more sensitive than they have a right to be with regard to fair criticism and reasonable disagreement. On the other hand, there were sections of the British Press which at one time went beyond fair and reasonable limits and seemed to delight in sneering at Nehru and his Government. They did not represent British opinion and their attitude was resented by Englishmen who have lived and worked in India, but they received a lot of attention in Delhi.

In spite of these incidents, the basic fact is that India relies on British help against any further attacks by China and to the ordinary man this far outweighs other considerations. Nevertheless these fluctuations in feeling make it clear that good relations require careful nurture.

It is unfortunate that one strand in the old cultural link between Britain and India has been snapped. For nearly two hundred years, British members of the Civil Services have studied the history, the languages, the ethnology, the flora and fauna and the art of India, and have contributed greatly to the knowledge of these subjects. They have, thereby, brought themselves and their country into close relationship with educated Indians. Their example has not been largely followed by the business community and, except for the missionaries, there are only a handful of Englishmen in India today with any deep interest in Oriental studies. The cultural traffic between Britain and India has in fact become one-way. The loss is serious and may become more so if, in the course of time, English is ousted from its position as the language of educated India. The leading politicians and the senior officials of India today were brought up to English ways of thought and the close understanding between Britain and independent India is partly the offspring of a common intellectual heritage. The next generation of Indian Ministers and officials will not share so fully in that heritage and there may be some weakening of the intellectual link between the two countries. Conscious effort will be necessary to maintain community of thought and feeling between Britain and India.

The U.S.A. impinged very little on India until the First World War, but in the following two decades or more, the American people were regarded with affection, as friends of freedom, who might be expected to press the supposedly reluctant English to grant self-government to India. This attitude suffered a reaction during the Second World War, when close contact with U.S.A. officers and soldiers showed that the psychological and emotional gap between Americans and the people of India was far wider than that which separated Indians from the British. The uninhibited manners of the G.I. were not understood, while on the other hand the average British Tommy made himself readily at home with all classes. Most outside observers will admit that at the end of the war the British stock stood higher than that of the Americans in India.

After the transfer of power, Chester Bowles did much to bring the U.S.A. closer to India, but his work was soon undone by the Indian dislike of Macarthyism and by the truculence of many American speeches on foreign affairs. Indians failed to understand that the American hatred of Communism was based on a passionate belief in the very same values which had long been cherished in India and which had inspired the Congress Party on the march to freedom. Indian politicians were therefore only too ready to equate America's dynamic approach to the Communist menace with aggressiveness. The position was made worse by the apparent inability of the U.S.A., in spite of the long years during which she remained isolated from world affairs, to understand Nehru's policy of neutralism. The gulf between the two countries was still further widened by Indian resentment at the military aid given by the U.S.A to Pakistan.

Towards the end of 1956, Indian feelings towards the U.S.A. appeared to undergo a rapid change for the better, as a result of the American reaction to the Anglo-French intervention in Egypt. The U.S.A. was considered to have supported the principle of peaceful negotiation and to have resisted the law of the jungle. Indian politicians began to believe that the American approach to world affairs was, after all, similar to their own, and Nehru's visit to the U.S.A. was expected to strengthen the new understanding. Within a few days of Nehru's return to India, however, the 'Eisenhower Doctrine' with regard to the Middle East was proclaimed. That doctrine – which apparently was not disclosed to Nehru during his American visit – was a complete negation of the neutralism in which Indians believe. It was, in fact, a renewal of the very declaration of war on Communism which had previously led India to distrust the foreign policy of the U.S.A. Since then, however – although it is obvious that the two countries approach world affairs from radically different points of view – mutual understanding has grown rapidly. The liberal approach of the U.S.A. to the problem of helping the underdeveloped countries has greatly impressed thinking Indians, and leading Americans on their part have begun to realise that neutralism does not mean pro-Communism. American policy in Cuba and Laos was not favourably regarded in India and American expressions of disapproval of India's invasion of Goa were not well received.

In 1962, however, the United States joined with Britain in rushing to the rescue of India from the Chinese threat, and that action and the continuing generosity of the United States in the matter of economic aid and the supply of food grains under P.L.480 have made a great impression on the Indian mind.

The attitude of modern India towards Russia is not easy to analyse. The first, instinctive reaction of educated people in India to the Bolshevik revolution was one of sympathy, but the complete suppression of liberty and disregard of human life to which it led soon destroyed that feeling, except amongst the young intellectuals who were attracted by the Communist creed. When the Second World War broke out, the shameless alliance of Russia with Hitler and her invasion of Poland repelled the Indian middle classes, since they instinctively desired the defeat of the Nazis, even though as good Congress men they felt bound to hold aloof from the struggle. They learned with relief of Russia's split with Hitler, and they followed with admiration the Russian resistance to the great Nazi military machine. Nevertheless, they had not forgotten the earlier episodes, and at the end of the war they were a little undecided in their attitude. The appreciation of the British generated by the transfer of power perhaps swung most of them into the camp of the Western democracies – but they had little contact with Russia and no need for any strong feelings about her.

As the years passed and the danger of a third world war appeared, many educated Indians became genuinely alarmed lest their close relations with Britain should involve them in it, and they clung firmly to Nehru's policy of neutralism, which we have already described. Their own concept of planning also gave them a certain fellow feeling with the Russians, who might be regarded as the originators of the idea of planning, and at the same time they were impressed with the great technical advances made by Russia. There was no emotional warmth towards Russia in the hearts of most Indians, but prudence suggested a degree of acquaintanceship with her. This called for some practical demonstration that India had no antagonism towards Russia, and in 1955 Nehru therefore accepted an invitation to Moscow. His visit was a tremendous success and led to a return invitation. Bulganin and Khruschev visited India in November and December 1955 and it was the writer's good fortune to be there at the time. The initial reception was one of spontaneous and sincere welcome, which faded noticeably as Khruschev continued to make bitter speeches against the British, whom most Indians today regard as friends. At the close of the visit it was clear that educated Indians were closer to England than they were to Russia, but there remained the awkward question as to which country could give India the economic help which she so greatly needed. It would be wrong to think of India in 1955 as in any sense pro-Russian, and observers in Delhi at the time of Nehru's return from Russia saw in him no signs of that enthusiasm which had bubbled over on his return from China in the previous year. Nevertheless India did not share the Western fear and suspicion of Russia and it seemed possible that she might well draw closer to that country if the West could not give India the help she needed in the Second Five-year Plan.

In 1956, however, there seemed to be a growing awareness in India of the ruthlessness and imperialistic character of Russian policy, and Russia's behaviour in Hungary towards the end of the year induced a feeling of revulsion in most educated Indians. The attempts of Communist propagandists to equate Anglo-French intervention in Suez and Russian action in Hungary convinced nobody, and Nehru's unwillingness to set these two episodes in their proper perspective led to vigorous protests from his countrymen. Russia's stock slumped in India and many Indians were embarrassed when Russia's offer of financial assistance for the purchase of machinery coincided with her brutality in Hungary.

During the last few years, however, Russia has played her cards in India with considerable skill. At the time of the Chinese attack she made her disapproval known, and articles in *Pravda* on this subject and on Kashmir excited so much admiration in

India that many public men omitted to notice that in the crisis of November 1962 Russia's help was confined to words. It was left to Britain and the U.S. to send military aid. Since then the widening rift between China and Russia has naturally induced a corresponding warmth of Indian feeling towards Russia. A few months after the main emergency was over, six MIG aircraft were supplied to India by Russia and at the same time the U.S.S.R. supported India's case in the Security Council.

Encouraged by these developments, India sent a mission to Moscow to seek further assistance and in due course plans were concerted for the production of MIG's in India with Russian aid. There has been some delay in getting the project started, but it has caught the Indian imagination and has perhaps overshadowed British and American help in such matters as the provision of transport planes, the plans for the Air Forces of Britain and the U.S. to hold air exercises in India, the supply of radar equipment and assistance from the West and the establishment of additional ordnance factories. Western military aid is perhaps taken for granted, whereas help from Russia is a matter for gratitude.

Economic aid will be discussed in a later chapter, but it must be said here that while the Russian contribution is considerably less than that of the West, it has been skilfully designed to take spectacular forms and has therefore made a considerable impact on the Indian mind. India today is far from being pro-Communist, but many of her leading citizens do regard Russia as the reliable Elder Brother.

The attitude of India towards Communist China has undergone a complete metamorphosis in the last two years. The feelings of friendship and admiration which the great majority of educated Indians entertained towards China in the early years of Independence have been replaced by suspicion, anger and an element of fear. The first unmistakable sign of Chinese aggressiveness appeared in 1950, when China invaded Tibet. In spite of her official protest, which China abruptly rejected, India was not greatly perturbed at this development. Tibet seemed remote and few Indians knew anything about that country. There were, therefore, only slight murmurings from a few far-sighted individuals when, in 1954, India recognised

China's sovereignty over Tibet in a Treaty, the preamble of which embodied Nehru's famous Panch Shila or five principles (of coexistence).

In March 1959 the flight to India of the Dalai Lama – a religious leader much venerated by Hindus – gave a rude shock to the public. The information regarding the ruthlessness and brutality of the Chinese in Tibet which now became available was confirmed by the findings of the International Commission of Jurists, and a revulsion of feeling against China was soon apparent. Anger mounted rapidly when towards the end of 1959 China began to encroach further on Indian territory. It is indeed doubtful whether before this time, many people in India knew of China's claims to territory traditionally included in India. No such claims were put forward by China at the time of the Panch Shila Treaty, but a few months thereafter China claimed the Barahoti area in the Uttar Pradesh and Chinese officials attempted to enter that area. India protested but did not take the matter seriously. In October 1954 Nehru paid a goodwill visit to China and when he drew the attention of the Chinese Government to some recently published Chinese maps which included within the Chinese border 50,000 square miles of Indian territory, he was told that they were merely reproductions of the old Kuomintang maps which the People's Government had had no time to revise. Chinese encroachments into the Uttar Pradesh territory continued, but when Chou En Lai visited India in November 1956, he apparently persuaded Nehru that China had no aggressive intentions and India continued to support China's claim to admission to the United Nations.

It nevertheless soon became clear that China claimed considerable areas in North East India where she refused to recognise the validity of the McMahon Line laid down in 1914 by representatives of Britain, Tibet and China, but never ratified by China – and also disputed the traditional location of that line on the ground. At the same time she claimed a large part of Ladakh and in 1957 Chinese soldiers arrested an Indian patrol party on normal routine duty in the Aksai Chin area of Ladakh. At about the same time the Chinese began to construct the Aksai Chin military road towards India.

In 1959, while encroachments into Ladakh continued,

Chinese forces also made incursions into the North East Frontier Agency and occupied the Indian frontier post of Longju. It is not necessary for our purpose to follow these moves in detail or to study the difficult question of the proper boundaries between India and China. It is sufficient to state that whereas in Ladakh the exact fixation of the boundary might reasonably give rise to dispute, no such problems should have arisen in the North East Frontier Agency. It is in any case clear that China was determined to enforce her claims by military measures and in all three sectors of the disputed frontier forcibly occupied areas which could not be claimed with any justification.

By 1962 China had occupied about 12,000 square miles in Ladakh and had made military dispositions which seemed to threaten the independence of Sikkim and Bhutan. Clashes occurred between Chinese forces and advanced Indian patrols in Ladakh and it is not impossible that probing operations by those patrols were the immediate cause of the large-scale Chinese attack in October 1962. Two facts must, however, be emphasised. First, wherever the exact location of the Indo-China boundary may be, the Indian patrols were within what was undoubtedly Indian territory; secondly, Nehru's complacency for some years over the Chinese attitude may imply a serious lack of judgment, but at least it exonerates India from any possible charge of truculence. The aggressiveness was all on one side.

In September 1963 the Chinese penetrated in force into the Tawang area of the North East Frontier Agency. On 12th October, Nehru announced that the Indian Army had been ordered to eject the Chinese from all Indian territory south of the McMahon Line, but on 20th October the Chinese launched a major offensive in the North East Frontier area as well as in Ladakh.

It was logistically impossible for India to defend Ladakh and by the middle of November it was for all practical purposes lost to India. The situation on the North East Frontier was wholly different and it was confidently expected that the Chinese would be held, if not driven back. In the event the Indian Army collapsed completely and the Chinese swept on to Tezpur within a few miles of the Brahmaputra. British nationals were evacuated from the North Bank, and when the writer was in Delhi on 20th November 1963, it was taken for granted by those responsible that the whole of Assam would soon be in Chinese hands. On the following day there occurred one of the most dramatic episodes in recent history. The Chinese announced a 'cease-fire' and declared their intention of beginning on 1st December to retire to twenty kilometres behind the line of control which existed in the North East Frontier Agency in November 1959 and to a corresponding distance behind the line of control in Ladakh as it was in November 1962. The Indian authorities not unnaturally suspected a trap, but the Chinese did in fact carry out their promise.

In the meantime, military stores and equipment from Britain and the United States were flown into Assam. Duncan Sandys, together with the Chief of the British General Staff, General Sir Richard Hull, and representatives of the Government of the United States of America arrived in India to concert measures for her defence. Indian pride was gravely hurt by what had happened and an exalted mood of determination to resist China appeared throughout the country. It led to a cessation of controversy and a closing of the ranks of the political parties, which unfortunately did not last long.

The motives of the Chinese withdrawal are a matter of speculation, but it is generally assumed that a major invasion of Assam was not part of the Chinese plan; that the local Commanders were amazed at the lack of Indian resistance and naturally overran their objectives; and that the immediate assistance given by Britain and the United States of America made it clear to Peking that a continuance of the operation might involve a world war which China did not want.

Another matter of speculation relates to the causes of the failure of the Indian Army. Naturally no satisfactory official statement on this subject has been made, but it is generally believed that while Indian troops were in no way personally inferior to the Chinese as fighting men, a defective Intelligence system, together with inadequate training in mountain warfare in the conditions of North East India and the lack of warm clothing and the other equipment necessary for this kind of campaign were responsible. It may be partly true that the whole tradition of the Indian Army from British times onwards had been to think in terms of the North West rather than the North East, but popular opinion in India put much of the blame on the shoulders of Krishna Menon, who, it was said, had demoralised the High Command of the Army. Be that as it may, he was forced to resign. It is always easy to look for scapegoats and some of Krishna Menon's bitterest critics forgot that Nehru and the Indian public alike had refused to recognise the Chinese menace until it was almost too late.

Since 1962, India has remained in a state of nervous tension, though her public men differ widely as to what is likely to happen next. There are some who believe that China will again attack India at some convenient time; others think that China will be content to keep India guessing; while yet others suggest that Burma may be the next victim of Chinese aggression. Three facts are, however, clear. First, China is now Public Enemy Number One; secondly, Chinese forces are deployed all along India's northern frontier where good military roads have now been built; and thirdly, India has been compelled to divert to military purposes resources which could otherwise have been devoted to economic development. The Panch Shila are dead as a door-nail.

The Chinese menace has, however, not produced much change in the feeling that the West should mind its own business about Asian affairs. That feeling was to some extent present even when India intervened, with beneficial results, in the Korean affair and was perhaps responsible for Nehru's complaint that the United Nations by 'sponsoring' the Korean war has lost the initiative in keeping the peace. As the years passed the 'Hands Off Asia' mood hardened and was emphasised when the U.S.A. proposed the establishment of SEATO. That body has more than once been denounced by Nehru and even such an anti-Communist paper as the *Eastern Economist* has commented that 'there is no doubt that what is foremost in the mind of educated India at the present time is that under cover of the Communist threat the Western powers are coming back with an alarming display of arrogance in their treatment of Asian nationalism'. The Chinese aggression has modified this feeling, but it is still true that if India had to choose between Communism and a return to 'colonialism', she would probably choose the former.

India's experience of intervention on behalf of the U.N. in the Congo has been unhappy, and she has been treated with discourtesy by the Congolese leaders. Nevertheless the attitude of the Press and the public to affairs in Indonesia and Algeria show that, except where India has a specific quarrel with a particular Asian country, Afro-Asian solidarity is still strong.

In view of the continuing threat on India's northern frontier, it is particularly unfortunate that in recent years her relations with Nepal have been strained. It is generally believed that in the early years of independence, Indian influence strengthened the forces which brought about the downfall of the Rana régime. If this is true, it would not necessarily have made India unpopular in Nepal, but that section of the Nepalese public which is politically conscious seems to have been convinced that India was continuing thereafter to interfere in her affairs. When in June 1959 King Mahendra established the first democratic government in Nepal, it might have been thought that there would have been a natural sympathy between the Nepalese Ministers and the Indian National Congress. That did not prove to be the case and the Nepalese Ministers repeatedly asserted that India was interfering with Nepal's foreign policy and encouraging subversive elements inside the country. Nor did relations improve when after eighteen months of democratic rule, King Mahendra dismissed his Ministers. Early in 1962 the news that Nepal had made an agreement with China for the construction of a road from Kathmandu, the capital of Nepal, to Tibet – just at the time when India was awakening to the Chinese menace – created anger in India. At the same time, a Nepal government controlled newspaper accused India of seeking to 'do a Cuba' on Nepal. During 1962 relations grew worse and in September a communique issued from the Palace of the King of Nepal frankly accused India of harbouring and abetting subversive Nepali groups.

Nepal was in fact undecided between fear of China – though it must be remembered that there are pro-Chinese elements in Nepal – and suspicion of India.

India's new Prime Minister, Lal Bahadur Shastri, who paid one goodwill visit to Nepal before he left the Nehru Cabinet, is determined to improve relations with Nepal and his Foreign

Minister, Swaran Singh, is about to visit that country with this object in view.

The relations of India with her immediate neighbours are not altogether happy. The position of Indians in Ceylon is somewhat complicated. When British investors began to undertake the economic development of Ceylon, the Sinhalese were neither inclined by temperament, nor compelled by necessity, to accept employment on plantations or in industrial establishments. Large numbers of Indians, therefore, went to Ceylon seeking employment as labourers. They did not settle down permanently in Ceylon, but as a rule returned to India for their annual holidays and continued to regard themselves as Indians.

The growth of nationalism in Ceylon, together with economic factors which have compelled the Sinhalese to look for employment in organised agriculture or industry, have led to resentment of the presence of these large foreign labour forces. There are also many Tamils permanently settled in Ceylon, outside the plantation areas. Since 1948 'Ceylon's Indians have been progressively debarred from citizenship and the franchise' and this matters more than previously in view of the recent suggestion that employment and the right to a rice ration in times of shortage may both be limited to citizens of Ceylon. An Indian by origin can only be regarded as a Sinhalese if he has been born in Ceylon and can prove that he has had a family connection with Ceylon for two generations. In many genuine cases it will be difficult to prove this, and the general belief in India is that Ceylon intends to make it as difficult as possible for persons of Indian origin to become Ceylon citizens. The Indian estimate is that, of the one million Indians in Ceylon, about half can expect to become Sinhalese citizens; about a quarter will perhaps be allowed to stay in Ceylon; and the remaining quarter million will have to return to India. Recently feeling between the Sinhalese and the Tamils in Ceylon has been exacerbated by the notification of Sinhalese as the sole official language of the country. In Ceylon as in India, the linguistic controversy has been the focal point of communal strifes and the position of the Tamils in Ceylon is very unhappy. Until a satisfactory solution of this problem has been found, it

o

is difficult to see how relations between India and Ceylon can improve.[1]

In the case of Burma, official relations are good. Neverthe-less Indians in Burma are neither happy nor popular. The simple truth is that the superior business capacity of the Indian merchant excites jealousy, particularly in view of the economic nationalism which is now so strong in Burma – so strong indeed as to amount almost to xenophobia.

Shastri has definitely made better feeling between India and her neighbours a main plank in his programme and he is per-haps better fitted than Nehru to bring about the much needed improvement.

In the seventeen years since the transfer of power, India has established herself as an important factor in world affairs, and can justly claim to have played a major part in preventing the struggle in Korea and Indo-China from developing into a major war. She still has no intention of aligning herself with the Western bloc, but will continue to be friendly with both Russia and the West while remaining resolute in her hostility to China.

[1] Since this was written, an agreement has been negotiated.

INDEPENDENT INDIA—ECONOMIC AFFAIRS

Chapter 17

The Economic Condition of India in 1947

A T THE END OF THE Second World War the Indian economy contained strongly contrasting elements of strength and weakness. War conditions had so stimulated development that India was officially classified as one of the eight major industrial countries of the world. Her productivity had gone up by leaps and bounds and she had a whole army of trained technicians. She had not only repatriated her sterling debt, but had, as a result of war-time production, accumulated substantial sterling balances. Last, but not least, rural indebtedness had been greatly reduced on account of the rise in grain prices, while the growing strength of labour and a more responsive attitude on the part of employers had led to an undoubted improvement in the conditions of life of urban workers. On the other hand, *per capita* income was still low even by Asian standards and population was increasing faster than the national income. Agriculture was unprogressive and India was dangerously dependent on substantial imports of foodstuffs. The lower middle classes were suffering severely from the increase in the cost of living and, in spite of growing industrialisation, middle-class unemployment was a grave problem.

In this chapter we shall examine these factors briefly and assess the favourableness or otherwise of the economic conditions under which India embarked on independence. It is natural to begin by considering the extent to which India, in 1947, could feed and clothe herself. Agriculture, though the most important, was in some ways the least satisfactory branch of the Indian economy. The efforts of the Agricultural Department and of every good District Officer, in the fifty years before the transfer of power, to improve methods of cultivation and to secure increased yields were, in the main, thwarted by social

213

and economic factors. The joint family system destroyed incentive; the continual fragmentation of holdings made scientific agriculture impossible; the use of cattle dung for fuel – itself the unavoidable result of ruthless tree cutting for generations – deprived the land of much needed nourishment; and the conservatism of the cultivator combined with his lack of capital to confirm him in the traditional practices. Here and there something could be done by seed selection or the use of artificial fertilisers, but as a rule, up to the Second World War a sense of hopeless indebtedness left the average cultivator with no real urge to better his lot. As a result of all these factors, yields remained low, as will be seen from the following table relating to the period before the war.[1]

CROP YIELDS (LB. PER ACRE)

	India	China	Japan	U.S.A.	World Yield
Rice	728	2,433	3,070	1680	1440
Wheat	811	989	1,350	990	840

From early in the twentieth century agricultural production failed to keep pace with the growth of population, while at the same time there was a tendency towards the replacement of wheat and, to a lesser extent rice, by the far less nutritious millets. During the same period there was also a decrease in the acreage under oil-seeds, which are of importance as the main source of fats for a large proportion of the population. Milk supplies were insufficient to help in producing a balanced diet. Although India has the largest bovine population in the world, Indian cattle are in general stunted and half-starved. Pressure of population leaves inadequate grazing land, fodder crops are not a normal part of the peasant economy and religious prejudice prevents the slaughter of diseased or useless cows. The bullocks are often not strong enough for work on the land and only a minority of cows give milk for human consumption. Even amongst that minority the yield is very low. Milk supply is thus hopelessly inadequate, and in 1947 the

[1] Taken from Radhakamal Mukherjee's Oxford Pamphlet – The Food Supply.

average Indian daily consumption, including the milk of buffaloes and goats as well as that of cows, was only a little over five ounces as compared with the pre-war average in Britain of $2\frac{1}{2}$ lb.

W. A. Ackroyd, Director of the Nutrition Research Laboratory at Coonoor, estimated, in 1944, that 30 per cent of the population was underfed in normal times and calculated that the poor villager in a certain area of South India received 1,700 calories per day as against requirements which would be not less than 2,500. Ackroyd was a first-class nutrition expert who rendered good service to India, but, in considering his estimate, it is reasonable to discount something for his zeal in the cause of feeding India. Vera Anstey, in a very balanced study of this subject, concluded that 'in a moderately good year India produces and retains within the country enough food to maintain the population in tolerable health and efficiency, assuming distribution to be approximately equal'. When allowance is made for the fact that monsoons are not infrequently deficient and that distribution is very far from equal, it is clear that at the time of the transfer of power the poorer sections of the population were underfed. Even to maintain this low level of nutrition, food grains had to be imported. Before the Second World War, India imported between one and two million tons of rice annually and the non-availability of Burma rice was one of the causes of the Bengal famine in 1943. Between 1939 and the end of the war, the growth of population must have increased India's need of food grains by between two and three million tons and in the year ending March 31, 1947, Rs.89 crores were spent on the import of food grains.

India on the threshold of independence was thus in the weak position of a primarily agricultural country unable to feed herself. This position was reached in spite of the fact that India had an irrigated area three times as large as that of the U.S.A. and larger than the combined total of any other ten countries in the world. Fortunately, the thorough knowledge of irrigation technique which had been acquired during the British period provided the foundation for the great river valley projects which were to figure prominently in the national plans of independent India. British administration had produced the conditions under which population rose so rapidly as to leave India with the difficult problem of feeding herself, but it had also shown how that problem could ultimately be solved.

The position with regard to cotton and jute was more satisfactory than that which obtained in food grains. Undivided India grew mainly short and medium staple cotton, and in spite of a decline in production of raw cotton in the ten years before independence, four-fifths of the cotton used by Indian mills in 1946–47 was indigenous and imports of cotton twist and yarn had practically ceased. The cotton textile industry is of particular interest, inasmuch as it was the first modern industry established and financed mainly by Indians, though British managers and technicians played an important part in it. In the early stages it had to cope with an unfair revenue policy imposed on India in defence of British interests, while at a later stage Japanese competition proved a severe trial. By 1914 India had become the fourth greatest cotton textile-manufacturing country in the world, but three-quarters of India's cotton textile needs were still imported. In between the two wars, fiscal protection helped the Indian cotton textile industry greatly, and in the last year before the Second World War imports of cotton textiles amounted to only 13 per cent of the total consumption of cotton cloth in India. By the end of that war, the position had still further improved. Imports of piece goods were negligible and, on the customary low basis of consumption of twelve yards per head per annum, India was practically able to clothe herself in 1947, though she still needed to import certain of the finer qualities of cloth.

Other important crops were jute and tea. India supplied practically all the world's requirements of jute and was the largest producer of tea. The place of these crops and the connected industries in the Indian economy is apparent from the following table of the principal exports in the year ending March 31st, 1947.

Commodity	Value of Exports (in £ million)
Jute yarns and manufactures	53
Tea	26
Cotton, raw and waste	21

Commodity	Value of Exports (in £ million)
Jute, raw and waste	14
Cotton yarns and manufactures	21
Hides and skins, tanned or dressed	14
Oils, vegetable, mineral and animal	3
Gums, resins and lac	9
Seeds (including nuts for oils)	3
Hides and skins, raw or undressed	6
Non-metallic mining and quarry products	3
Spices	3

We may sum up the position of agriculture and the connected industries in 1947 by saying that they provided the major part of India's earnings of foreign exchange; that India could more or less clothe her people from indigenous products; but that her great weakness was an apparently inescapable, though marginal, dependence on the import of food grains.

In industry, the progress achieved by 1939 was more striking than in agriculture. In the standard book on modern Indian economic history, Vera Anstey has described the decline of India's indigenous industry under the early free-trade régime of the British Government, and has explained how it was only towards the end of the nineteenth century that the rise of the jute, cotton, tea, iron and steel and engineering industries began to make up for what had been lost. Early in the twentieth century the Government of India embarked on a positive policy of encouraging industrial progress and India was therefore in a condition to take advantage of the economic stimulus of the First World War. Still more deliberate efforts were directed to this end after that war. A new tariff policy, together with the activities of the Provincial Industries Departments, combined with a considerable influx of British capital to produce rapid development. The following indices of output of the main industries illustrate the progress achieved:

	1925	1931	1937
Cotton mill industry	100	111	152
Jute mill industry	100	81	90
Sugar refining	100	128	584

	1925	*1931*	*1937*
Iron and steel industry	100	84	113
Paper industry	100	119	168
Cement industry	100	121	222
Coal industry	100	92	103

Even during the slump of the early 'thirties, although prices and profits fell considerably, industrial output continued to expand. The Second World War gave a great fillip to this process of development, and the historian of the Supply Department of the Government of India rightly says that the war years witnessed 'an industrial transformation which, under normal conditions, could not have taken place in twenty-five years'. In spite of the non-co-operation of the Indian National Congress in the war effort, India became one of the major arsenals of Britain and her allies and in the process developed a productive capacity which was to stand her in good stead in the early years of independence.

At the end of the Second World War it was recognised that the Government must continue to play an active part in economic development and a large number of industrial panels were set up to prepare plans for future progress. These panels observed, in 1945 and 1946, that in some important industries production had declined since the end of the war. Perhaps the main reasons for the decline were, first, the fact that the energy of the war years had been dissipated; secondly, that raw materials were in short supply; thirdly, that costs of production had again begun to be of importance; and fourthly, that labour in India was in the same difficult mood as in so many countries after the war.

It would, therefore, not be correct to assess independent India's industrial strength by war-time statistics. It is fairer to work on the basis of facts in 1947, after the war effort had produced its inevitable reaction. We have already considered the older industries such as tea, jute, cotton on which India's prosperity so largely depended, but must briefly refer to the more modern industries. The most important of them were coal – in which India had for some time been normally self-sufficient and had indeed a useful export surplus; paper and cement, in which she could produce about half her needs; oil, indigenous production of which was far short of requirements; and iron and steel, in which India was nearly self-sufficient, largely because consumption was very low. The author of the *Board of Trade's Economic Survey of India for 1949* observes that, if consumption of steel was taken as an index of industrial growth, it would reveal a 'lamentable feature in the industrial expansion of India', and he supports that statement by the following table.

(In million tons)

(*1*) Year	(*2*) Production	(*3*) Imports	apparent consumption regarded as total of Columns (*2*) and (*3*)
1914	neg.	1·29	1·29
1929	0·40	1·25	1·65
1933	0·48	0·33	0·81
1939	0·78	0·28	1·06
1947	0·89	0·05	0·94
1948	0·85	0·19	1·04

In non-ferrous metals, India was fairly well advanced. She dominated world markets in mica and had important export surpluses of manganese ore and gypsum, though she was to lose much of the latter to Pakistan on partition. In gold and aluminium and certain other important minerals she was more or less self-sufficient.

Considerable progress had been made in engineering. Light engineering industries, in general, were advancing rapidly and India could manufacture about one-quarter of her requirements of sewing machines and hurricane lamps. Developments in the manufacture of oil engines were hopeful. On the other hand, India's output of machine tools was not more than 10 per cent of her requirements and even this covered only the simpler types.

In the field of heavy chemicals, in 1947 productive capacity for sulphuric acid about equalled demand, but production of caustic soda was negligible and India could produce only about one-quarter of her requirements of soda ash. Somewhat similar conditions prevailed as regards fertilisers.

It is perhaps not necessary to pursue this subject in further detail. It is clear that India's industrial capacity had been greatly expanded by the end of the Second World War and, so far from having the 'colonial economy' which Britain is

sometimes alleged to have fostered, India had sufficient industrial capacity to provide a firm foundation for her further
economic development. Two comments of a general nature
must nevertheless be made. The first is that, except in the
case of the plantation industries, the overwhelming proportion
of India's industrial production was for home consumption.
The second general observation relates to the great extent to
which Indian industry at that time depended on imports oɩ
machinery, machine tools, chemicals, metals, electrical goods
and vehicles. Any severance of communications in a major
war would have brought her industry to a standstill by depriv-
ing her of the tools of her trades.

In industrial and commercial organisation India was reasonably well equipped. The managing agency system, though it
had long been regarded by Indian politicians as outmoded, still
provided the hard core of many of the old-established industries. It made available an *expertise* which few separate
tea, jute, or cotton companies could have otherwise afforded and
its financial support gave stability to managed companies in
difficult times. Moreover, it gave confidence to the small
middle-class Indian shareholder, who would invest in a particular concern, not on the basis of any study of its finances or
productive capacity, but in the knowledge that a British
managing agent was associated with it, or that some well-known
industrialist had money in it. By the end of the Second World
War the habit of industrial investment had, in fact, become well
established and a surprisingly large proportion of shares in Indian
public companies was held by Indians of the middle classes.

The growth of public companies between the beginning of
the First World War and independence is shown by the following table.

Year	*Number*	Paid-up Capital (*crores of rupees*)
1916–17	2,306	85·0
1921–22	4,095	1,92·1
1927–28	4,108	2,04·9
1933–34	5,736	2,02·1
	(India ex Burma)	
1938–39	6,859	2,13·0
1945–46	10,129	3,23·0

In 1946, partly as a reaction against war-time speculation and partly on account of the serious disorders in the country and the uncertainties in the political situation, a serious decline in share values set in. Confidence was still further undermined by the 'socialist' budget of Liaquat Ali Khan in the Interim Government, and at the time of the transfer of power the capital market was in a state of almost complete stagnation. This was, however, a passing phase and India had, in fact, become investment-minded.

In banking and insurance, British companies had not only furnished India with adequate facilities, but had also set the pattern to which enlightened Indian opinion expected Indian companies to conform. It must unfortunately be admitted that these expectations were frequently disappointed and, except for a few first-class companies, Indian insurance acquired such a bad reputation that a few years later the Government of India decided to nationalise life insurance. Indian banking had grown on rather sounder lines than life insurance and was an important element in the economy at the time of the transfer of power.

At the end of the Second World War India's financial position in the world was sound. For many years before the War she had enjoyed substantial favourable balances of trade, but, on the other hand, she had had to pay interest and amortisation charges on debt, to remit profits on British and foreign investment, to meet shipping, insurance and similar charges and to pay pensions and leave salaries for British officers. During the war, imports were necessarily cut down, exports were stimulated, and the balance of trade became even more favourable than before. India was able to purchase the Indian railways, to repatriate nearly all her external debt and to accumulate large sterling balances in England. Large sums were required by the British Government for war expenditure in India, and under the Indian Reserve Bank Act, the Bank was bound to issue rupees in unlimited quantities in exchange for sterling deposited at its credit in London. These sterling deposits amounted at the beginning of 1947 to over £1,200 million. In some British quarters there was a demand that this debt should be scaled down – since it had been spent at least partly for the defence of India – while Indians, on the other hand, claimed that 'this balance to the credit of India in London largely represented blood, sweat and tears on the part of India's masses who were forced to live in sub-human conditions (through a lack of consumer goods) so that the grist would be forthcoming for the mill of allied defence'. Without necessarily accepting this argument, the British Government rightly decided that it must honour its debts.

It would be wrong to regard the whole of the sterling balances as being available for development, since an acute shortage of consumer goods had to be made good. Nevertheless, India was left with what should have been the nucleus of a valuable development fund. Unfortunately, in the early post-war years, the necessity of importing food grains on a consider-able scale, together with a certain lavishness in expenditure on the import of other commodities, led to a substantial deficit in the balance of payments. By the time of the transfer of power, India was drawing rather heavily on her overseas resources, and, like the rest of the sterling area, was continuing to run a deficit balance with the dollar area.

In this and other respects, 1947 has rightly been described as 'a bleak economic year in India'. Nevertheless, there were great elements of strength in India's economic position. The sound orthodox finance of British Finance Ministers over a long period had laid firm foundations and India was in a good financial condition to go forward with the heavy tasks of independence.

At this stage, however, India was partitioned and the effects on the whole economy were profound. At the outset, Pakistan presented almost the perfect example of the 'colonial economy', while India, though primarily an agricultural country, had made considerable progress in industrialisation. The levels of wealth and the stages of development in the two countries were thus so different that even if political relations had been good, customs barriers, separate currencies and different economic policies would have been unavoidable, though normal trade could have continued. Unfortunately, political stresses and strains produced long periods when ordinary trade between India and Pakistan was gravely handicapped.

Perhaps the most serious economic effect of partition on India was in the matter of food grains. In normal years the surplus of rice in what was to become West Pakistan, had nearly balanced the deficit in East Bengal, while West Pakistan also had a substantial surplus of wheat. It so happened that 68 per cent of the irrigated area of undivided India went to Pakistan and, according to C. N. Vakil, yields of rice and wheat in India were only 750 and 650 lb. respectively as against 900 and 850 lb. in Pakistan. India, with a slightly larger population in proportion to area than Pakistan, and with a much larger urban population, found herself with a greater shortage of food grains than had been experienced by undivided India. A somewhat similar situation prevailed in regard to livestock, since the better milk-yielding cattle in India were in Sind and the West Punjab. Vakil calculates that, with a population only one-quarter that of India, Pakistan's milk production in 1947 was nearly half that of India and, though one may doubt whether the data to justify so precise a conclusion exist, the broad fact is beyond dispute. It must be accepted, then, that India's ability to feed herself was substantially lessened by partition.

Almost equally serious was the effect of partition on the Indian textile industries. While all the jute mills of the sub-continent were located in what had become India, nearly 80 per cent of the raw jute was grown in East Pakistan. India was thus faced with the dilemma of choosing between a dangerous dependence on East Pakistan for raw jute supplies, or growing jute herself in not wholly suitable conditions and using, for this purpose, land badly required for food production.

In the cotton textile industry India was also in difficulties. Of the 394 cotton textile mills of the sub-continent, only fourteen were located in Pakistan, which nevertheless produced 40 per cent of the raw material, including some of the best varieties of American-type medium-staple cotton. At the same time, the Indian mills were deprived of an important market in West Pakistan, where *per capita* consumption had been higher than elsewhere in undivided India. In both these ways, therefore, the Indian textile industry was badly hit by partition.

In general industry, on the other hand, India's resources were largely unimpaired, and indeed relatively strengthened by partition. All the iron ore, manganese and mica and nearly all the coal of the sub-continent were located in India. All the paper mills and glass factories, practically all the heavy chemical plants (except a large soda ash factory and two sulphuric acid plants) and 80 per cent of all production of cement, paint and matches were located in India, though in some cases the raw materials came partly from Pakistan. All the primary producers in the iron and steel industry were in India, though there were foundries and rolling mills in Pakistan. Unlike Pakistan, India was fairly well advanced in structural engineering, and had plans for the manufacture of locomotives, while her manufacture of simple electrical goods and appliances had grown rapidly during the war. A small industry for the manufacture of diesel engines had also been started. In the leather and tanning industries, on the other hand, the loss of the superior skins and hides from Pakistan lowered the quality of Indian production and the prohibition of cow slaughter led to further deterioration.

Partition thus left India fairly well off in the matter of industrial establishments and, what was even more important, there were a considerable number of experienced Indian industrialists and financiers who could be expected to underwrite great schemes of development in self-governing India. The chief difficulty arose from the migration to Pakistan of a large number of Muslim mechanics. The railways alone lost 83,000 Muslims in this way, most of whom were drivers, firemen, blacksmiths, coppersmiths and the like. It is true that 73,000 non-Muslims in Pakistan opted for the Indian railways, but they consisted largely of clerical and administrative personnel. On the East India Railway the shortage of drivers after 1947 amounted to 45 per cent and coal loadings from the mines to the railways had therefore to be reduced by half. In industry as a whole, managerial, administrative and superior technical personnel were available to meet requirements, but there was a serious shortage of mechanics. On the organisational side, partition created little difficulty for India, since banking, insurance and the managing agency system were all better developed in India than in Pakistan.

In the field of Government finance the position was less satisfactory. It is true that the revenue of India *per capita* was considerably higher than that of Pakistan, and that the budget gave no cause for anxiety. On the other hand, India's export capacity was considerably reduced by the loss of a certain proportion of her raw materials, while at the same time the fact that she was deprived of some of the richest grain-bearing areas of undivided India made it necessary to import increased quantities of foodstuffs. Moreover, India had to pay higher prices for raw jute than in pre-partition days. It was clear that in the earlier stages of independence she would have to face a deficit balance of payments and draw on her sterling reserves.

These difficulties, however, were likely to be temporary and India's economic position was basically sound. Her resources were vast, she had a considerable fund of technical and managerial skill, and important sections of her people were in a dynamic mood. Britain had, in fact, left India well equipped for industrial progress.

P

Chapter 18

Economic Policy 1947–64

OR A WHOLE generation before the transfer of power,
members of the Indian National Congress had been nur-
tured in the belief that the poverty of India was the result
of British rule and they were confident that independence
would release the energies of the people and lead rapidly to
prosperity. India would, in fact, achieve in a few years the
progress which had taken a century or more in Europe, but
this could only be brought about by discipline and careful
organisation of resources. 'Planning' was thus to be the corner
stone of the new economy.

It was also part of the Congress faith that India had suffered
from the principles of the 'colonial economy'. The production
of raw materials, which served the purpose of the rulers, had
been regarded as her proper role, and industrial development
had been retarded. To an objective observer this may seem a
somewhat distorted picture, but it was the foundation of
economic thought amongst the rank and file of the Congress
Party in 1947. Indian industry must, therefore, be developed
at all costs and agriculture could take care of itself.

There were, however, two schools of thought as to the right
lines of industrial development. There were the Gandhians,
who were justifiably afraid that India might suffer the social
evils which attended the Industrial Revolution in England and
therefore pinned their faith to the expansion of cottage industries; and there were the modernists, who recognised that
a country without highly developed large-scale industries could
not count in the modern world. It was perhaps a foregone conclusion that the latter school would triumph, though lip service would still be paid to cottage industries, which might
indeed have their place in a transitional economy.

Some of those who thought in terms of large-scale industry

oversimplified the problem. It seemed to them mainly a matter of replacing British by Indian industrialists, and there were prominent Parliamentarians who looked for a solution in the utilisation of the sterling balances for compulsory purchase of British industries in India. Practical responsibility soon destroyed the belief in any such facile solution, and outside observers were surprised at the rapidity with which the Indian Cabinet realised the difficulties attendant on a development policy. Quite early in the new régime. Nehru said frankly, 'We require not only money, but what is far more important, trained human material; in fact, that is the only thing in the ultimate analysis, whether it is industry or in any other department of life, and let us admit that we have not got a sufficient quantity of that trained human material in any aspect of life today.' A little later the Prime Minister continued in the same realistic tone, 'We must increase our production; we must increase our national wealth and the national dividend and only then can we really raise the standard of living of our people. We may here and there make some adjustment by a more equal distribution of existing wealth – but ultimately more wealth can only come from production of more types and kinds of goods.' This was indeed a far cry from the unpractical approach of pre-independence days.

Unfortunately, the Punjab massacres, the problem of Kashmir and the routine business of organisation resulting from partition, absorbed most of the energies of the Indian Government for a time and it is perhaps remarkable that they were able to formulate an industrial policy as early as 1948.

Under the old Government of India Act, which was in force until the transfer of power, British commercial interests had been protected from various forms of legislative and executive discrimination. Those safeguards naturally disappeared after August 15, 1947, and in view of the attitude of certain Indian politicians at that time, many British business men were uneasy about their future. There was some discussion amongst them as to the desirability of asking His Majesty's Government to negotiate a Commercial and Establishments Agreement with the Government of India, but after much thought they came to the conclusion that reliance on the good intentions of India would be more advantageous than treaty protection. The apprehensions were nevertheless real and were indeed an aspect of the doubts felt by all business men, British and Indian, as to the attitude of the new Government of India towards private enterprise. These doubts had been strengthened by the report of the Economic Programme Committee of the All India Congress Committee which was published at the beginning of 1948, and which envisaged a large measure of State ownership of industry, as well as limitation of dividends, division of surplus profit between the workers and the shareholders and the abolition of managing agencies.

It was therefore with great anxiety that the business world awaited the Industrial Policy Resolution of April 6th, 1948. The Resolution recognised that a mere redistribution of wealth would not serve India's purpose and that the fundamental need was for the expansion of production. To that end the State must play a progressively active role in the development of industries, though 'for some time to come' the State should concentrate on new units of production, instead of undertaking nationalisation of existing units. Industries were to be divided into certain categories, in the first of which there would be a Government monopoly. This category included armaments and railway transport and certain other industries. In the second category, which included coal, iron and steel, shipbuilding and mineral ores, the State was to be exclusively responsible for new undertakings, though existing enterprises would be allowed to run for ten years, after which the situation would be reviewed. The third category covered the rest of the industrial field and this was left open to private enterprise, though even within this sector Government proposed to undertake the regulation and control of certain basic industries, including heavy machinery and machine tools, textiles, nonferrous metals, minerals and cement.

The Resolution was undoubtedly more reassuring to the capitalist than the crude and ill-considered socialism of the Economic Planning Committee's Report and some observers regarded it as a deliberate attempt by Nehru to encourage private enterprise, as far as was politically possible. Others, however, were unhappy about the reference to 'postponement of nationalisation for some time' and to the ten-year period after which the private sector was to be reviewed. They felt that business men who had been told to come up for sentence in ten years' time would have little interest in development, or in putting fresh money into industry, and there is no doubt that a great many Indian business men did feel extremely apprehensive of undertaking long-term investments. They were also disturbed at a statement in a later part of the Resolution 'that labour's share of profits should be on a sliding scale, normally varying with production'.

The Resolution then went on to deal with foreign capital, but the relevant paragraph was not very enlightening. The matter was clarified and amplified in the Prime Minister's statement in the Constituent Assembly a year later. The Prime Minister began by explaining that the disappearance of foreign domination had changed India's attitude on this subject, and he now wished to encourage foreign capital investment in industry, not only for its own sake, but because of the technical and industrial knowledge it would bring with it. He laid it down that, as a rule, the major interest in a new undertaking should be in Indian hands, though each case would be dealt with on its merits. Non-Indians could be employed where necessary in posts requiring technical skill and experience, but Indians must be trained for such posts as quickly as possible. He went on to declare that, subject to foreign exchange considerations, remittance facilities would be provided for foreign enterprises and they would, in other respects also, receive the same treatment as Indian concerns.

If this statement had been interpreted literally, its emphasis on majority Indian shareholding might have been a deterrent to foreign investment, but most British business men regarded it as a deliberate encouragement of foreign capital and were heartened by it. The condition regarding Indian participation in the shareholding was, in practice, interpreted with considerable flexibility in the ensuing years.

The three main points in the Resolution were those relating to a government monopoly in some industries, to the regulation of certain other industries, and to foreign capital, and Government now proceeded to give effect to the Resolution on all three points. With regard to the first head, they soon embarked on the manufacture of locomotives at Chittaranjan and sulphate of ammonia at Sindri, as well as on the construction of telecommunication equipment in association with a British company. The second point – regulation of basic industries – led in 1949 to the passing of the Industries (Development and Regulation) Act. The most important sections of the Act were those which empowered Government to assume control of a mismanaged industry and provided for the licensing of all new industries within the scheduled list. A Central Advisory Council was set up to assist in carrying out these functions and this Council soon found itself concerned with the third point of the Resolution – the conditions of operation of foreign capital. Ministers had frequently re-affirmed India's need of, and desire for, foreign capital, but of more practical importance was the body of doctrine gradually built up by the Government of India and the Central Advisory Council. The first principle laid down was that a foreign new-comer must be concerned primarily with manufacture rather than trade. The Commerce Minister had, indeed, stated publicly that India needed no help in the sphere of trade and that new foreign participation in trade would not be welcome. Secondly, the Council ruled that foreigners would, as a rule, only be allowed to start a new industrial enterprise if existing productive capacity in that field had proved to be inadequate, or where the proposed investment would help to save foreign exchange by increasing exports or reducing imports. Thirdly, adequate provision must be made for the training of Indian personnel for senior posts, both administrative and technical.

When these criteria were satisfied, the Government were not unduly rigid with regard to the 51 per cent participation by Indian capital and it soon came to be realised that if a proposed industrial venture would be of value to India, the promoters could, within reasonable limits, negotiate as to capital holdings. On the other hand, the test of adequacy of productive capacity was applied strictly and in such fields as pharmaceuticals a number of applicants were refused permission to manufacture. The non-Indian new-comer could, in fact, operate where India needed help, and nowhere else. In such industries as iron and steel, the reservation of the initiative to Government was not observed too rigidly. The Commerce Minister

T. T. Krishnamachari[1] – a believer in private enterprise subject to governmental control – was perhaps mainly responsible for the flexibility in this matter and private concerns in the iron and steel industry were, in fact, allowed to expand, and even to erect new plant.

The policy was thus to encourage private enterprise generally and to welcome foreign capital within a field that was not unduly restricted. Ministers were at pains for some years to explain away that part of the Industrial Policy Resolution which seemed to convey a distant threat of nationalisation, and in 1952 even K. C. Reddy, a Minister generally regarded as a thorough-going Socialist said: 'If a choice was given to me to nationalise the existing steel industry and to set up in the alternative a State steel industry, I would unhesitatingly go in for the new plant to be set up instead of frittering away the resources in nationalising the existing industry.' This attitude was maintained for some years until, in 1954, the growing left-wing tendencies of the Congress Party produced a change of emphasis. Before dealing with that change, we must refer to the import and tariff policies of India in the early years of independence.

The import policy of the Government of India in the last two years before the transfer of power was perhaps unwisely generous. Luxury goods were imported on a lavish scale, even from dollar areas, and severe encroachments on India's foreign exchange resources took place. This error was corrected by the Interim Government just before Independence Day and necessary restrictions on the import of luxury and semi-luxury articles and even almost essential consumer goods were imposed.

By June 1948, the new restrictions had produced the desired result and it was again found possible to liberalise imports. This liberalisation was essential to counter inflation, but it was criticised by Indian manufacturers. The Government made it very clear, in February 1949, that they did not regard import restrictions as a means of affording protection to particular industries and that the foreign exchange position should be the only criterion by which to determine the level of imports. In spite of this view, when in 1951 an unfavourable

[1] He became Commerce Minister in 1952.

foreign exchange situation again necessitated more rigorous import control, it was obvious that, in fixing priorities, regard must be had to indigenous production. Moreover, the concept of planning which was given concrete form in 1950, clearly meant that limited foreign exchange resources must be directed into the most important channels. The Government of India nevertheless stood by their declaration that import control was not to be a method of protection and in the following years, whenever the foreign exchange position permitted, imports were liberalised.

Tariff policy followed the lines that might be expected in a mainly agricultural country striving to achieve a rapid increase in industrial production. Industries connected with defence were naturally to be protected, while other industries were to be eligible for protection if they were likely to develop sufficiently, within a reasonable period, to be able to dispense with protection thereafter. This principle has, on the whole, been applied wisely and fairly, and objective observers must admit that protection has assisted in the development of Indian industry, both before and since independence. It has been accompanied by attempts to enforce satisfactory standards in the protected industries. Tea chests provide a good illustration of the Government's determination to improve the quality of home-produced goods. Before the Second World War the tea industry imported the bulk of its tea chests. During the war recourse had perforce to be had to a certain proportion of indigenous chests, but when after the war the use of a high proportion of locally manufactured chests was made obligatory, the tea industry rightly protested, in view of the poor quality of most Indian tea chests. Its protests were brushed aside, but at the same time the Government took steps to see that indigenous production was improved, and today the quality of Indian tea chests is considered by tea producers to be on the whole not unsatisfactory.

From about 1954, Indian economic thought and policy seemed to undergo a new orientation which was disturbing to all business men, Indian or British. Three different factors combined to produce this change. In the first place it was partly the result of adult suffrage and the consequent strengthening of the left-wing element in the Congress Parliamentary Party after the elections of 1952. Secondly, an important section of Indian economists and intellectuals had come to the conclusion that it was impossible for private savings to accumulate at a sufficiently rapid rate to make the implementation of the Five Year Plan possible through private enterprise, and since they were not willing to infer that the plan was unreal and needed curtailment, they were forced to regard the public sector as the main source of development. They did not demand that the private sector should be abolished, but their view that it would be only of secondary importance lent considerable strength to the doctrinaire Socialist group within the Congress Party. Thirdly, there was the belief of many middle-class people that a measure of Socialism was the only possible protection against the threat of Communism. These factors enabled the hard core of determined Socialists, including some members of the Cabinet, to force their views on the party and the shift to the left in the economic policy of the Congress was unmistakable.

The first outward manifestations of the stronger trend towards Socialism appeared in 1954 in connection with the proposal for the construction of a steel plant at Durgapur on the basis of Indo-British collaboration. The matter was, to some extent, complicated by a profound difference of approach between two important members of the Indian Cabinet. Steel production was at this time the concern of both T. T. Krishnamachari, the Industries Minister, and K. C. Reddy, the Minister of Production, and no two men could be more different in their approach to economic problems. Krishnamachari, or T.T.K. as he is affectionately called by all who know him, had been a business man and believed that India had need of private enterprise. He looked therefore to the capitalist to play a major part in the development of the steel industry. Under his influence, the clause in the 1948 Industrial Policy Resolution which confined new developments in steel and connected industries to the public sector had been relaxed in practice. He encouraged B. M. Birla, a member of the greatest family of industrialists in India, to enter into discussions with British steel manufacturers with a view to forming an Indo-British steel manufacturing consortium. Reddy, on the other hand, was a confirmed Socialist, who insisted that all new steel development must be in the hands of the State. In the end, Reddy's view prevailed and when negotiations between Birla and a British group had advanced some way and looked hopeful, the Indian Cabinet called them off and insisted that, though British private capital would be welcome in a steel consortium, the Indian element must be publicly owned. British steel interests showed flexibility in their approach and, in due course, a scheme for Indo-British co-operation in the construction of a steelworks was accepted. The rejection of Birla's proposal on grounds of principle was nevertheless regarded by Indian business men as a sign that Socialism was to be the order of the day.

Shortly after this episode, the new pattern of thought led to the removal from the constitution of clauses which many business men had regarded as a protection against acquisition of their property, for purposes of nationalisation or otherwise, without adequate compensation. During the discussions on this amendment, Nehru gave an exposition of his views on compensation, which was profoundly disturbing to the business community. He said: 'It never occurred to me that Government should take over anything without paying compensation.

'If we are aiming at changes in the social structure, then you cannot think in terms of giving what is called full compensation. First, because you cannot do it. Secondly, because it would be improper to do it, unjust to do it, and, thirdly, it should not be done even if you can do it.

'If we give full compensation, the "haves" will remain the "haves" and the "have nots" the "have nots". . . . Therefore, in any scheme of social engineering you cannot give full compensation.

'I can imagine or conceive of a thing whereby in the case of a slum no compensation might be necessary or desirable. Leaving that specific case out, generally speaking compensation in all these cases will be paid according to the constitution, according to our general practice.'

Undoubtedly Nehru's object was to make sure that vested interests should not stand in the way of slum clearance and other measures of social justice, but the principle enunciated by him has wider implications and was received with acclamation by the rank and file of the Congress Party.

The shift of thought was given outward expression at the

annual session of the Indian National Congress at Avadi in January 1955. At that session it was for the first time laid down explicitly that the object of planning must be the establishment of a socialistic pattern of society. Some of the leaders of the party were still a little hesitant about this and seemed to take some comfort from the distinction between socialism and a 'socialistic pattern of society', but the Budget for 1955–6 was generally recognised as a full-blooded socialistic budget. The Finance Minister declined at that time to lay down a ceiling on personal income, but he made drastic increases in taxation in the higher-income groups. There is nothing necessarily ominous about increases in taxation in any country, but all observers in Delhi regarded these increases as the direct result of the Avadi Resolution, rather than of revenue needs.

At the annual session of the Indian National Congress at Amritsar in February 1956, the goal was defined more clearly. The hesitance of the previous year had gone, the 'socialistic pattern' was replaced frankly by 'Socialism' as the guiding principle and one member of the Indian Cabinet made it very clear that 'the dropping of the last two letters from the word 'socialistic' was deliberate and not inadvertent'. Another Minister laid it down that the goal of a Socialist society must be achieved within a measurable time. The official resolution stated that 'the conversion of the Imperial Bank of India into a publicly-owned and publicly-managed State bank, and the recent nationalisation of life insurance, are significant steps towards the establishment of a Socialist structure'. Lip service was paid to the continuing need for the private sector, but the deprecatory references to the profit motive, the condemnation of disparities between one class and another, and the demand in the Presidential address for a ceiling on personal incomes, set the tone of the session.

The Government of India did not surrender entirely to this trend in economic thought and when, in order to remove the uncertainties which had been created in the minds of investors, they issued the Industrial Policy Resolution of 1956 it did not differ radically from that of 1948. Indeed it went a little further in the direction of encouraging the private sector, and within the category of industries allotted to that sector, Article 10 stated that 'It would be the policy of the State to facilitate and encourage the development of these industries in the private sector'. Reference was also made to the possibility of assisting them with finance or by fiscal measures. Sir Theodore Gregory sees in this Resolution the turning-point between the earlier dogmatic attitude and the 'pragmatic approach' of which Indian economists were to write and speak frequently two or three years later.

In fact the terms of the Resolution were so wide that emphasis on either the public or private sector could be justified. For the first year or so after the passing of the Resolution, the bias was strongly in favour of the public sector. This is well illustrated by the treatment of the mining industries. In April 1956 the Centre directed State Governments not to grant any further coal prospecting licences to private parties and to ask colliery companies to surrender the leases of areas not yet worked. The Minister of Natural Resources declared that he proposed 'to prevent the expansion of coal mines under the private sector', and under the Second Five Year Plan, out of the additional twenty-two million tons of coal to be produced, twelve million were to be in the public sector. This decision had unfortunate effects on the Indian economy, since the public sector failed lamentably to do what was expected of it, but it was typical of the doctrinaire approach popular at the time. A similar attitude was manifest in the dealings of the Government of India with the oil industry and in the passing of an Act which purported to curtail seriously the right of mining companies in general to renewal of their leases.

As the years passed the difficulties experienced by the public sector, together with India's need to encourage foreign investment, led to some diminution of the prejudice against the private sector and by 1960 it was generally reported by business men that Government was becoming a little more realistic in its outlook. Nehru indeed expressed impatience at the controversy over the public and private sectors and went so far as to say 'I want to encourage private enterprise because I think it desirable to encourage every way that helps a nation's growth and production'. Nevertheless, there can be little doubt that the general trend of thought inside the Congress Party continues to be towards a Socialist State.

This does not mean that the stage was set for wholesale nationalisation of industry. The financial requirements of the Third Five Year Plan were clearly going to strain the resources of the nation and leave so little margin for the acquisition of existing enterprises that nationalisation, if carried out at all, would have to be highly selective and little attention was paid to the wild men of the party, who talked as though the public sector could become all-embracing in the near future. Confiscation was not in the air and in the cases of nationalisation affecting foreign interests so far – The Imperial Bank, Life Insurance and the Kolar Gold Fields – fair compensation was paid, though it must be stated that in the Kolar Gold Fields proceedings a reasonable award had to be forced on the Mysore Government by the Government of India.

An outward manifestation of the new Socialist trend was the establishment of the State Trading Corporation. The entry of Government into a wide range of highly technical industries may possibly be justified on the practical ground that capital for them would not otherwise be forthcoming. Few economists, however, except those committed to the idea of the Socialist State, would approve of the continual encroachment of the State Trading Corporation on the private domain. Although the statement of the objects of the Corporation was very comprehensive, it was understood at the time of its establishment in 1955 that it was primarily intended to handle trade with the Iron Curtain countries, and it is admitted on all sides that such a Corporation was necessary for this purpose. Its sponsor, T. T. Krishnamachari, saw in the Corporation a useful instrument of practical policy. It was, however, received with acclamation by that large section of Congress back benchers who believe that trade can be run better by the State than by private enterprise and that middle-men are only parasites who ought to be eliminated. This view soon led to the granting to the Corporation of a monopoly in the trade in cement. The argument used to support this development was simple. The cost of imported cement was higher than that of cement produced in India. It was considered only just to equalise the price of all cement, irrespective of its origin, and this it was claimed could only be done by allowing the Corporation to assume control of the internal as well as the import trade. A few years later the import of cement was discontinued, but the Corporation still continued to handle the internal trade and did not reduce its price to the consumer. The Estimates Committee of Parliament pointed out that 'It was most inappropriate that in addition to the considerable revenue raised by levy and high excise duty, Government should have taken advantage of its monopoly in raising additional revenues by fixing high prices for cement'. As Sir Theodore Gregory puts it, the State Trading Corporation is being used as 'an extra Parliamentary source of taxation'.

Apart from cement, the Corporation soon had a monopoly of the import of caustic soda, raw silk and soda ash and of the export of iron ore and a 50 per cent monopoly of the export of manganese ore. In September 1960 Nehru declared that 'we must progressively investigate more and more avenues of State trading' and it was only the determination of S. K. Patil, the Food Minister, that prevented the assumption by the Corporation of all trade in food grains.

A gradual expansion of the activities of the State Trading Corporation is highly probable, since its ideological attractions are strengthened by its revenue-raising capacity and Indian business men today are very apprehensive with regard to this aspect of the Socialist trend of Indian economic thought.

Their fears have been strengthened by the creation of ancillary Government Corporations such as the Mineral and Metal State Trading Corporation and by the great potential for investment of the State-owned Life Insurance Corporation, the scope of which was greatly expanded in 1963 by the decision of Government that the Corporation would enter the field of general insurance.

A second factor tending towards the Socialist State is the control-mindedness of the Government of India. Every business man is painfully aware of the complicated structure of rules and regulations by which he is hemmed in on every side, but it will serve our purpose if we refer briefly to Government controls with regard to Company Law and labour.

The English Company Law in the main follows the principle that it is for the shareholders to decide how their money should be spent, and that it is only necessary for the law to ensure that the relevant facts are placed fully before them. In India, Government have departed entirely from this principle. The assumption seems to be that the shareholders do not know what is good for them. They must be protected not only against the Directors, but against themselves. Under the Act of 1955 the remuneration of Directors is limited by statute; a Company cannot appoint Managing Agents without the approval of Government; and the Company Law Administration intervenes in a very large number of matters which in England would be entirely within the competence of the shareholders. Many reasons are officially adduced to justify this network of regulations, but the fact is that India today enjoys control for its own sake.

A similar control-mindedness is apparent in the labour policy of the Central Government. The statutory fixation of minimum wages and the assumption by Government of power to refer any industrial dispute to a Tribunal whose findings are binding illustrate this tendency and they have the unfortunate effect that neither employers nor labour are forced to learn by experience the value of collective bargaining. Unions thus have had no need to develop along healthy lines. There are exceptions to this general statement and in one or two states the Government concerned has been wise enough to stand aside and allow employers and employees to hammer out long-term collective agreements, but in other States Ministers have either been far too ready to refer every dispute to a Tribunal or have frankly allied themselves with labour in so-called Tripartite Conferences at which employers have been simply dragooned into doing what they are told. Recently this attitude has led to two decisions which are almost certainly unsound. In the first place the Central Government has imposed a so-called profit sharing bonus scheme in which a guaranteed minimum bonus is paid whether the employer makes a profit or not; and secondly, in the case of the Tea Industry, an interim wage increase entirely unjustified by any change in the cost of living, has been forced through by a Wage Committee under Government direction. These actions are, of course, all part and parcel of the belief that Government knows best.

It is obvious that the concept of planning necessitates a certain measure of Government control, but it is equally clear that the Government of India is very control-minded and indeed regards controls not as temporary measures but as a part of the permanent pattern of Indian economic life. They are indeed a step on the road towards the Socialist State, at which the Congress Party aims. The interpretations of this general ideology by the left and right wings of the Party differ widely and this difference was clearly revealed at the Bhubaneswar Session of the Congress in January 1964. K. D. Malaviya proposed a resolution calling for a more rapid advance to socialism than was contemplated in the official resolution which he himself was seconding, and in company with B. Patnaik he demanded the nationalisation of banks. As might be expected Krishna Menon supported the left wing view, but Shastri and Kamaraj – the men who really count today – would deviate neither to the right nor to the left, and secured the passage of the original middle of the road resolution. That resolution lays down that the basic objective of the Party is 'the establishment of a socialist state based on parliamentary democracy'. Perhaps the real division inside the Party is between the pure theoreticians and the men who actually have to run the business of government. Certainly Shastri and T. T. Krishnamachari are firm believers in the mixed economy and as long as men of their calibre are in charge of the economy, there will be plenty of scope for private business in the specified but very wide field.

The policy of India today is based not only on the belief in Socialism, but also on a widespread economic nationalism. That sentiment is strong in almost every Asian country and has in general expressed itself in three ways. First there is the demand that industry shall, in the main, be owned and controlled by nationals of the country concerned; secondly there is insistence that such nationals shall fill superior posts in industry, whoever the shareholders may be; and thirdly, there is the reservation to the country's own citizens of important sections of its trade. In all these matters India has been more moderate than some of her neighbours. She has interfered little with existing non-Indian industry, and except to some extent in the matter of taxation, foreign business men have not suffered serious discrimination. We have already seen that India has not been illiberal in her attitude towards foreign participation in new ventures, and that a foreign investor proposing to establish an industry which India considers important, can within reasonable limits make his own terms as to the proportion of the equity capital to be held by him. It was a little disturbing, therefore, two or three years ago, when the Minister for Industries, Manubhai Shah, indicated that a tightening up of this matter was proposed and suggested that in general the foreign investor should be satisfied with 25 per cent participation. It soon appeared that this statement need not be taken too seriously and experience has shown that each case will be judged on its merits and that flexibility will be greater in practice than in theory.

With regard to the remittance of profits by sterling investors, India has been most reasonable and the assurance given by the Prime Minister in April 1949, that remittance facilities would be maintained has been fully honoured. On the other hand, during much of the period under review India has been unduly restrictive in regard to the payment of royalties and consultancy fees to foreign industrialists, but there are signs that a more practical view is now beginning to prevail.

The second important aspect of economic nationalism relates to the increased employment of Indians in superior posts in all branches of trade and industry. India naturally attaches great importance to this development, but, unlike Pakistan and Ceylon, she has not enforced a policy of Indianisation by statute, nor has she required visas for the entry of British employees into India. She has been content to achieve her aim by negotiation with British and other foreign companies. This makes documentation somewhat difficult, but the broad outlines of the picture can easily be drawn.

The leaders of British business have unreservedly recognised the right of Indians to expect a full share of superior employment in industries operating in their own country, and for some years the increasing recruitment of Indians to superior posts has been taken for granted by all progressive British firms. The Government of India, on the other hand, have recognised that it is right for a British-owned firm to have a British head and that this necessitates continued recruitment of British assistants. The Government have also taken the view that they are concerned only with the overall problem and not with the filling of particular posts. If a particular industry falls behind in recruitment, the help of the President of the Associated Chambers of Commerce – who is the leader of the British

Q

business community for the time being – is taken and an approach by him to the defaulters nearly always produces the desired result. Indianisation is, in fact, being facilitated by the general expansion of business, and the overall progress will be seen from the following figures of employment in British – or foreign-controlled companies on salaries of Rs.1000 per mensem and above.

Year (as on 1st January)	Indians	Non-Indians
1954	3455	7008
1955	4139	6810
1956	4862	6566
1957	5906	6025
1958	6959	5652
1959	7916	5304
1960	9113	4809
1961	10,229	4364
1962	11,535	4001
1963	12,434	3570

It is perhaps unfortunate that towards the end of 1960, the Minister for Industries, Manubhai Shah, made a statement which at first rather disturbed the British community. It was to the effect that within a short time there would be practically no non-Indians in posts carrying salaries of less than Rs.2,000 per mensem. As young British assistants are not normally paid as much as this in their early years, this statement if taken literally, would have prevented the recruitment of young British mercantile or general assistants. The Minister has since made it clear that this was not the intention of Government and since Government recognise that it is right for a British business to have a British national at its head if it so wishes, the recruitment of young men from Britain must continue, though not on a large scale.

It seems likely that progressive Indianisation would have been achieved without Government intervention, partly because many British companies themselves consider this policy to be correct, and partly because the high rates of taxation and the ever-increasing cost of living make it difficult to secure and retain the services of well-qualified British young men. It must, however, be remembered that it takes as long to make a manager as to train a technician and perhaps India's greatest shortage today is of trained managerial and administrative personnel. It would pay India to encourage young British men to take up such posts, but this would be politically difficult. Nevertheless in 1964 the Finance Minister took the bold step of granting special taxation reliefs to expatriates and thereby demonstrating India's desire not to drive away foreign personnel.

A third manifestation of Indian nationalism is the reservation of particular fields of business – or increased shares in them – to Indians. It has already been made clear that foreign newcomers will not be allowed in trade as distinct from industry. Apart from this there is constant pressure on exporters to ship by Indian Lines and recently the British and Indian Shipping Lines are understood to have agreed to the allocation to Indian Lines of a particular percentage of all cargo between India and Britain. A similar desire to secure for India a larger share in the services ancillary to industry has led to compulsion on the Indian tea industry to divert to the Calcutta auctions a considerable percentage of its tea formerly sold in the London auctions.

It may well be doubted whether these artificial constraints will benefit the Indian economy in the long run, but in the early years of self-government of any underdeveloped country they are psychologically inevitable. British concerns have accepted them with a good grace and in the knowledge that in these respects India has been more considerate than some other newly independent countries.

Chapter 19

Economic Progress 1947-64

HE FIRST two or three years after the transfer of power
were discouraging for those who had hoped for an
immediate spurt in economic activity. The slump in
industrial production, which had begun in 1946, became even
more marked in the first year of independence. A partial
revival in 1948 was followed by further deterioration in the
two following years and pessimists began to believe that the
expansionist spirit of pre-independence days had already
evaporated. This gloomy view failed to take account of the
temporary nature of some of the factors which had retarded
development, chief amongst which were the breakdown of
law and order over a wide area in 1947, the dislocation of trade
resulting from partition, the economic war between India and
Pakistan in 1949 and the uncertainty of Indian business men
at that time as to the future economic policy of the Government
of India.

By 1951, some of these adverse factors had disappeared or
diminished in strength, and at the same time the Government
of India set itself to work not only to increase the *tempo* of
development, but also to direct it into the channels which
would be most profitable to the nation as a whole. National
planning began to be accepted as the sure foundation of prosperity, and ambitious targets for increasing production and
for raising the standard of living were fixed by the Planning
Commission. Whatever may have been the purely economic
value of the plan, its psychological impact was tremendous.
Once again Indians began to believe that the burden of poverty
could be lifted, and in the pursuit of this aim a new spirit of
co-operation between the public and the Government was
born. That spirit has produced striking results and it is impossible to travel round India today without feeling that the

country has entered a new, dynamic phase. In the towns, industrial progress is sometimes overshadowed by the problem of unemployment and by the serious economic difficulties of the middle classes. In the villages, on the other hand, the signs of a rise in the standard of living are unmistakable, even though this improvement is not easily capable of statistical demonstration.

As agriculture still provides 50 per cent of the national income and occupies half the working population, it must come first in our brief survey of economic development. Agricultural progress since the transfer of power has been substantial. As we have seen, India was an importer of food grains even before the Second World War, and partition so increased her dependence on the outside world that in the three years ending in 1951, her average annual imports of food grains amounted to about three and a half million tons. It could reasonably be assumed that, by 1956, the population would have increased by another twenty million and an additional three million tons of food grains would be required if the current standard of consumption were to be maintained. Allowance had also to be made for the undernourished classes, and the authors of the First National Plan therefore fixed 7.6 million tons as the target for increased annual production by 1956. The achievement of this target was essential in order that foreign exchange might be released for industrial development.

Indian politicians at this time had exaggerated ideas as to the area of genuinely cultivable land not actually cultivated, and the first efforts at increasing production were directed mainly towards the extension of the area under food grains. Much marginal land, which the ordinary cultivator had been wise enough to leave alone, was brought under cultivation and average yields per acre of the principal crops were considerably lower in 1951 than in 1947. This was soon realised, and more attention began to be given to improved methods of cultivation. In some paddy areas, particular emphasis was laid on the introduction of the so-called Japanese system. There was nothing new in principle about this method. It was based on the same plan of careful seed selection, ruthless destruction of poor plants, greater use of artificial fertilisers in the seedling stage, and proper spacing between the plants, which the various

agricultural departments had long advocated, but more intensive efforts than previously were made to educate the cultivator in these matters. At the same time, facilities for the supply
of good seeds and of fertilisers were multiplied and cheapened,
and numerous demonstration plots were laid out in the villages.
Irrigation works were given high priority.

These measures produced impressive results in the first few
years. Fluctuations from season to season make progress
difficult to measure, but three-year averages of the official
figures of production of all food grains show that by 1955
the normal level of production was about 66 million tons as
compared with 52 million tons in 1951. Thereafter there was
some flattening in the curve of progress, but the upward trend
was soon resumed and recent figures suggest that 80 million
tons may now be regarded as a normal outturn.

There is considerable lack of accuracy about Indian agricultural statistics, and at a time when the work of subordinate
officials is judged to no small extent by the results of their
activities in connection with the Grow More Food Campaigns,
inaccurate reports are likely to err on the optimistic rather than
on the pessimistic side. Nevertheless a reliable outside authority
has estimated that the true average rate of gain over the past
eight or nine years has been about 2.6 per cent. It is a little
ironical that in spite of India's creditable achievement in this
direction, she is still unable to feed herself even in a normal year.
The deficiency is due partly to a rate of increase of population
greater than previously anticipated and partly to the fact that
over the period since the transfer of power standards of living
have risen and important sections of the population, though
still inadequately nourished by Western standards, do in fact
consume more food grains than they formerly did. In this sense
India's difficulties are the measure of her success. The Asoka
Mehta Foodgrains Enquiry Committee in a very careful study
of this subject, estimated that for the foreseeable future India
would need to import from two to three million tons of food
grains annually, and it is satisfactory to note that the U.S.A. has
undertaken to supply seventeen million tons of food grains to
India during the period of the Third Five Year Plan.

In an average year imports are thus able to restore the
balance between supply and demand, but even a relatively

small decline in production in a particular year results in shortages and prices shoot up rapidly. In 1962-3 climatic conditions were adverse in five important food producing States. The outturn of rice and wheat was 3.7 million tons below that of the previous year, and though this was to some extent offset by an increased production of other foodgrains, the total shortage was in the neighbourhood of 2.2 million tons and foreign exchange difficulties prevented India from increasing imports by a corresponding figure. Prices rose rapidly and in the case of rice reached almost record heights. The tight credit policy adopted by Government compelled holders of stocks to unload part of them and this together with the release of Government stocks eased the price of wheat, but no such action was possible in the case of rice.

In 1963-4 similar conditions prevailed and at the end of January 1964 rice prices were 10 per cent higher than at the beginning of 1963. The normal cold weather seasonal decline did not take place and the anticipated shortage not only led to hoarding by middlemen and retention by farmers, but also caused some State Governments to follow an unduly restrictive policy in the matter of foodgrains exports to other States. Towards the middle of the year something like panic set in and the price of cereals reached levels of 164.7 as compared with a base of 100 in 1952-3. The opposition, particularly the Communists, naturally exaggerated the shortages and belaboured the Government, and equally naturally Government painted the picture in less sombre colours than the facts warranted. In reality famine conditions did not prevail, and the rise in prices was the most serious aspect of the situation.

It is clear that even the increase in production of more than 50 per cent in the past twelve years or so has not been sufficient to put India in a safe position in the matter of food.

Nearly all observers agree that in recent years far too little energy has been put by State Governments and district officers into Grow More Food Campaigns. Any rapid increase in food production must depend not on new vast irrigation works, but on small local scale schemes, and in spite of the faith which Nehru placed in village self-help, these schemes will only succeed if they are pushed by the local officials. So far very few

State Governments have given agricultural development the highest priority in their efforts.

As regards other crops, the desire for self-sufficiency has led to strenuous attempts to increase production of cotton and jute. In cotton the result has been most satisfactory, particularly since much of the increase is in the long-staple varieties which India so badly needs. Jute presented a more intractable problem. Many outside observers felt grave doubts as to the wisdom of planning for any great expansion of jute cultivation, and argued that conditions in West Bengal were not suitable from the point of view of quality, yield or availability of water for retting. Nevertheless the jute crop has risen by over 30 per cent in the last decade. Oil seed production has risen by 20 per cent in the same period and the sugar-cane crop has increased by 60 per cent. Agricultural progress as a whole must be regarded as fairly satisfactory.

Closely connected with agricultural development are the great irrigation and power schemes which formed a main feature of the First and Second Five Year Plans. When independent India took stock of her position in 1947, electrical development was extremely backward. Generating capacity was negligible by comparison with that of Japan or the U.K., and even that limited capacity was not fully used. Only one in every two hundred villages with a population of below 5,000 had been electrified – yet the importance of electrification both for tube-well irrigation and for cottage industries, was obvious. A second fact which the new leaders of India had to consider was that, in spite of the great development of irrigation during the twentieth century, only about six per cent of the annual flow in the rivers was utilised for irrigation. It was, therefore, natural that the planners should think in terms of great storage dams which could be used for the generation of electricity as well as for irrigation. At this time, the Tennessee Valley scheme had caught the imagination of educated Indians and there was, therefore, a great demand for the initiation of multi-purpose river schemes with the least possible delay. It was realised that five years was too short a time for the completion of such projects and a long-term plan, aimed at doubling the area under irrigation within twenty years and simultaneously generating seven million kilowatts of power, was accepted. The most important of the multi-purpose schemes which were initiated at this time were the Bhakra-Nangal project on the Sutlej, the Damodar Valley scheme and the Hirakud dam project (which was intended to form part of a series of dams for the integrated development of the Mahanadi Valley). The schemes were bold and imaginative and, in spite of unexpected technical setbacks, considerable progress has been made.

Since then a number of hydro-electric and thermal schemes have been taken up and electrical capacity has been more than trebled since 1947. Unfortunately some of the authorities concerned underestimated both the time likely to be required for the completion of projects and the probable rate of growth of demand. Whereas some years ago it was to some extent necessary to create installed capacity in order to stimulate demand, today there are serious power shortages in all the most important towns. This situation is seen at its gravest in Calcutta – undoubtedly the worst administered of the great cities of India. Some years ago the West Bengal Government, obsessed with the belief that the public sector – in this case the Damodar Valley Corporation – would be able to meet all Calcutta's electrical needs, prevented the Calcutta Electric Supply Company from importing the plant which they considered necessary for expansion. The Damodar Valley Corporation fell far below its target for supply of power and the resulting overstrain on the Company's installations, coupled with unlucky accidents, resulted in 1961 in a serious breakdown in power supply and many services had to be cut for several months. On a smaller scale, over-optimism has similarly bedevilled power planning in other areas too and shortage of power has certainly retarded development in the Third Plan period. Nevertheless much progress has been made, though village India is still in the kerosene lamp stage, and only 2½ per cent of the towns and villages with populations of less than 10,000 have an electric supply.

In irrigation, the fine work done by the British has been worthily continued, though progress could have been faster but for the tendency of the planners to rely unduly on large-scale and necessarily long-term projects. Of the thirty-eight million acres which are to be irrigated from major and medium schemes started during the first two plans, only about one-quarter were in fact irrigated by the end of the Second Plan. Even when irrigation facilities have been made available, there is often considerable delay in the villages in constructing water courses and field channels. According to the National Council of Applied Economic Research, in the case of major and medium irrigation schemes the gap between available facilities and actual utilisation is rapidly increasing and it had reached $4\frac{1}{2}$ million acres by the end of 1962–3. Various State Governments have therefore passed legislation empowering the State to construct the village irrigation channels themselves and recover the cost from the beneficiaries. It still remains to be seen if this will bring about an improvement, but it has been realised that it is a mistake to neglect simple and even primitive methods, such as those involving tanks, tube wells and small storage dams, of which the cultivator is very ready to make use.

Industrial progress is more difficult to describe in general terms and must be treated under three heads, namely, the public sector, the private sector and cottage industries. Official figures do, however, show that industrial production in 1959 was 22 per cent greater than in 1955 and if we exclude the traditional industries – cotton textiles, tea and jute – the increase was about 50 per cent. From 1959 onwards the rate of progress has been slower than was expected – the hoped for acceleration of an acceleration has not taken place. Foreign exchange difficulties have necessitated import restrictions which have in some cases made it impossible to manufacture to capacity, while in other cases lack of demand has slowed down development. The heavy burden of taxation after the Chinese attack and the nervousness created at times by the extreme doctrinaire socialists in the Congress Party, have also had their effect.

This must not obscure the fact that in absolute terms development has been remarkable, or that during the period of the first two Five Year Plans industrial production as a whole increased by about 40 per cent. In the first two years of the Third Plan, factory production has risen by 14.5 per cent.

This increase in production is to a great extent to the credit of the private sector. Many of the projects in the public sector are by their nature bound to be slow in completion and, moreover, they have nearly all fallen behind their time schedules. Over-optimism in estimating construction times and underestimation of costs have indeed characterised most of India's planning in the sphere of public enterprise.

This must not lead us, however, to belittle what has been done. The first important achievement in the public sector was the Chittaranjan locomotive factory, which was the fulfilment of the imaginative vision of two railway officers during the British period. The factory is impressive and India is now self-sufficient in steam locomotives, though some component parts of them still have to be imported.

The next most important development in the public sector was the Sindri fertiliser factory. After the usual teething troubles, the factory is working well and now produces over 300,000 tons of ammonium sulphate annually. India, however, is at last becoming fertiliser minded and even with the additional fertiliser plants now in operation or under construction Indian production will not meet the needs of the country.

Other schemes in the public sector followed in quick succession. Mention of machine tools, a heavy machine building plant, telephone cables, antibiotics, insecticides and newsprint will illustrate the wide range of the industries covered and it is only necessary to refer in detail to steel and oil. Steel is of particular interest as exemplifying foreign collaboration with the Indian public sector. The Durgarpur steel plant has been constructed by contract with a consortium of British firms; the Bhilai project has been carried out under an agreement with the U.S.S.R.; while the Rourkela plant has been constructed under contract with the German firms of Krupp and Demag. When these plants are in full operation, India's production of steel will be 6 million tons annually as compared with $1\frac{1}{2}$ million tons at the beginning of the Second Five Year Plan. Naturally enough it has been impossible to keep to the time table, and full production will not be achieved until two or three years later than the scheduled date. Outside observers have been very critical of the administrative arrangements for the new steel plants. There is said to have been too much centralisation and too little attention to costs, and the lack of efficient, experienced Indian managers and senior technicians has proved a considerable handicap. Recently there have been signs of improvement. Fortunately the Government of India have recognised the necessity of continuing to employ foreign personnel, but do not find it easy to get them. In spite of these difficulties the wisdom of constructing these three steel plants cannot be questioned and the ultimate saving in foreign exchange will be considerable.

Development of the oil industry has been seriously hampered by the insistence of Government for a long time that the expansion of refining and distribution of oil should be confined to the public sector. In 1953 the Assam Oil Company – a subsidiary of the Burmah Oil Company – struck oil in the Nahorkatiya area of Assam. After much haggling and intransigence on the part of Government, in 1959 a new company, Oil India Ltd – in which the equity capital is held one-third by Government and two-thirds by the Burmah Oil Company – was formed to develop the new field and to build the pipeline for conveying the oil to two new refineries which are being constructed by Government with assistance from Russia and Rumania. At the beginning of the Second Plan, India's annual requirements of oil amounted to 7 million tons of which only 400,000 were available from local production. The Nahorkatiya field is expected ultimately to produce from $2\frac{1}{2}$–5 million tons annually, so that even with the rapid growth of consumption, nearly half of India's needs will then be met from the local production. The new refineries will increase India's capacity by about 50 per cent to a figure of $8\frac{3}{4}$ million tons in terms of crude petroleum – roughly equal to her present needs.

Exploration for oil was retarded for some years by the reservation of new concessions to the Oil and Natural Gas Commission in the public sector. In 1959 the unwisdom of this policy of exclusion was realised and foreign companies were invited to apply for concessions. In May 1961 an agreement between the Government of India and the Burma Oil Company opened up a large area in Assam for prospecting and development by the joint venture – Oil India Limited – referred to above. It is reasonable to hope that this more practical approach of Government will be continued.

In spite of high taxation and other discouragements, the private sector is abounding in vitality and expansion is taking place rapidly, partly under the influence of protection and partly as a result of the growing habit of collaboration between

British or foreign and Indian industrialists. Another important factor is the psychological change which has occurred amongst Indian business men. Many who were formerly only traders and financiers are now becoming industrially minded. There has been a great diversification in industry during this period and development has been well balanced.

Industries of particular importance to India's development are those concerned with engineering, heavy chemicals, metallurgy and cement. In all these fields remarkable progress has been made and in the engineering field the main point of interest is the very wide range of products now being manufactured on a considerable scale. The heavy chemical industry, too, has developed rapidly in the last few years and there has been a considerable increase in the production of sulphuric acid, caustic soda and soda ash. Nevertheless, substantial imports are still necessary and further expansion is planned.

The demand for cement in the Third Five Year Plan will be almost unlimited and the satisfactory progress which has been made in this industry is of the utmost importance to the whole economy. Production has increased from $2\frac{1}{2}$ million tons in 1950 to 7 million tons in 1959, and to nearly nine million tons in 1962-3.

In cotton textiles, development has to some extent been complicated by political considerations and the consequent determination of Government to foster the handloom industry, even at the expense of the mills, if necessary. Restrictions were placed on any increase in the number of looms in cotton mills and the production of mill-made dhoties was limited. In spite of these restrictions, the total production of cotton cloth and yarn appears to have grown more rapidly than domestic consumption. Overstocking in the mills resulted and when export markets also contracted, production necessarily declined. It is nevertheless 33 per cent higher than in 1950.

The increase in sugar production up to 1961 was a natural continuation of a process started many years ago when heavy protection was given to the sugar industry. Production became equal to India's total demand at present rather low consumption levels, and India became an exporting country. Unfortunately this progress was not continued. The controlled prices at which the mills were allowed to buy cane from the growers appears to have been fixed too low. The area under cultivation declined and at the same time a larger proportion of the cane was sold to the manufacturers of *gur* instead of to the mills. Production of sugar has therefore declined. Government are nevertheless determined to export and there is a suggestion that they may take over some sugar mills for the purpose of manufacturing sugar for export. With the general rise in the standard of living, the demand for sugar will grow and still further expansion of the industry will be required. The unsatisfactory features of this industry are the low yields of cane per acre – less than one-quarter of that in Japan – and the low extraction rate.

It is not possible here to pursue the details of industrial development further. It is clear that progress has been more than satisfactory and that private enterprise has played a notable part in it, in spite of the fluctuations of Government policy and the discouraging statements of individual Ministers, which have at times seemed to suggest that private enterprise would have only a short lease of life. Foreign aid has also been of importance in stimulating industrial growth and it should be recorded that from 1951 to 1964 external loans and grants towards development in India amounted to over £3000 million.

Cottage and small-scale industries have a double aspect. On the one hand they are part of the Gandhian tradition and an expression of India's determination to avoid the social evils of the Industrial Revolution in Europe. On the other hand, they are of importance in the transition phase, when neither agriculture nor large-scale industry can provide anything like full employment. In the early days of independence there was a good deal of sentimentalism and loose thinking about this subject. Scientific inquiries by such bodies as the Ford Foundation have led the Government to change its attitude to some extent, but there is still a tendency in some quarters to believe in limiting the productive capacity of large-scale industries where they compete with cottage industries.

This is not surprising, in view of the fact that cottage industries employ about twenty million people, a quarter of whom are engaged in the handloom industry. Apart from spinning and weaving, the coir, sericulture, vegetable oil, soap and match industries are of importance. Expert committees and boards were set up some years ago to assist in the development of small-scale industries and the policy has been to arrange production programmes, to teach improved techniques and to make capital grants for the provision of modern equipment. Financial and technical assistance is provided by the Central Government and a National Small Industries Corporation endeavours to obtain, for the village industries, Government contracts for handmade goods. Credits to small units are granted by the Corporation; machinery and equipment are made available on hire purchase terms; weavers and other producers' co-operative societies have been organised in most States; and assistance is given in marketing the products of village and small industries. The increasing availability of electrical power is likely to change the character of some of the village industries, but attempts to develop small-scale units as ancillaries to large-scale industries have not so far been successful. On the whole the movement for the development of village and small-scale industries must be recognised to be of value, even on strictly economic considerations, in the present transition period of the Indian economy.

The general expansion of the economy must necessarily to some extent be limited by availability of transport and it must be admitted that the present situation is not satisfactory, though the freight carried by Indian railways today is some 75 per cent higher than in 1938, while the passenger miles operated per year are nearly three times the pre-war figure. At the end of the war the Indian railways, which had played a significant part in the war effort, were badly run down and in the first three years of the First Five Year Plan rehabilitation was slow. In the fourth and fifth years, and during the Second Five Year Plan, more rapid progress was made, but the supply of wagons was still quite inadequate and long delays in booking were not infrequent. In the last two years there has been considerable improvement and this is particularly noticeable in the availability of wagons for coal. Moreover, over 400 miles of new lines have been constructed and more than 1000 miles of the track has been doubled in the last two or three years. Electrification and dieselisation have also gone ahead rapidly. Road transport, however, is far from satisfactory. Road construction is not proceeding as fast as could have been hoped, and the desire of some State Governments to nationalise road transport is seriously discouraging the growth of private road services.

Inland water transport is of great importance in East India, but the principal river carriers are finding it hard to make ends meet in the face of rising labour and other costs. The Government of India has recently granted them a loan for the modernisation of their fleet, but the position will remain precarious for some time. If they ceased to operate, the effect on the economy of eastern India, and on India's strategic position would be serious.

In the services ancillary to commerce, such as banking, shipping and insurance, there have been great developments in the last few years. The banking system is rightly described by the United States Department of Commerce as one of the most highly developed aspects of the Indian economy. It consists of the Reserve Bank, which performs the normal functions of a Central Bank, the Government-owned State Bank and ninety-four scheduled banks – which with the State Bank account for deposits worth over Rs.1500 crores against the Rs.200 old crores with the foreign banks and relatively small non-scheduled banks. The remarkable growth of the banking system can be seen from the fact that deposits today are roughly twice as high as in 1949 – though it must be remembered that part of the increase arises from the deposits of U.S.A. counterpart funds against the cost of foodgrains imported under Public Law 480. The sharpness of the shock administered to the public by the failure of the Palai Central Bank in 1960 is the measure of the high standards now expected from Indian banking, and it can safely be said that India today is well served by her banking system.

In insurance, development has on the whole been less satisfactory. There are a few highly respected and well-run insurance companies, but there are many smaller concerns which have achieved expansion at the expense of soundness or integrity. It was mainly for this reason that the Government of India nationalised life insurance in 1956 and few impartial observers were prepared to quarrel with that decision.

The development of Indian shipping has not proved as easy as was hoped, but from the shipper's point of view, British and foreign Lines provide ample facilities for transport overseas. Indian tonnage has increased rapidly in recent years and at the end of 1959 Indian vessels of gross tonnage 437,000 were engaged in overseas shipping, and ninety-five Indian vessels with a gross tonnage of 307,000 were carrying India's coastal trade – all of which, except that in petrol, is in fact in Indian hands. By 1964 India's total tonnage of shipping had reached 1.3 million tons. Recent attempts to divert traffic from the railways to coastal shipping have failed, and one outside authority has attributed the failure partly to the fact that their monopolistic position enables Indian shipping companies to be very unenterprising.

A further indication of the economic expansion that has taken place during the last few years is given by the growth of capital investment in public companies from Rs.323 crores in 1945–6 to Rs.566 crores in 1950–1 and Rs.978·6 crores[1] in 1962.

We must now consider how all these changes have affected India's foreign exchange position. India has, except in 1950–1, had a consistently adverse balance of trade since the transfer of power. A brief analysis of the position from 1947 to 1956 will be of interest. The large sterling balances accumulated by India during the War gave her a feeling that she could afford to be lavish in making up the wartime shortage of miscellaneous commodities and in the first year of independence she had a moderate adverse balance of trade. In 1948–9, poor harvests, together with the partial failure of the Government's grain procurement policy necessitated large imports of foodstuffs and the adverse balance of trade rose to nearly Rs.218 crores. In the following year the food situation improved, devaluation stimulated exports, the dollar deficit was practically wiped out and the exchange controversy almost put a stop to imports from Pakistan. The adverse balance of trade therefore fell to Rs.93 crores, while in 1950–1 the international demand for primary commodities led to an increase in the value of Indian exports by over Rs.100 crores and a small favourable balance of trade was achieved. The next year, 1951–2, witnessed remarkable changes. The world demand for jute and jute manufactures continued strong and the report of the Department of Commercial Intelligence and Statistics shows that exports rose to

[1] Provisional vide *India 1960*.

R

nearly Rs.733 crores. Unfortunately, imports also rose by over Rs.300 crores. Several successive monsoons had partially failed and heavy food imports were necessary, while at the same time raw cotton had to be imported on a considerable scale. The adverse balance of trade reached the alarming figure of Rs.221 crores. A drastic effort was then made to reduce imports and the deficit was reduced to about Rs.83 crores in the following year and to Rs.41 crores in 1953-4.

In the following year prices for Indian primary commodities – particularly tea – were satisfactory and at the same time exports rose in volume. Export earnings increased by Rs.52 crores, but imports rose by rather more than this on account of a general liberalisation of import policy, together with heavy imports of industrial raw materials. The deficit increased to Rs.85 crores and in the following year rose still further to Rs.105 crores.

This somewhat dreary recital of statistics is of value only in showing the instability in India's balance of trade as a result of two factors. In the first place she has been in the weak position of a primarily agricultural country unable to feed herself.

The value of her average annual imports of food from 1949 to 1955 was over Rs. 120 crores.

Secondly, as an exporter of primary products and a heavy importer of raw materials, spare parts and machinery, she was and is particularly vulnerable to fluctuations in the terms of trade.

From 1956 onwards the position became somewhat artificial. The U.S.A. began to supply food grains under P.L.480, at little cost in foreign exchange to India. Foreign aid and loans began to be forthcoming on a considerable scale, but at the same time India embarked on a somewhat grandiose National Plan. The net result was a rapid deterioration in her foreign exchange resources. Her sterling balances, which stood at Rs.820 crores in July 1949, had fallen to Rs.681 crores by July 1956. By November 1956 India's total foreign exchange reserve had fallen to Rs.543 crores. Since this included the necessary backing for the Indian currency, it could not be regarded as large in view of India's ambitious development programme.

It was no doubt this fact which led the Government of India in 1956 to amend the Reserve Bank of India Act. As that Act stood, reserves in the form of foreign securities and gold had to be held to the extent of forty per cent of the note issue. Under the amended Act, the Bank was only required to hold a flat minimum of Rs.400 crores of foreign securities and Rs.115 crores in gold. In the words of a contemporary observer, 'a substantial proportion of the existing foreign exchange reserves will be released from their present somewhat static statutory function and the way cleared for progressive expansion of the note issue, if this is found to be desirable'.

A little later the Reserve Bank gold reserves were written up from about £30 million to about £88 million, and the proportionate backing of gold and foreign securities for the note issue was further reduced. In spite of these measures a serious crisis occurred in 1957. By October of that year the reserves had fallen to about Rs.327 crores as against Rs.582 crores twelve months earlier. The decline continued and the latest official figure of the Reserves is Rs.96.61 crores – a sum which must be regarded as inadequate in relation to the size of the economy and in view of the continuing unfavourable balance of trade. It is clear that the economy would stagnate if help from friendly countries came to an end. Fortunately there is no risk of any such discontinuance.

The Government of India are nevertheless resolute in their determination to increase India's exports, but this presents many difficulties. The main earners of foreign exchange are the traditional Indian exports – jute goods, tea, cotton and cotton textiles, oilcakes and vegetable oils, iron and manganese ores, and leather goods. In all these fields other nations are competing with increasing keenness, and demand is limited. Government through the enthusiastic medium of Manubhai Shah, the Minister for Trade, are bringing great pressure on those concerned in these industries to expand production, but do not always realise that increased production may even result in lower prices and diminished foreign exchange earnings. Attempts are being made to induce the newer industries to export, but in many cases production costs are too high and the goods are uncompetitive. In spite of these difficulties, India's export earnings have risen from Rs.714 crores in 1962–3 to Rs.795 crores in 1963–4.

As worrying as this rapid drawing down of the reserves was

the realisation two or three years ago that there had been little or no co-ordination between the spending Ministries and those responsible for watching India's foreign exchange position. It was known that very heavy commitments had been made, but it was impossible even to guess at their magnitude. Officials and politicians alike were seized by a mood of depression and self-reproach. Desperate attempts to secure long-term credits on a sufficient scale were only partially successful and Draconian remedies were clearly required. Foreign travel allowances for Indian nationals and all forms of foreign expenditure were brought under close scrutiny, whilst fresh efforts were made to boost export earnings. A contemporary commentator accurately conveyed the mood of the time when he stated that the terms in which the spokesmen of the Finance Ministry explained the various measures taken were 'greatly reminiscent of the inspiring words with which the Commander of a beleaguered garrison addresses his forces'.

By the early months of 1958 this mood of extreme pessimism had been replaced by a more sober appreciation of the situation. It was realised that the Indian economy would not break under the strain, but that on the other hand the crisis would be more prolonged than had been expected. Foreign loans and credits would have to be repaid in due course and the Finance Minister recognised frankly that India's position in 1961 might well be more difficult than it was in 1958. Credits for three or four years would, in fact, not greatly help, since they merely put off the day of reckoning.

There was nothing mysterious about the origin of the crisis. The financial assumptions underlying the Second Five Year Plan were unsound and India was inevitably led into an orgy of over-spending. The difficulties were, in fact, built into a Plan based not on India's earning capacity, but on abstract calculations of her needs. It is now clear that India's export earnings are not at present adequate to supply her current needs of foreign exchange for the maintenance of existing industry. Fortunately, the rest of the world came generously to the rescue with aid and loans and the crisis passed.

Two major causes of anxiety nevertheless exist. The first is unemployment, which will be discussed in the next chapter, but the second and perhaps even greater worry, is the fact that

India has apparently entered on a period of serious inflation. In its report for 1963–4 the Reserve Bank stated that the rise in the wholesale price index had been larger than any year except one since the beginning of the First Five Year Plan. Since then there has been a further increase of fifteen points – the base year being 1952–3. Rapidly increasing population, and a shortfall in foodgrains production have been important causes, but to these must be added the large-scale expenditure by the Central and Provincial Governments. This has not in the main been due to the needs of defence, but to development plans not sufficiently closely related to the real economic capacity of the country, and to the resulting deficit financing over a period of years. Inflation is regarded by many competent observers as the greatest threat to India's welfare today.

Unfortunately, data by which one could judge the effect of all these developments on the real national income or assess the change in the standard of living are not available, but the statement of the Planning Commission that in the period of the first two Plans *per capita* income has risen by 16 per cent is worthy of belief and in spite of the causes of anxiety just described economic progress since the transfer of power must be regarded as satisfactory.

Chapter 20

The National Plans

IT WOULD BE difficult for any Englishman, even if he
were a thorough-going Socialist, to understand the place
that comprehensive, economic planning now occupies in
the minds of Indian politicians and administrators. The necessity of planning has indeed become a dogma and anybody rash
enough to question it, or to suggest that, in the long run, unfettered private enterprise might produce better results, would
at once be labelled a reactionary and regarded as lacking in
social conscience. The foundation of the dogma is the belief
that, with a planned economy, India can, within a decade or so,
raise her productive capacity to that of Western countries and
yet avoid the social evils which accompanied the Industrial
Revolution in Europe. India has rejected the doctrine that
inequality is the condition of progress, and aims simultaneously
at an expansion of production and an equitable distribution of
wealth. In the First Five year Plan the Planning Commission
thus expounded its philosophy: 'In the industrially advanced
countries, broadly speaking, the emphasis of planning is on a
correction of the shortcomings of the system of private enterprise through changes which would secure a more equal distribution of the benefits of economic development. For countries relatively underdeveloped, the problem is to promote
rapid development and, at the same time, to see that the benefits of this development accrue to all classes of the community.
The last half-century has witnessed a widening of social ideals.
The economic system is now expected to provide, in increasing
measure, freedom from want and from insecurity, not to a few
but to all. The problem of economic development under
modern conditions has, therefore, a social complexion quite
different from the one that countries, say, in the nineteenth
century had to face. First, there is now a greater sense of

urgency; secondly, there is a greater awareness of, and insistence on, certain basic values. Economic progress is therefore
interpreted to mean much more than the building up of an
efficient apparatus for production of material goods; it means
also the provision of social services, the widening of opportunities for the common man and social equality and justice.
Such all-round progress cannot be attained without planning.'

When the Planning Commission was set up in 1950 it had
to face a situation in which prices in India had risen since 1939
faster than income, *per capita* consumption of food grains was
lower than before the war, the housing shortage was acute, and
the relief and rehabilitation of over seven million displaced
persons was a major and apparently insoluble problem. The
Commission's first task was, therefore, to strike a balance between present and future needs and it soon realised that
'maximum production, full employment, lower prices, greater
equality of income – all these cannot, under certain conditions,
go together'. It rightly decided that, in spite of the widespread
belief that under a 'colonial economy' the primary need was
the expansion of industry, its first task was to deal with the
shortage of food and raw materials and to counter inflation,
and it formulated a plan in which 44 per cent of available
resources was to be devoted to the improvement of agriculture, irrigation and power, and community development, while
only 8·4 per cent was to be allocated to industrial development.

Planning, as understood in India, is the complete reversal
of ordinary commercial practice. The business man takes stock
of his resources, including credit, and does what is possible
within the limits thus imposed. The planner, on the other
hand, begins by considering what is desirable, and fixes targets
accordingly. The authors of the First Five Year Plan thus began
from the assumption that *per capita* income must be doubled
in about twenty years. This led to the conclusion that 'the rate
of saving as a proportion of total national income will have to
go up from 5 per cent in 1950–1 to 20 per cent by 1967–8'
and, although it was recognised that this would involve hard
work and austerity, it was taken for granted that it could be
done.

This somewhat doctrinaire approach did not condition the Plan as much as might have been expected. The planners had to learn a new technique and, moreover, they had to produce their Plan in an impossibly short space of time. They were therefore glad to take a large number of isolated schemes prepared by different authorities and give them some kind of cohesion. The Plan was, indeed, little more than an aggregate of separate proposals each of which had been considered practicable by some body of experts and was given a suitable priority. Certain predictions were then made as to probable achievements within the five-year period and they did not have to be related very closely to the theoretical target of a doubling of income in twenty years. It is now generally agreed that the priorities were right, but that the predictions were generally inaccurate. The rise in national income was seriously underestimated; the prediction of the probable rate of expansion of the economy and the *tempo* of execution of many important planned projects had little relation to reality; and in the first three years the expected adverse balance of payments would not have occurred but for several crop failures.

It is not possible to discuss the First Five Year Plan in detail and we need only note that the agricultural section of the plan was remarkably successful; that, on the whole, the public sector fell below its target; that progress in iron and steel and in the heavy electrical industries was disappointing; and that investment in the private sector was close to the estimate. The private sector, in fact did, its job; the public sector did not. National income is reported to have risen by 18 per cent during the period of the Plan, and though there is room for doubt as to the reliability of the calculations on which this conclusion rests, the evidences of progress are abundant. Nevertheless, much of the justification for the belief in planning must lie in the possibility of moderately accurate prediction of the rate of development, and, judged by this test, the case for planning in India was not yet proven.

We must now turn to the Second Five Year Plan. It laid down four objectives – namely, an increase in the national income of about 25 per cent; rapid industrialisation; a large expansion of opportunities of employment; and the reduction of inequalities in income and wealth. Each of these objectives must, of course, modify the other. For example, it was recognised that the expansion of heavy industry – which is perhaps India's greatest economic need – would absorb much capital without any commensurate increase in employment. Nor would it, in the immediate future, enlarge the supply of consumer goods. Undue concentration on this aspect of development would thus run counter to the social concept underlying the Plan. Some counterbalancing weight had to be placed on 'labour intensive' industries.

The outstanding features of the Plan were its emphasis on the public sector, its bias in favour of industry rather than agriculture and its considerable magnitude. The first of these characteristics was a natural expression of current Indian thought and the Planning Commission correctly expressed the general will when it declared that 'the basic criterion for determining the lines of advance is not private profit but social gain. Major decision regarding production, distribution, consumption and investment . . . must be made by agencies informed by social purposes'. The logic is in fact inexorable. Once the premise of planning is admitted, State control in all important departments of the economy is unavoidable and private enter· prise is likely to be relegated to a subordinate role. Here the planners found themselves up against a delimma. They felt bound to write down the importance of the private sector and yet they dared not discourage it unduly – for in the First Plan, as the *Eastern Economist* put it, 'the volume of over-fulfilment in the private sector has greatly exceeded the under-fulfilment of the public sector'. They compromised by providing for industrial investment of only Rs. 2,300 crores[1] in the private sector as against Rs.3,800 crores[2] allotted to such in investment in the public sector. They also stipulated that the exploitation of minerals and 'basic or capital goods industries which are major determinants of the rate of growth of the economy' must be a matter for the State.

In the First Plan period the progress of agriculture had been greater than that in industry and in the Second Plan the emphasis was therefore deliberately shifted. The share of agriculture together with the allied subjects of irrigation and

[1] About £1725 million
[2] About £2850 million.

power in the total expenditure proposed in the public sector was reduced from 43·2 per cent to 30·8 per cent and a little later even this figure was lowered to 29·7 per cent. The reduction was not quite as serious as might have appeared, since better means were proposed for the implementation of the agricultural programme. The community development organisations, which had originally been intended mainly to provide social amenities in the villages, were now geared to the task of increased food production and much attention was to be given by them to the education of farmers in improved methods of agriculture. It is nevertheless clear that agriculture received insufficient attention in the Second Plan. Few, however, would quarrel with the decision to erect three steel works, or to establish heavy electrical machinery and heavy chemical plants, since these projects will not only save foreign exchange in the long run, but are also necessary to the ultimate development of India as a modern industrial country. Generally speaking, the priorities laid down in the industrial sector were sound and the planners did not commit the mistake made by the early Russian planners of neglecting consumption goods. Apart from the increase in food grains production which they proposed, they provided for an increased production of 100 per cent in bicycles, 35 per cent in sugar, and similar increases in other articles in common demand.

Many objective observers considered the scale of the Second Plan too large in relation to India's financial and administrative resources. Here the Planning Commission was faced with a difficulty inherent in planning. Once the Government of an underdeveloped country makes itself responsible for economic development as a whole, it is bound to be in a hurry. It cannot turn round to the poor man and ask him to be patient. It is in fact led on willy-nilly to spend beyond the real capacity of the country, and inflation and foreign exchange difficulties are bound to arise. In the Second Plan an expenditure of Rs.4,800[1] crores was proposed for the public sector, but only half of this sum was reasonably in sight and the remainder was left to be covered by deficit financing, or external assistance or in some unspecified way. A serious weakness in the Plan was the uncovered deficit in foreign exchange and it is not surprising

[1] £3,600 million.

that India soon ran into the troubles which have been discussed in an earlier chapter. Here we need only say that in 1958 the foreign exchange reserves fell to dangerously low levels; that the Western countries performed a rescue operation; and that steps were taken to reduce the size of the Plan. The proposed expenditure of Rs.4,800 crores in the public sector, which had in the meantime been raised to Rs.5,100 crores[1] was now cut down to a hard core of essential projects estimated to cost Rs. 4,500 crores[2]. the remaining schemes being postponed.

The physical progress achieved under the Second Plan has been discussed earlier in this book. It is sufficient to note here that if allowance is made for the increase in prices during the Plan period, expenditure in real terms was from 80–85 per cent of that originally proposed. Iron and steel plants cost considerably more than had been assumed, but on the other hand administrative difficulties or shortage of foreign exchange curtailed outlay on some important projects.

It is obvious that India made a great leap forward as a result of the Second Five Year Plan and even an 80 per cent success in a plan which many critics, including the present writer, considered over-ambitious, is a remarkable achievement. At the end of the period, however, several disappointing features had to be recognised. In the first place the development of the economy had so increased India's need of imports that her foreign exchange earnings were insufficient to maintain existing industry and she was left entirely dependent on the help of friendly nations for the foreign exchange element in any further development. Secondly, according to official statistics, the increase in national income during the period was a little less than twenty per cent as compared with the target of twenty-five per cent set by the Planning Commission. Even this increase was offset by a growth of population more rapid than had been anticipated. It is now estimated that over the period of the two Plans, real *per capita* income has risen at the rate of 1½ per cent per year.

Thirdly, the problem of unemployment loomed larger in 1961 than in 1956. At the time of the Second Plan it was assumed that additional non-agricultural employment would be found

[1] £3825 million.
[2] £3375 million.

for eight million people. In fact only six and a half million new urban jobs are said to have been created and since the population has risen more rapidly than the planners had estimated, the seriousness of the situation is obvious.

Another cause of anxiety is the fact that domestic savings have fallen well below the planners' target. It is beginning to be clear that in poor countries earnings will be used to buy rather than to save and it is perhaps for this reason too that the borrowing programmes of the Central and State Governments fell behind schedule.

This catalogue of anxieties might well give a wrong impression of the position and prospects of India and it is necessary therefore to emphasise the remarkable nature of the progress recorded in earlier chapters. India is indeed far better equipped for the future than was the case at the time of the transfer of power. A colossal task nevertheless awaited her as she embarked on the Third Five Year Plan which we must now describe.

That Plan is rightly regarded as merely a phase of an ambitious long-term programme, the aim of which is to raise *per capita* income from its present level of Rs.330 per annum to Rs.530 by 1976 and at the same time to ensure that thereafter India will not be dependent on outside assistance for further development. This would involve a spectacular leap forward at the end of which India would, for example, produce 18 million tons of steel, 170 million tons of coal and 125 million tons of food grains annually, and would have more than doubled her export earnings.

The Third Plan followed the usual principle of jobbing backwards – the planners began by fixing the target and then decided what resources had to be made available. The starting point was indeed the assumption that *per capita* income must increase by 17 per cent over the next five years. To this figure the Planning Commission applied certain projections of population growth prepared by the Central Statistical Organisation and arrived at a conclusion that national income needs to rise by at least 30 per cent during this period. Previous guesses by the Central Statistical Organisation as to the growth of population have been so hopelessly wrong that it is difficult to feel much confidence in the present forecast. It was, however, the best basis that the planners had at their disposal and they proceeded to construct a plan which should, they considered, result in an increase of 34 per cent of National income if all the programmes included in the plan were completed in time. Here a note of realism appeared and since 'many difficult conditions' had to be fulfilled they reduced this figure to 30 per cent.

The outstanding characteristic of the Plan is its Socialist bias. 'It is a basic premise,' we are told that 'through democracy and widespread public participation, developments along Socialist lines will secure rapid economic growth and expansion of employment, as well as equitable distribution, reduction of disparities in income and wealth, and prevention of concentration of economic power.' This bias makes itself felt in three ways. In the first place we are told explicitly that, though the private sector has a large contribution to make 'the role of the public sector in the development of the economy' will become ever more dominant, and it is in accordance with this principle that out of a total planned expenditure of about Rs.12,000 crores, Rs.8,000 crores is allotted to the public sector – and even this figure does not include expenditure by municipalities and other local bodies. Secondly, the authors of the plan have returned to the concept of the ceiling on income, which Nehru appeared to have discarded some time ago. It is true that for the time being they accept a high ceiling, but as low incomes rise the ratio between the lowest and the highest is to be reduced. Thirdly, they do not conceal their anxiety at the fact that rapid economic development enlarges opportunities for well-established firms to expand their size and enter new fields of enterprise. Here the bogey of 'concentration of economic power' looms large – though to some schools of thought the undue expansion of the public sector might seem to involve the most dangerous possible concentration of economic power – and everything must therefore be done to encourage new *entrepeneurs*, medium- and small-scale enterprises and co-operative organisations. All these objects are to be achieved by governmental powers of control and regulation and particularly by such instruments as licensing, financial aid to industry, taxation of wealth and capital gains, and stricter legislation regarding the management of companies. The plan in fact implies an increasing measure of governmental control over industry and it is clear that Indian large-scale industrialists will be tolerated rather than welcomed. In view of the need for foreign exchange, the foreign capitalist may enjoy a warmer reception.

The physical targets in the plan are reasonable in the sense both of being modest in relation to India's needs and of being within her capacity to achieve, if finance and superior manpower are available on an adequate scale. In contrast to the Second Plan, greater emphasis is now rightly put on agriculture. Of the total expenditure in the public sector, the allotment to agriculture and community development has been raised from 11 per cent to 14 per cent, but what is more important is the statement that in this field 'whatever is physically practicable, should be made financially possible'. Progress in agriculture depends perhaps more on administration than on finance and it may well bc that the sum allotted is the maximum that could be properly used. For some time Indian thought on the subject of agriculture was somewhat confused by the unrealistic statement of the Ford Foundation Team that by 1966 India would need and could produce 110 million tons of food grains annually. The Planning Commission has adopted as its target the more modest figure of 100 million tons. Even this is probably too high. India's real needs by 1966 have been estimated by a competent authority at 95 million tons and unless fertilisers and water supplies on a larger scale than that proposed can be provided – and unless, too, some State Governments show more energy in this matter than they have hitherto done – it is unlikely that production can exceed 95 million tons.

The soundness of the priorities between other sectors of the economy is more open to doubt. Some authorities consider that the proposed scale of expansion of steel production is unncessarily large and that in any case sufficient coking coal for the production of 10 million tons of steel by 1966 may not be available. They maintain that it would pay India better to cut down her steel production plans and concentrate rather more on the development of the engineering industries.

This, however, is very much a matter of opinion and more serious criticisms are those relating to transport, electricity and coal. The inadequacy of the transport system in several important areas is only too obvious to industrialists, and it is to be regretted that the Planning Commission did not recognise the necessity of a more rapid development of roads and road transport. Equally serious is the fact that the Commission's provision for the development of electrical power was far short of probable requirements. In the case of coal, the production target was reasonable, but nothing in the detailed plan suggests that it will be reached. These criticisms, however, do not alter the fact that the broad outlines of the plan were sensible.

It is now necessary to see to what extent the results so far achieved have justified the planners in their expectations, and fortunately we have available a Mid-Term Appraisal prepared by the Planning Commission in November 1963. The Commission admit frankly that the first two years of the Plan were a period of slow economic growth and that whereas the Plan postulated an increase of 30 per cent in the National Income during the Five Years, the actual increase in the first two years was only 5 per cent. This shortfall is due to failure to reach the targets in almost every sector of the economy, but the most significant instance of this failure is in agriculture. Foodgrains production was expected to rise from 79 million tons at the beginning to 100 million tons at the end of the period. In actual fact it has declined and was only $77\frac{1}{2}$ million tons in 1962–3. Adverse climatic conditions were partly responsible for this setback, but shortage of nitrogenous fertilisers, unwillingness of cultivators in many areas to pay for irrigation facilities, failure of local authorities to construct minor irrigation works, together with the general lack of drive by State Governments have played an important part. Apart from this failure it is the writer's view that the target was quite unrealistic and that there was never any chance of production reaching 100 million tons by 1966.

In oil-seeds and cotton, progress has been more satisfactory than in foodgrains, but even here the figures fixed by the Planning Commission are not likely to be attained.

A shortfall in agriculture alone would seriously affect predictions of *per capita* income, but unfortunately industrial development too has disappointed the authors of the Plan. Industrial production increased by 6.5 per cent and 8 per cent in the first and second years respectively, against an average of 11 per cent envisaged in the Plan. Shortages of power, transport and coal

were an important factor, and in view of the recent improve-
ments in those sectors some acceleration of industrial production may be possible in the remaining years of the period, but
it is improbable that the target will be even approximately
reached. The Commission point out that one bright aspect of
the situation is the fact that the main failures have been in consumer industries, while much better results have been achieved
in the producer goods and basic industries – notably steel,
aluminium, machine tools and fertilisers.

Even in these fields, however, the expectations of the Commission are not being fulfilled. In the case of finished steel, for
example, as a result of delays in the expansion of the three steel
plants, output at the end of the period is now estimated at
5.8 million tons against a target of 6.8 million tons, while
production of fertilisers is not likely to reach more than 50 per
cent or 60 per cent of the figure put forward in the Plan. In
coal, the private sector is likely to fulfil its task, but production
in the public sector will probably be short by 25 per cent.
Fortunately, the fact that industry is not developing as rapidly
as was hoped will lessen the demand for coal, and the Planning
Commission believes that the supply will meet the demand.

It is not necessary to follow this enquiry into other industries,
but it may be said generally that achievement will be a good
deal below the targets. As the National Council of Applied
Economic Research puts it, there will be a spillover into the
Fourth Plan. The Council goes on to remark that if performance
be judged against the task set, the private sector has done better
than the public sector.

The publication of the Mid-Term Appraisal created a quite
unjustified gloom in Indian political circles. The failure to reach
the high targets set was allowed to obscure the remarkable
progress which had occurred. The writer has always regarded
the objectives put forward by the Commission as quite impossible of attainment, but when he has pressed this view on
Ministers and officials the answer has invariably been that if you
ask people to jump over the moon, they will at least get off the
earth. This is perhaps psychologically unsound, for it takes no
account of the depression and demoralisation which result
when the moon is found to be out of reach.

So far we have only examined the physical objectives of the

Plan. We must now look at its financial aspects. Although the actual projects in the public sector were estimated to cost Rs.8,000 crores, the Commission have, with proper caution, only proposed expenditure of Rs.7,500 crores in that sector. Of this sum Rs.6,300 crores is on account of investment, while Rs.1,200 crores relates to current outlay including staff, subsidies and the like. In the draft outline of the Plan, circulated for public opinion last year, resources for the public sector were estimated at Rs.7,250 crores and it is difficult to resist the feeling that the increase to Rs.7,500 crores was the result, not so much of any new discovery regarding resources, as of a desire to include in the Plan schemes which had been pressed upon the Commission from one quarter or another.

Apart from new taxation and foreign aid, a sum of Rs.3,040 crores was to come from existing sources of revenue as follows:

Balance from current revenues	Rs.	550 crores
Contribution of railways and other public enterprises	Rs.	550 crores
Loans and small savings	Rs.	1,400 crores
Provident Funds, Steel equalisation fund and miscellaneous capital receipts	Rs.	540 crores

The first of these items then appeared reasonable in view of the buoyancy of the revenues in recent years, but the estimate has been invalidated by the increase in military expenditure necessary in order to ward off the Chinese threat. The National Council of Applied Economic Research, in a careful study of this subject, suggeest that instead of a surplus of Rs.550 crores from current revenue there will be a deficit of Rs.79 crores, and they also express the view that railways and other public enterprises cannot contribute more than Rs.450 crores. The steel and fertiliser plants will yield less in the early stages than the Planning Commission has assumed, and the unwillingness of State Governments to increase their charges for electricity is also an adverse factor. The estimates for loans, small savings and miscellaneous capital receipts cannot be discussed in detail here, but there is some ground for thinking that they are reasonable.

s

Even if all these forecasts are fulfilled there still remains a gap of Rs.4,460 crores. The Planning Commission assumed that Rs.2,200 crores would be met from rupee receipts corresponding to external assistance. They then proposed to raise Rs.1,710 crores by additional taxation, leaving Rs.550 crores to be covered by deficit finance. With this addition, tax revenues would, according to the Commission's estimates, amount to 11·4 per cent of the national income at the end of the planned period. Theoretically this is not an excessive proportion, but three factors have to be borne in mind. In the first place the estimates of national income at the end of the period have proved to be too optimistic. The tax revenues will probably amount to a higher proportion of national income than that estimated. Secondly, since the cost of general administration and non-Plan expenditure is almost certain to rise – and since defence expenditure has increased considerably and may increase further – by no means all of the additional tax revenue will be available for the purposes of the Plan. Thirdly the popular pastime of 'soaking the rich' has now exhausted its possibilities. If fresh revenue is to be raised on a significant scale it can only be by means of indirect taxation, or a considerable increase in the taxation of land, or a lowering of the minimum taxable level so that the better-paid wage-earners are brought into the net. Measures of this kind are bound to be unpopular, but Government has had the courage to make significant increases in indirect taxation.

Since the Plan was promulgated, production costs have increased considerably and it is also clear that in many cases, even on the basis of costs then prevailing, expenditure was underestimated. The National Council of Applied Economic Research assume a general cost increase in Plan projects up to date of about 25 per cent.

All these considerations suggest that deficit financing is likely to be higher than Rs.550 crores, though not necessarily so high as to strain the economy unduly. What will happen in practice is that the Five Year Plan will be implemented in seven or eight years.

India's requirements of foreign exchange for the period of the Plan have to cover not only the requirements of the Plan itself, including those of the private sector, but maintenance imports for the ordinary purposes of commerce and industry as well as for projects initiated during the Second Plan period. The total requirements were estimated at Rs.5,750 crores, excluding the import of food grains from the U.S A. under Public Law 480 for which no foreign exchange is demanded (except for part of the freight). As against this expenditure the Commission estimated that export earnings during the period would amount to Rs.3,700 crores as compared with Rs.3,053 crores in the Second Plan period; that a net loss on capital transactions of Rs.550 crores must be deducted from this figure; and that external assistance amounting to Rs.2,600 crores would be required.

Expert opinions differ greatly as to whether the estimate of exports is realistic. The present writer is inclined to regard it as over-optimistic in view of the uncertainties in the world situation in respect of India's major exports, namely, tea, jute goods and cotton piece goods. It is at least clear that in the case of the tea industry a target has been set which the trade regards as quite unrealistic – first because producers cannot reach it and secondly because the tea manufactured could not be sold if the target were reached. A prudent business man would reduce the estimated figure of export earnings considerably. India's net requirements of external aid may thus exceed Rs.2,600 crores.

Since the success of the Third Five Year Plan will depend largely on India's ability to fill this gap, it is necessary to consider in some detail how external finance is likely to be obtained. The three main possible sources are foreign private investment; the raising of a loan in the City by the Government of India; and loans from Institutions such as the World Bank or from friendly countries. Private investment has up to now been predominantly British in origin. Until recently, in the absence of an insurance treaty protecting her nationals against blockage of remittances, U.S.A. private business was not much interested in India. In the last year or so there has been a considerable modification in that attitude, but it can perhaps be taken for granted that if there is to be foreign investment on any significant scale, it will be from British sources. We must therefore assess the favourable and unfavourable factors as they present themselves to British investors. Bull points are : the political stability of India; her economic soundness; the scope for profitable business provided by a rapidly expanding economy; the reservoir of potential managerial ability; and India's good record in the matter of remittance of profits and repatriation of capital. Discouraging factors are: the leftward drift in economic thought and the growing belief in controls; the unwisdom of much of India's labour policy and the resulting rise in costs of production; and the heavy incidence of personal taxation. Such taxation may not affect the investor directly, but an overseas investor will always expect to have a number of his own nationals in superior employ in the business. Further British investment in India will thus partly depend on the attractiveness of that country as a field of employment for British personnel. A distinguished Indian industrialist, who has been for many years in close contact with British business men, recently expressed the opinion that a large proportion of them, particularly in the middle ranks, were uneasy and dissatisfied, and there can be little doubt that this statement is correct, even though British people in India enjoy many amenities not available to their countrymen at home and are treated with friendliness by their Indian colleagues. Their uneasiness is solely political and economic in its origin. They are nervous of left-wing tendencies in Indian economic thought – including, for example, the threat of the imposition of a ceiling on incomes – and at the same time they feel that the present incidence of personal taxation makes it impossible to save sufficient for retirement in comfort at the age when British people normally find it necessary to leave tropical climates. It is true that crushing taxation is the lot of the corresponding classes of society in Britain, but men of energy and ability do not embark on life in the tropics, with all its disadvantages of family separation and climate, unless it offers reasonable prospects of financial gain. The Government of India have already recognised the existence of this problem to some extent by their tax concessions to short-term foreign technicians, and more significantly in the Finance Act 1964 by the educational allowances for tax purposes given to non-Indian nationals. It is indeed clear that a contented British business community employed in India would remove one of the deterrents to further British investment.

Any such investment would clearly not be in the old-established industries, such as tea, jute, collieries and the like. It would be concerned with highly technical industries where there is still a real need for Western skill and knowledge and it may be that the pattern of future British investment in India will be found in partnerships between the subsidiaries of great British engineering concerns and Indian governments or public companies. On the whole conditions for this kind of collaboration are favourable and it is becoming common.

The second possible source of funds from abroad is to be found in loans raised by the Government of India in 'the City'. Here a difficulty arises from the non-applicability to such loans of the Colonial Stocks Act, but, if that obstacle can be overcome, there is no obvious reason why such loans should not be a success. The credit of the Government of India is good and the fair treatment accorded to life insurance and the Kolar Goldfields at the time of nationalisation should also help.

The main source of external finance, however, must be loans from the World Bank, and from friendly countries. The World Bank has already endorsed the Third Five Year Plan as being in the main sensible and the response so far from the consortium of the U.K., U.S.A., West Germany, Canada, Japan and France is most encouraging.

Unless radical and unforeseen changes in the world economic or political situation occur, it is reasonable to guess that foreign private investment and foreign aid together will not fall far short of the estimated requirement of Rs.2,600 crores. Unfortunately the cost of important projects has risen during the planned period. Unless India resolutely postpones some of her schemes and keeps strictly to the limit of Rs.2,600 crores, she will therefore be in trouble. The probability, however, is that it will be in the field of internal rather than external finance that she will experience her greatest difficulties. The Government of India have faced up to this problem and the cutting down of the Plan is at present under consideration.

The internal finance of the Plan is of course linked with the problem of how to counter the inflationary tendencies which the Planning Commission recognise as inherent in a Plan of this nature. The Commission advocate a complicated five-fold policy. Prices of essentials are to be controlled, partly by statutory regulation, but mainly by Government marketing and buffer stock operations; exports of some commodities are to be subsidised at the expense of the home consumer; certain commodities in short supply are to be the subject of physical allocations; excess purchasing power is to be mopped up by taxation; and above all the Reserve Bank's policy of selective credit control, together with restriction of the total credit created by banks, is to be continued. The prices of some non-essentials must nevertheless be allowed to rise, if only as a means of controlling consumption. All that is lacking in this complicated scheme is a body endowed with the super-human foresight and wisdom which would be necessary to operate it. Price control is more difficult in India than in most countries and neither before nor after the transfer of power has it ever been effective. Inflation is already causing great anxiety and it may be taken for granted that the forces which have resulted in a steady increase of prices during the Second and Third Plan periods will operate still more strongly during the next two or three years.

One other aspect of the Plan calls for brief mention. Perhaps the most serious weakness of the Second Plan was its failure to make any impression on the problem of unemployment. The working population increased faster during the period than had been estimated, and the development schemes gave employment to over two million people less than the Commission had anticipated. The backlog of unemployment at the end of the Second Plan was thus nine million as compared with the Commission's earlier estimate of 5·6 million. During the next five years it is reckoned that the addition to the labour force will be of the order of seventeen millions, while the Plan will only provide additional employment for about 14 millions. The situation at the end of the Third Plan will thus be worse than at the beginning, and when to this is added the ever-growing number of persons who are only partly employed, the gravity of the problem is obvious. The Commission suggests the organisation of rural works programmes providing work for perhaps a hundred days a year and the intensification of village industries. Schemes of this kind, however, will encroach on resources required for the Plan itself and too much must not be expected of them. The Commission therefore take the line that in all construction projects 'where mechanisation does not lead to significant economies, preference must be given to labour-intensive methods of construction', and for this purpose they recommend that a Committee of senior officers should examine all decisions to choose machinery in preference to men.

It is difficult to quarrel with this recommendation in principle, but there is a serious danger that political influences will lead to its interpretation in a reactionary sense and employers who in recent years have tried to rationalise their industries, will appreciate the reality of this fear.

As regards unemployment amongst the educated classes, the Commission evidently and understandably feel helpless and all that they can do is to express the pious belief that as the rural economy develops there will be increased opportunities of employment for these classes.

There are, indeed, many grounds on which armchair critics could assail the Plan. They could for example argue that the Plan is based on optimistic assumptions as to finance and as to the availability of superior manpower; that it tends to ignore or minimise the administrative difficulties that will arise; that it makes inadequate provision for the development of power, transport and communications; that it relegates to an inferior role the private sector which alone has justified expectations in the past; that it pays insufficient attention to the probable inflationary effects of the vast expenditure proposed; last but not least that it will inevitably lead to an all-embracing system of controls and regulations, which may damp down initiative and retard the very processes that the Plan is designed to stimulate. Its proper implementation would demand an almost infinite degree of collective wisdom and its underlying philosophy is the extreme form of the belief that 'the gentleman in the Secretariat knows best'.

These criticisms do not mean that the Plan is bad, or that India would be better without it. In the present stage of India's development, when resources are inadequate to do all that is desirable, there must clearly be a system of priorities, and such a system is in fact the hard core of the Plan. There is nothing sacred about the five-year term set for its accomplishment. That term may well have to be considerably extended. The Plan is of value because, subject to a few qualifications, its priorities are right and because it will help to maintain the enthusiasm and determination on which India's development must depend. If it is worked in a spirit of flexibility, if care is taken neither to discourage private enterprise nor to deprive it of necessary resources, and if at the same time India tries to provide an attractive field for the investment of foreign capital, India will go ahead fast. Apart from its importance to India, the success or failure of the Plan is of great interest to the outside world, since it provides the first opportunity to watch the operation on a vast scale of a Socialist experiment conducted by men who believe in freedom. If by some probable mischance the Plan were to fail completely, India would be more likely to surrender the belief in democratic freedom than to abandon the idea of planning, but the impressive advance under the First, Second and Third Plans leave one with no misgivings on this score.

Chapter 21

Social Progress

A LTHOUGH INDIAN social progress is to some extent a by-product of economic development, certain aspects of it require separate treatment. Its foundation is the fact that ordinary folk in India are awakening to an awareness of their own backwardness and to a consciousness of their own needs. Amongst those needs, better education and improved medical and public health facilities perhaps loom largest in their minds, but there are other public activities included in the somewhat unsatisfactory term 'welfare', to which prominence is given in the National Plan. Education, health, welfare and labour matters will be discussed briefly in this chapter.

We have already seen that, by the middle of the nineteenth century, English had become the medium of instruction in the secondary and university stages. Education had taken on a purely literary bias, which may have suited boys of first-class ability, but led many others to flounder along, memorising text-books of which they understood little and learning only to despise manual work. In primary schools a surprising amount of good work was done by schoolmasters whose salaries were much less than the wages of domestic servants, but who were often much respected in their villages. Manual training of any kind was rigorously excluded from the curriculum. In the twentieth century many District Officers strove to break down the exclusively academic character of education and to introduce handicrafts, practical agriculture, and other extra-academic activities, but such changes were frequently resisted by parents as not likely to lead to government employment, which had become the accepted goal of education. It was perhaps unfortunate that in most Provinces the delegation to District Boards of the responsibility for primary education cut the primary schools off from any contact with the members of the Indian Educational Service, who were the only educationists with any Western background and so postponed the introduction of modern methods. A further trouble was that only a small proportion of boys passed right through the primary schools. In Bengal, for example, in the early 'forties of this century, 93 per cent of those who entered primary schools left before reaching the top class. Compulsory Primary Education Acts had been passed in certain Provinces, but their introduction in any district depended on the readiness of the District Board or other local authority to introduce an education cess. In most areas the public was not prepared to pay and the acts became a dead letter. Even where compulsory education was introduced, it was found impossible to enforce it. The education of girls was even more backward than that of boys and progress was retarded by the social prejudice which in many areas made it difficult for girls to attend school after they had attained puberty.

At the university level, numbers rather than high standards became the aim in the twentieth century and numerous good high schools insisted on being converted into inefficient colleges. By the beginning of 1947, university students in British India numbered over 229,000. In many cases the academic standards were very low and most graduates had a deplorably narrow range of interests. They could not be regarded as educated men – a fact which has often been obscured by the existence of a number of very brilliant Indians who would have held their own intellectually anywhere in the world.

Despite the efforts of individual officers, the British had been less successful in the sphere of education than in any other department. A self-governing India thus had a great task ahead of her in this field. As regards primary schools, Gandhi had fought strenuously in the Wardha Education Conference of 1937 for a more practical bias in instruction and had advocated a basic education through a profit-making vocation such as spinning, weaving, tailoring and so forth. This idea was accepted by the Congress Party and, though the suggestion that vocational activities must pay for the cost of running the schools has been dropped, 50 per cent of the primary schools to be established under the Second Five-year Plan were to be of the basic education type, while in the remaining 50 per cent the teaching of handicrafts was to be introduced. It is not known how far this object has been achieved, but the writer regards this proposal with peculiar satisfaction in view of the fact that thirty years ago, in a remote district of Bengal, his attempts to give a more practical bias to primary and middle school education were frustrated by the opposition of the parents.

Unfortunately lack of funds has made it impossible to implement the directive principle of the Constitution that universal compulsory primary education should be introduced by 1960. By the end of the Second Five Year Plan, 60 per cent of children between the ages of six and eleven were receiving primary education, while nearly 23 per cent of those between eleven and fourteen years of age were under instruction. In the Third Plan facilities for the free education of all children between the ages of six and eleven are being provided, and in theory such education will be compulsory. In fact, however, only 40 per cent of girls in this age group now attend school, and though this compares favourably with the figure of 20 per cent ten years ago, the Planning Commission does not expect more than 60 per cent of girls to be receiving primary instruction by 1966. It does reckon that by then all boys between six and eleven years of age will be attending school. Although it is in one sense unfortunate that the initial target has not been achieved, it is important not to multiply schools faster than trained teachers can be made available and the time-lag may therefore be a blessing in disguise. Many primary school teachers are still either completely unqualified or inadequately trained, and though training facilities are to be increased considerably in the Third Plan it will be a long time before this defect can be completely remedied.

In secondary education determined attempts are being made to diversify the curriculum. When the writer was a District Officer it always seemed to him that, under the deadening influence of the memorising of textbooks which was characteristic of the average high school and the monotony of which was broken by no outside interests or hobbies, the average boy became progressively duller as he went up the school. It is therefore satisfactory that the planners have proposed the introduction of gardening, music, military training and other extra-academic activities, as well as courses and lectures tended to widen the interest and sympathy of secondary-school teachers. In the Third Plan it is proposed to put much more emphasis on science teaching, but here again the lack of adequately qualified teachers is a serious brake on progress.

As might be expected in a plan aimed largely at industrial development, technical education has received a good deal of attention. Provision has been made for many more technical schools, as well as for stipends and scholarships and for the encouragement of research. In this branch of education progress has been satisfactory.

In the sphere of university education it was recognised by the Planning Commission some years ago that any further expansion in numbers was undesirable and that emphasis must be on higher standards and greater selectivity in the admission of students. This has turned out to be only a pious aspiration and the increase in the number of students in universities and colleges from 630,000 to 1,300,000 in the last ten years seems to have been accompanied by a further decline in the already low standards. There can be little doubt that education in India under the British was top heavy. Many students not intellectually equipped to benefit by advanced education nevertheless went to the universities and found themselves uneducated and unemployable at the end of their course. Since the transfer of power the situation has become even worse. There are fifty-four universities and over one thousand colleges, but many of them are seriously overcrowded and indiscipline is rife. It is a pity that the Government of India have not had the courage to limit admissions to universities to those really fit for them.

In the Second Plan a good deal of attention was given to what is called social education. Some years ago the Congress Party came to the conclusion that in a country where three-quarters of the adult population were illiterate, it was not possible to wait and let juvenile education cure this defect in course of time. Adult education must therefore be organised and many earnest attempts in this direction were made by Congress volunteers and, in some Provinces, by paid village workers. The results were on the whole disappointing and there was a marked tendency for an adult who had barely learned to read to relapse into illiteracy. The Planning Commission therefore came to the conclusion that the concept of adult education must be widened to include not just book learning but education in citizenship and the use of leisure. They decided that this could best be done by linking the basic primary schools with the life of the neighbourhood. As an experimental measure, one primary school in each district was to be developed into a school-cum-community centre. Apart from ordinary primary instruction, the activities of the centre were to include lectures, classes and courses for adults, the training of women in handicrafts, and library facilities. These centres required specially trained teachers and a certain number of basic training colleges with demonstration schools attached to them were organised for this purpose. This work, however, has scarcely gone beyond the pioneering stage and it is still too early to judge its possibilities.

This idea linked up naturally with the village community projects and with the General Welfare Programme. The work of the Central Social Welfare Board and connected bodies is too varied to permit a summary, but three branches of its activities deserve notice. The first is the provision of financial or technical assistance to voluntary organisations concerned with the welfare of women, children, delinquents, the mentally and physically handicapped and others in special need. In work of this kind, there is inevitably a great deal of waste and inefficiency and a certain amount of window dressing, but competent observers nevertheless consider that useful results are being obtained. A second branch of the work is concerned with the initiation of projects to enable women workers and others to supplement their income. In Delhi, for example, under a scheme of this kind, 500 middle-class housewives are earning as much as a rupee a day in centrally-organised cottage industries. This is but an example of what is happening in many parts of India. A third activity of the Board consists in training welfare personnel, who are sent into the villages as *Gramsevikas*[1] to spread modern ideas of hygiene and child welfare, to teach simple arts and crafts and generally to bring the practical enlightment which the villager now seeks. Work of this kind can, of course, easily degenerate into

[1] Literally, those who serve the village.

meaningless routine or even laziness, but the organisers believe that there is sufficient enthusiasm to keep up the momentum and, in the words of V. T. Krishnamachari, 'to change the outlook of the sixty million families living in the countryside, arouse enthusiasm in them for new knowledge and new ways of life and fill them with the ambition and the will to live a better life'.

Gram *sevikas* were expected to play an important part in the Community Development projects, the theory underlying which was that a limited number of rural areas would be taken up for the intensive development of agriculture, animal husbandry, co-operative societies and rural industries, and that as funds and man-power became available the number of villages covered would be increased. Closely allied to this movement Government proposed to build up what was called *Panchayati Raj;* that is to say local popularly elected bodies at village, block and district levels would be associated with and made partly responsible for development work. It was indeed part of the theory that these local organisations would help to prepare plans at block level, and the State plans would then to a considerable extent be the aggregations of the block plans. The whole scheme is indeed an outward expression of Nehru's fervent belief that progress must come from the people rather than from government. Many friends of India, including the writer, doubt if social consciousness is anything like sufficiently developed to make this possible, but it has been enthusiastically adopted by the Congress Party as established doctrine.

As might be expected, practice has diverged considerably from theory. In those areas where some exceptionally public spirited non-official has taken the lead – or where a zealous official, more interested in economic development than in the Nehru democratic ideal, has brought pressure to bear – good results have been achieved. In many other areas, however, there has been a good deal of make-believe and in such areas the replacement of the authority of the official by ineffective local bodies may retard progress for a time. It remains to be seen whether or not, in India as a whole, there will be such an awakening of social consciousness as a result of these schemes as to compensate for any temporary retardation of development.

An aspect of *Panchayati Raj* which was prominent in Nehru's mind was the development of co-operative agriculture. He continually stressed the fact that Indian agriculture was still primitive; that the individual cultivator had neither the resources nor sufficient land to enable him to adopt modern methods of farming involving tractors and other mechanical appliances, and that it was essential, therefore, for the cultivators in each locality to join together in communal ownership of the instruments of intensive production. As a matter of economic theory this may be sound – though it would represent a trend directly opposite to the individualist farming which led to the great improvement of English agriculture after the period of enclosures – but so far it has made little appeal to the Indian peasant. It is indeed doubtful if anything short of the totalitarian methods employed in Russia and China will induce Indian cultivators to take to co-operative farming. Co-operative sale or credit societies are another matter, and some of them are very successful.

The Planning Commission has naturally put much emphasis on measures for the improvement of medical and public health services. Here it was possible to build on firmer foundations than in the case of education, since a great deal of first-class work had been done during the British period. India, indeed, was in the forefront of the fight against malaria, cholera, smallpox, plague and other tropical diseases, and in some cases the results achieved in the twentieth century were spectacular. Nevertheless, finance was always a limiting factor and though mortality, and above all infant mortality, rates had come down spectacularly in the twentieth century, medical facilities and public health resources at the time of the transfer of power were still woefully inadequate.

In 1946 a Committee under the chairmanship of Sir Joseph Bhore surveyed India's medical needs. It found that, in spite of the great improvement to which we have referred, mortality rates were still more than twice those of Australia or New Zealand and that India ranked high as one of the largest reservoirs of infection in respect of cholera, smallpox and plague. The Committee observed that there was one doctor to every six thousand inhabitants of India, as against one per thousand in England, and that the situation as regards nurses was even worse. It proposed that steps should be taken to provide one doctor for every two thousand of the population by 1971, and had to recommend an even more radical step-up of the supply of nurses by that date. It rightly attached even greater importance to preventive than to curative measures, and, in addition to a great increase in hospital facilities, therefore proposed the establishment of a network of health units throughout the country. The Committee's plans were ambitious – though not more so than circumstances required – and involved the expenditure of Rs.600 crores in the first ten years, including amortisation charges on capital expenditure.

When the Planning Commission prepared the First Five-Year Plan it found its resources hopelessly inadequate for all that had to be done, and one of the spheres in which it economised was health. It was, in fact, only able to provide Rs.131 crores for health purposes, and even that modest sum included Rs.83 crores for the development of curative and other preventive facilities. Naturally, progress was much slower than the Bhore Committee had anticipated. The number of hospital beds rose only by 10 per cent in the period of the First Five Year Plan and the increase by the end of the Second Five Year Plan was about 40 per cent as compared with 1950. As regards doctors, the Bhore target has evidently been discarded as too ambitious and even in 1966 there will be only one doctor for every 6,000 inhabitants. In the categories of nurses, midwives and the like, progress is falling still further short of the Bhore Committee's estimates of India's needs. Good work has been done by enthusiasts, but the inadequate scale of provision for the improvement of public health is well illustrated by the fact that, even on the most optimistic assumptions, the number of health assistants and sanitary inspectors employed in 1961 is only 7,500, although it is estimated that 20,000 are needed. The planners have done well within the limits of their resources, but they are discovering, as their British predecessors discovered before them, that the gap between what is desirable and what is practicable in an underdeveloped country is very wide.

Progress in the department of health in the last three decades before the transfer of power was as rapid as funds permitted and it is perhaps unlikely that the pace can be greatly accelerated now or that improved medical facilities can do much more than keep pace with the growth of population. Considerable importance is attached therefore to the family planning campaign launched by the Government of India. It has not yet made much impact on the great mass of the people and it is only in one or two areas that the campaign can be said to have been reasonably successful. Social prejudice against it is strong amongst large sections of society, but a greater difficulty, arises from the costliness of the methods normally practised. Statisticians differ considerably in their estimates of the present rate of growth of population, but according to the Economic Survey for 1964 the rate has risen from 2 per cent in the fifties to about 2.3 per cent now. It would be unwise to assume that there would be any significant slowing down in this rate during the period of the Third Five Year Plan.

Not the least important aspect of social progress is that connected with the welfare of labour and here those concerned were confronted with a serious difficulty. The great export industries, on which India's earnings of foreign exchange so largely depend, grew up at a time when, because food was cheap and India's standards of living deplorably low, wages of labour were also low. These industries have thus developed on the basis of cheap production and have to compete with other industries which have grown up on a similar foundation in other Asian countries. Any radical improvement in the remuneration in conditions of labour today may raise costs of production in India above the level of her competitors. This danger is well illustrated by the case of the tea industry, where East African producers are able to land tea in the U.K. so much below the cost of production of Indian tea that they can regard falling markets with relative equanimity. There is thus a danger that India may lose important markets in certain commodities, in which case the last state of her labour forces will be worse than the first. The Government of India is thus faced with a dilemma. It tends in practice to ignore it and to concentrate on securing higher remuneration for labour without much regard for the economics of industry or for the possibility that India's competitors may under-sell her. In these matters India is very sensitive to criticism in the International Labour

T

Organisation and this factor, together with the growing power of labour, strengthens the tendency we have described.

In great industries such as the tea industry, in the second quarter of the twentieth century employers themselves took the initiative in protecting the standard of living and providing better amenities for their employees. In this move British employers were noticeably in the lead. In some industries, however, a new responsiveness to labour demands was slow in growing. The Government of India had, therefore, to decide between letting the process of collective bargaining redress the balance between the employer and employee, or itself regulating wages and conditions. On a long view it might have been better to let trade unions feel their strength and learn to use it with restraint, but this would have involved a period, perhaps extending over many years, during which, under Indian conditions, repeated strikes would undoubtedly have led to violence and chaos. At the same time, such a situation would have offered useful opportunities to the Communists.

Shortly before the transfer of power, the Interim Government, therefore, followed the example of some of the Provincial Governments and embarked on a policy of fairly stringent control of labour relations. That policy is now an integral part of Indian thought and law. We need not discuss it in detail here, but need merely note, first, that in some industries minimum wages are in force, and, secondly that when industrial disputes occur they are in many cases referred to tribunals, whose findings are binding. A large body of case law covering all aspects of relations between employers and employees has thus grown up with no specific statutory foundation and, as might be expected under such circumstances, contemporary economic theories and feeling have played a large part in its evolution. In some States, labour has been made to feel that any claim, however preposterous, is worth advancing, since there is a reasonable expectation that Government will refer it to a tribunal and a fairly good chance that the tribunal will award at least some part of the claim. It is considered by some observers that the tribunal procedure has, in fact, encouraged disputes instead of settling them and has made it unnecessary for unions to learn the lesson of responsibility in the hard and only way. This is particularly important in view of the lack of leaders of high calibre in the trade union movement in India and it would be fair to state that, whatever its success in other branches of activity may have been, the Indian National Congress has signally failed to assist the trade union movement in developing along healthy lines. As a result of the lack of any such development, and of the undue weighting of the scales by Government against employers, discipline has become undermined, retrenchment on rational grounds has become difficult and labour problems are one of the strongest obstacles today to industrial development. On the other hand, it must be admitted that the Government of India and the State Governments have succeeded in raising the standard of living of labourers and securing better conditions for them and that this constitutes an important credit item in their balance sheet of social progress.

Chapter 22

An Assessment

THREE ASPECTS of modern India are of absorbing interest today. In the first place it is the most successful example of a Parliamentary democracy in the East; secondly it is the scene of the greatest experiment in Socialism ever conducted in a freedom-loving country; while thirdly, it is the only great country wholly outside either of the international blocs. Each of these aspects must find its place in our assessment of modern India.

Although adult suffrage has long been an essential part of Congress policy, after the transfer of power many of the party leaders were frankly apprehensive of the first General Election in independent India, when 175 million electors, the majority of whom were illiterate, would have to elect members of Parliament from a bewildering medley of twenty-two effective parties. The apprehensions proved to be groundless. The elections were as orderly as those in the United Kingdom. The uneducated public was not swept off its feet by the extremists, either of the right or the left; and a Parliament truly representative of the thought and feeling of ordinary Indians came into being. That Parliament, as we have seen, works somewhat differently from its counterparts in other parts of the world, but it satisfies the three most important tests of a democratic legislature. It is highly sensitive to public opinion; it is the vigilant guardian of the rule of law; and it commands general respect. Contrary to the expectations of many friendly observers before the transfer of power, the Parliamentary system seems firmly entrenched in Indian political life.

During Nehru's lifetime the democratic character of the Indian Government was sometimes obscured by the astonishing personal ascendancy of the Prime Minister and by the readiness of all his colleagues to subordinate their views to his. This situation was apt to give the casual Western observer the impression of dictatorship in the making. In reality, however, Nehru's power sprang largely from his closeness to the masses. More than any other Congress leader, he was the true mouthpiece of the ordinary man at his best and when he preached neutralism or Socialism he was expressing what was already in the hearts of the people. Before the transfer of power, British friends of India often asserted that democracy was not suited to the Indian psychology. It is possible that it would have been nearer the truth to say that the process of determining the public will in India might differ from that in Britain. All who have lived in India know how often at the end of a village gathering, lasting perhaps for many hours, the issue is settled, not as as in England by a show of hands but by a somewhat mysterious process of arriving at general assent. It may be that, in the larger context of Indian national life, democracy will operate, not by a process similar to the British two-party system, but by the wise selection of a leader to whom the public will give unbounded confidence and who will use Parliament as a forum in which to expound policy. This form of democracy requires a leader of Nehru's calibre if it is not to degenerate into tyranny, and there was therefore well-justified anxiety as to who in due course would succeed Nehru. Fortunately the present Prime Minister, Lal Bahadur Shastri, is a liberal-minded gentleman, too modest to aim at dictatorship and yet by no means lacking in moral fibre or the power to command.

It is still an open question whether or not, now that the old guard of the Indian National Congress is disappearing, that party will divide naturally into a right and left wing and the Indian Parliament will then conform more closely to the British pattern, with Conservatives and Socialists as alternative parties in power. The Swatantra Party is presumably gambling on a split of this kind, but unfortunately most Indian businessmen, who would have been the natural nucleus of the Conservative Party, seem to have abandoned any serious attempt at playing an effective part in politics. At the moment there are moderate conservatives in the Cabinet, but amongst Congress back benchers the right wing is weak. Unless the Swatantra Party achieves an unexpected success in the elections it looks as though the political battle of the future will be between a left wing Congress and the Communists. It may be assumed that the latter party will continue to receive backing from abroad, and it must not be taken for granted that the confusion amongst the Communists resulting from the Chinese attack will endure for ever. All thoughtful Indians are conscious of the factors in the social and economic life of the country which may predispose towards Communism and many of them regard the present Socialist trend of Congress policy as the best defence against that danger.

In the meantime, the stability and peace of India present a happy contrast to the chaos in countries farther east. It is true that in the big cities the possibility of disorder is never very far away and that there are States which show a lamentable unwillingness or inability to take swift and stern action against violence and intimidation. It is also true that at times communal and inter-State bitterness disrupts the tranquillity of India. and that there have been very unhappy instances of this tendency this year. Nevertheless, in general, law and order are well maintained and the ordinary citizen has a sense of security. Above all the Government of India is strong and determined to allow no subversive movement to become dangerous.

The relative orderliness of India is in no small measure due to the soundness of the administrative foundations laid by the British. Indian members of the old Imperial Services and particularly of the Indian Civil Service, faithfully maintain the old tradition, and the standard of ability, industry and integrity at top level in the Delhi Secretariat is fully equal to that of Whitehall.

There is weakness in the middle levels of the official hierarchy, where the loss of British officers led to unduly accelerated promotion, and in some cases to the appointment to particular posts of men not altogether fit for them. Fortunately, the quality of the young recruits to the Indian Administrative Service is excellent and, provided the young men are not discouraged by the somewhat niggardly terms which the Government of India now offers to its superior staff, they will serve India well. In the States the weak links are more numerous and in the old princely States there are large administrative gaps still unfilled. There is much public talk of corruption in some of the States, and though it is always difficult to assess the accuracy of general allegations of this kind, there is no doubt that there has been considerable deterioration in this respect in recent years.

Perhaps the chief administrative danger is that the modern doctrines of planning and control will compel the services to take on more than they can perform. Already the strain imposed on men of real ability is great and the planners must be careful lest they raise it to breaking point. Nevertheless, it can fairly be claimed that Parliamentary forms of Government, operating through a British type of Civil Service irremovable except for misconduct, are working well.

The second most interesting aspect of modern India is that of the great Socialist experiment, which can only be explained against the general background of the awakening of the East. After centuries of acquiescence in things as they were, Asia is at last conscious of the poverty, ignorance and general backwardness of many of her people and she attributes these at least partly to foreign rule. This does not necessarily imply a failure to recognise the benefits that the West has brought to Asia, but this belief springs from a conviction that foreign rule, however good, must be spiritually debilitating and that under it the energies of the best men are not fully released. When India attained her freedom she experienced an exaltation of the spirit which was manifest to the friendly observer and in that high mood she looked, with new eyes, alike at her own deficiencies and at the defects in Western economic organisation. She resolved once for all that she would end poverty and ignorance, without undergoing the evils which resulted from the Industrial Revolution in Europe. She was convinced, too, that by borrowing modern techniques she could telescope into the space of a generation the progress painfully achieved in the West in the course of a century or more. A reasonable impatience is the keynote of modern India. The inevitability of gradualness makes no appeal to her. Solutions which would produce a sound and prosperous economy at length of days, or which would involve a temporary increase of the disparities between classes, receive short shrift at the hands of India today.

In this mood of impatience her leaders have looked at China and Russia as examples of determined planning for progress.

They were until recently impressed with the signs of activity in China and are still full of admiration for the immense technical progress of Russia, and they have perhaps not realised fully the discontent and the backwardness of the peasants in those countries. Nevertheless, they see in Communist countries elements which they do not like. The absence of freedom, the rejection of the rule of law and the enslavement of the mind are contrary to the sense of values that they have acquired from the West or inherited from their own past. They believe that they can achieve the same success as Russia, without following the political pattern of that country. This leads them to believe in planning and in an economy which, though retaining a considerable measure of individual freedom, will in its broader aspects be controlled. In their view, the needs of the State rather than the profit motive must condition development. The National Plan has therefore become the focal point in Indian economic thought – it is the touchstone by which everything else will be judged.

We have already called attention to the unsound elements in the National Plan and to the air of unreality about some of its assumptions and estimates. It does nevertheless provide the psychological pressure necessary for rapid progress and the Planning Commission can take pride in India's remarkable advance during the last ten years.

The dispositions of the planners, and the general trend of political and economic thought in India, all point to Socialist solutions of the problem of poverty. Nevertheless, the Government still feel that private capital, Indian and foreign, may possibly be necessary and that institutional investment or aid from abroad might be deterred by too rapid implementation of left-wing economic doctrines. Their Socialism is thus qualified by a pragmatic approach. Capitalism may continue within limits provided it can make the stipulated contribution to planned development. The Indian capitalist as such has no friends in Indian political life today, or indeed amongst the public; he is on ticket-of-leave for a while, ready to come up for sentence if authority is dissatisfied with him. Free private enterprise in the old sense is disappearing and the survival or otherwise even of the controlled capitalism of the new age will depend on the capacity of the private sector to fill the role assigned to it. If the Plan succeeds, this kind of mixed economy may be allowed to continue – but what if it fails? The answer to this question has been put strikingly by Guy Wint.

'Whichever country shows the more impressive economic progress, India or China, is likely to be accepted as the social, and perhaps the political, leader of Asia. All the countries of South Asia are watching the competition. At present, though there is plenty of sympathy for Communism, the intelligentsia of most of these countries may have a bias in favour of free systems. But they are not indissolubly attached to them. The prime interest is in material advance. If it appears, from the result of the test in India and China, that by sacrificing freedom there can be a quicker advance materially, much of the intelligentsia will not hesitate to turn Communist. Even in India itself this may happen. If, on the other hand, the progress under the liberal system is striking – if the Colombo Plan achieves its results – there will be an immense strengthening of the confidence in liberal and democratic ideas.'

The determined neutralism in international affairs, which is the third important feature of modern India, has already been discussed in some detail and it is only necessary here to emphasise three points. In the first place, it was not something imposed on India by the commanding personality of Nehru. It sprang from the combined effect of philosophy, historical factors and present circumstances and it was accepted as a dogma by the great majority of educated Indians in the first decade of independence. Of late its character has considerably changed. Non-violence as a creed has been discarded and Nehru has frankly declared his readiness to use force in defence of India's interests where necessary. The invasion of Goa has lent reality to this declaration and the Chinese attack has added greatly to its significance.

Secondly, India is genuinely determined to keep clear of international military groupings and her neutralism is not a cloak for partiality to the Communist countries. It is true that her relations with Russia are now good, but the hostility of her people to China is unmistakable. Thirdly, this neutrality is not

U

regarded by India as in any way incompatible with loyal membership of the Commonwealth. India is, in fact, a good Commonwealth member. She fulfils her obligations as a member of the sterling area and her treatment of United Kingdom citizens living and working in India is exemplary.

Her attitude has recently become to some extent complicated by the increased tension between herself and Pakistan. Nehru's rejection of the plebiscite as an appropriate method of settling the problem of Kashmir not unnaturally exacerbated feelings in Pakistan. In India, on the other hand, there was a growing apprehension of the development of Pakistan's military strength. The Chinese attack and the military backing given by Britain and the U.S. to India have radically changed the picture, and whereas a few years ago India was apprehensive of the growing strength of the Pakistan Air Force, today the boot is on the other foot. The tension between India and Pakistan will vary from time to time, but it is unlikely to disappear in the foreseeable future, and may periodically become dangerous. In Indian eyes it seems to strengthen the case for neutralism.

This desire to keep out of international groupings, and at the same time to proclaim a kind of Monroe doctrine with regard to Asia, has not hindered India from playing a notable part in the settlement of Far Eastern problems. An India which fourteen years ago was inexperienced and diffident in foreign affairs, today counts for a great deal in international politics, and this vigour in world affairs is but the natural outcome of the dynamic spirit which the West can claim to have brought to India, and which self-government has intensified immeasurably.

Appendix

STATES AND UNION TERRITORIES IN INDIA

State	Area (Sq. Miles)	Population (1961 census)	Capital
Andhra Pradesh	106,286	35,983,447	Hyderabad
Assam	78,529*	12,209,330*	Shillong
Bihar	67,196	46,455,610	Patna
Gujarat	72,245	20,633,350	Ahmedabad
Jammu and Kashmir	86,023	3,560,975	Srinagar
Kerala	15,002	16,903,715	Trivandrum
Madhya Pradesh	171,217	32,372,408	Bhopal
Madras	50,331	33,686,953	Madras
Maharashtra	118,717	39,553,718	Bombay
Mysore	74,210	23,586,772	Bangalore
Orissa	60,164	17,548,846	Bhubaneswar
Punjab	47,108	20,306,812	Chandigarh
Rajasthan	132,152	20,155,602	Jaipur
Uttar Pradesh	113,654	73,746,401	Lucknow
West Bengal	33,829	34,926,279	Calcutta
Nagaland	6,366	369,200	Kohima

* Includes North East
Frontier Tract

Union Territories

Andaman and Nicobar Islands	3,215	63,548	Port Blaire
Dadra and Nagar Haveli	189	57,963	Silvassa
Delhi	573	2,658,612	Delhi
Goa, Daman and Diu	1,426	626,978	Panjam
Himachal Pradesh	10,885	1,351,144	Simla
Laccadive, Minicoy and Amindivi Islands	11	24,108	Headquarters: Kozhikode
Manipur	8,628	780,037	Imphal

Pondicherry	185	369,079	Pondicherry
Tripura	4,036	1,142,005	Agartala
OTHER AREAS			
North East Frontier Tract[1]	31,438	336,558	Headquarters: Shillong

[1] The North East Frontier Tract is administered by the Ministry of External Affairs, with the Governor of Assam acting as the Agent of the President.

Bibliography

1. *For the period up to August 15, 1947*
A full bibliography will be found in *The British Impact on India*
by the present writer, but the following books will probably be
sufficient for the general reader:

A Survey of Indian History   K. M. Panikkar
A Short History of India   Moreland and Chatterjee
The Legacy of India   Edited by G. T. Garratt
An Outline of the Religious Literature of India   J. N. Farquhar
History of British India   P. E. Roberts
India   Valentine Chirol
Our Heritage   Humayun Kabir
The Transfer of Power   E. W. R. Lumby
Discovery of India   Jawaharlal Nehru
Transfer of Power in India   V. P. Menon
India Today   Frank Moraes
Punjabi Century   Prakash Tandon

2. *For the period after the Transfer of Power*
(a) There are very few authoritative books on this period yet
    and the story is mainly to be found in the files of newspapers
    or in Government reports.
(b) Books recommended are:
    The Story of the Integration of the States   V. P. Menon
    Danger in Kashmir   Josef Korbel
    Two Nations and Kashmir   Lord Birdwood
    India Changes   Taya Zinkin
    Britain and India   Maurice and Taya Zinkin
    The Government and Politics of India   W. H. Morris-Jones
(c) Government of India Reports of particular interest are as
    follows:
    White Paper on Hyderabad 1948
    White Paper on Indian States 1948

White Paper on Indian States 1950
Report of the States Reorganisation Commission 1955.
(d) For economic affairs, the most important documents are the First and Second and Third Five-year Plans and the Progress Reports of the Planning Commission. The Board of Trade's Overseas Economic Surveys of India, published in 1949 and 1952, are of great value for this period. The annual numbers of the *Eastern Economist* will also be found of considerable use.

Investment in India   U.S.A. Department of Commerce
(e) Three excellent books on Indian constitutional development may be consulted:
Constitutional Development in India   C. H. Alexandrowicz
The Republic of India   Alan Gledhill
Parliament in India   W. H. Morris-Jones

Maps

INDIA AND PAKISTAN
INDIAN UNION STATES MAY 1960
INDIA FROM MAY 1960

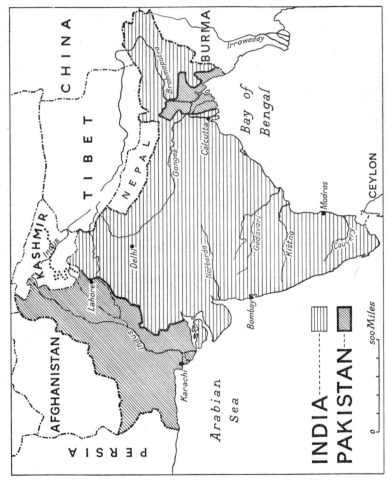

KASHMIR BORDER—the dotted line demarcates that portion of Kashmir in Indian possession from that part possessed by Pakistan

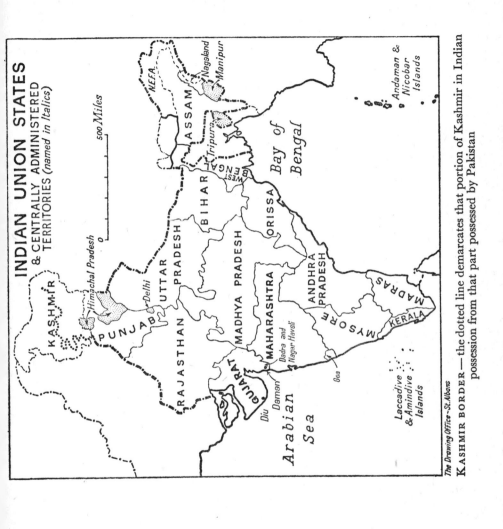

INDIAN UNION STATES
& CENTRALLY ADMINISTERED TERRITORIES (named in Italics)

500 Miles

0

NEFA

ASSAM

Nagaland

Manipur

Tripura

WEST BENGAL

BIHAR

ORISSA

Bay of Bengal

Himachal Pradesh

KASHMIR

Delhi

PUNJAB

UTTAR PRADESH

RAJASTHAN

MADHYA PRADESH

MAHARASHTRA

Dadra and Nagar Haveli

ANDHRA PRADESH

MYSORE

KERALA

MADRAS

GUJARAT

Daman

Diu

Goa

Arabian Sea

Laccadive & Amindive Islands

Andaman & Nicobar Islands

The Drawing Office—St. Albans

KASHMIR BORDER — the dotted line demarcates that portion of Kashmir in Indian possession from that part possessed by Pakistan

Index

*Printed in Great Britain by
Cox & Wyman Limited,
London Fakenham & Reading*